DATE			

BY ADRIENNE RICH

Collected Early Poems
1950–1970

An Atlas of the Difficult World:
Poems 1988–1991

Time's Power: Poems 1985–1988

Blood, Bread, and Poetry: Selected Prose 1979–1986

Your Native Land, Your Life

The Fact of a Doorframe: Poems Selected and New 1950–1984

Sources

A Wild Patience Has Taken Me This Far

On Lies, Secrets, and Silence: Selected Prose, 1966–1978

The Dream of a Common Language

Twenty-one Love Poems

Of Woman Born: Motherhood As Experience and Institution

Poems: Selected and New, 1950–1974

Diving into the Wreck

The Will to Change

Leaflets

Necessities of Life

Snapshots of a Daughter-in-Law

The Diamond Cutters

A Change of World

What Is
Found
There

W·W·Norton & Company

NEW YORK · LONDON

What Is Found There

NOTEBOOKS ON POETRY AND POLITICS

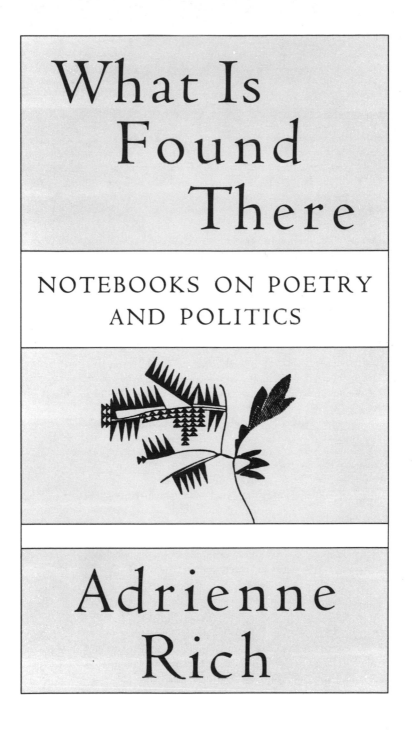

Adrienne Rich

Grateful acknowledgment is made for permission to quote from the works of Gloria Bolden, Jacqueline Dixon-Bey, and Mary Glover in *INSIGHT: Serving the Women of Florence Crane Women's Facility*, Coldwater, Michigan.

Portions of this book first appeared in *The American Poetry Review, Hungry Mind Review, The Kenyon Review, Parnassus,* and *PMLA*. I was fortunate to be able to present parts of the final draft as the McGill Lecture at the University of Southern California, for the Hellgate Writers' Workshop in Missoula, Montana, for the Iowa Writers' Workshop, and as the 1993 Paul Zweig Lecture for Poets House, New York.

Jacket art: *T-5* by Judith Larzelere (1986). Collection of Kenneth Kronenberg. Photo: Jan Bindas Studios, Boston, Massachusetts.

First Edition

The text of this book is composed in Bembo 270
with the display set in Centaur.
Composition and manufacturing by The Haddon Craftsmen, Inc.
Book design by Antonina Krass.
Stenciled book ornament by William Addison Dwiggins.

Library of Congress Cataloging-in-Publication Data

Rich, Adrienne Cecile.
What is found there: notebooks on poetry and politics
/ Adrienne Rich.
p.   cm.
ISBN 0-393-03565-4
1. Rich, Adrienne Cecile—Notebooks, sketchbooks, etc.
2. Politics and literature.   3. Poetry.   I. Title.
PS3535.I233W45   1993
818'.5403—dc20   93-9912
ISBN 0-393-03565-4

W. W. Norton & Company, Inc., 500 Fifth Avenue, New York, NY 10110
W. W. Norton & Company Ltd., 10 Coptic Street, London WC1A 1PU
1 2 3 4 5 6 7 8 9 0

Contents

It is difficult
to get the news from poems
            yet men die miserably every day
                        for lack
of what is found there.

—William Carlos Williams,
"Asphodel, That Greeny Flower"

Dead power is everywhere among us—in the forest, chopping down the songs; at night in the industrial landscape, wasting and stiffening the new life; in the streets of the city, throwing away the day. We wanted something different for our people: not to find ourselves an old, reactionary republic, full of ghost-fears, the fears of death and the fears of birth. We want something else.

—Muriel Rukeyser, *The Life of Poetry*

. . . what, anyway,
was that sticky infusion, that rank flavor of blood, that
poetry, by which I lived?

—Galway Kinnell, "The Bear"

Sometimes we drug ourselves with dreams of new ideas. The head will save us. The brain alone will set us free. But there are no new ideas waiting in the wings to save us as women, as human. There are only old and forgotten ones, new combinations, extrapolations and recognitions from within ourselves—along with the renewed courage to try them out.

—Audre Lorde, "Poetry Is Not a Luxury"

Preface

This book is about desire and daily life. I began it because I needed a way of thinking about poetry outside of writing poems; and about the society I was living and writing in, which smelled to me of timidity, docility, demoralization, acceptance of the unacceptable. In the general public disarray of thinking, of feeling, I saw an atrophy of our power to imagine other ways of navigating into our collective future. I was not alone in this perception, but I felt it with a growing intensity, especially as the Cold War, which had occupied so much of the political horizon of my life, began to unravel. It seemed that a historic imaginative opportunity was passing through and that, in the stagnation and dissolution of public life, it might be grasped at weakly, if at all. Some people, indeed, spoke of claiming a "peace dividend," of turning the billions of Cold War dollars toward curing the social lesions within our borders, even toward creating, at last, a democracy without exceptions, that was really for us all. But the major (in the sense of most visible and audible) conduits of public dialogue in the United States have had little aptitude—or use—for framing such visions, or the policies that might emerge from them.

I knew—had long known—how poetry can break open locked chambers of possibility, restore numbed zones to feeling, recharge desire. And, in spite of conditions at large, it seemed to me that poetry in the United States had never been more various and rich in its promise and its realized offerings. But I had, more than I wanted to acknowledge, internalized the idea, so common in this country, so strange in most other places, that poetry is powerless, or that it can have nothing to do with the kinds of powers that organize us as a society, as communities within that society, as relationships within communities. If asked, I would have said that I did not accept this idea. Yet it haunted me.

And so this book reflects the time and place in which it has been written: an alleged triumph of corporate capitalism in which our experience—our desire itself—is taken from us, processed and labeled, and sold back to us before we have had a chance to name it for ourselves (what do we really want and fear?) or to dwell in our ambiguities and contradictions. It reflects the undertaking, by one kind of artist, to see and feel her way to an understanding of her art's responsive and responsible relationship to history, to her contemporaries, and to the future. I have never believed that poetry is an escape from history, and I do not think it is more, or less, necessary than food, shelter, health, education, decent working conditions. It is as necessary.

In a different kind of society, the struggle I was experiencing might seem perplexing, either because the repression of the artist took such unmistakable and ruthless forms, or because art was assumed to be as integral to daily life as roads, laws, literacy, clean air, and water. I know that "capitalism" is an unfashionable word. "Democracy," "free enterprise," "market economy" are the banners now floating above our economic system. Still, as a poet, I choose to sieve up old, sunken words, heave them, dripping with silt, turn them over, and bring them into the air of the present. Where every public decision has to be justified in the scales of corporate profits, poetry unsettles these apparently self-evident propositions—not through ideology, but by its very presence and ways of being, its embodiment of states of longing and desire.

This is one poet's book, one citizen's book. But, in fact, poetry is always being created anew, in new places, by unforetold hands and voices. In this, it is like the many movements against demoralizing power. We don't know where either will come from. This is a story without an end.

—Adrienne Rich
February 1993

What Is
Found
There

I

Woman and bird

January 1990. I live on a street of mostly older, low-lying little houses in a straggling, villagelike, "unincorporated" neighborhood between two small towns on the California coast. There are a few old palms, apple, guava, quince, plum, lemon, and walnut trees, here and there old roses, climbing a fence or freestanding. One garden boasts an ancient, sprawling prickly pear. An elementary school accounts for most of the traffic, mornings and midafternoons. Pickup trucks and boats on trailers sit for days or weeks or months in front yards; old people and children walk in the road, while the serious traffic moves along the frontage road and the freeway. It's an ordinary enough place, I suppose, yet it feels fragile, as condominiums and automobile plazas multiply up and down the coast.

Around the house I live in there are trees enough—Monterey pines, acacias, a big box elder, fruit trees, two Italian cypresses, an eastern maple—so that mockingbirds, finches, doves, Steller's jays, hummingbirds are drawn to come and feed on plums and ollalieberries, honeysuckle and fuchsia during the warm months of the year. There's almost always a gull or two far overhead. Somebody keeps chickens; a rooster crows at dawn.

Today I returned from an errand, parked the car behind the house. Opening the car door I saw and heard the beating of enormous wings taking off from the deck. At first I thought: a very big gull, or even a raven. Then it alighted on the low roof of the house next door, stretched its long body, and stood in profile to me. It was a Great Blue Heron.

I had never seen one from below or from so near: usually from a car window on a road above a small bay or inlet. I had not seen one many times at all. I was not sure. Poised there on the peak of the roof, it looked immense, fastidious, apparently calm. It turned a little; seemed to gaze as far into the blue air as the curve of the earth would allow; took a slow, ritualistic, provocative step or two. I could see the two wirelike plumes streaming from the back of its head.

I walked quietly into the garden toward the fence between the two houses, speaking to it in a low voice. I told it that I thanked it for having come; that I wanted it to be safe. I moved backward again a little to look at it better. Suddenly it was in air, had flapped out of sight.

It would be easy to call this apparition "dreamlike," but it did not feel so. After some moments I went into the house. I wanted to be sure I could name what I had seen; to stay with what I had seen. I pulled from the bookcase a guide to Pacific Coast ecology. The color plate of the Great Blue Heron confirmed my naming.

Then, as I sat there, my eye began to travel the margins of the book, along the names and habitats of creatures and plants of the 4,000-mile Pacific coastline of North America. It was an idle enough activity at first, the kind that sometimes plays upon other, subterranean activities of the mind, draws thinking and unfiltered feelings into sudden dialogue. Of late, I had been consciously thinking about the decade just beginning, the last of the twentieth century, and the great movements and shudderings of the time; about the country where I am a citizen, and what has been happening in our social fabric, our emotional and sensual life, during that century. Somewhere beneath these conscious speculations lay a vaguer desire: to feel the pull of the future, to possess the inner gift, the un-sentimentality, the fortitude, to see into it—if only a little way.

But I found myself pulled by names: Dire Whelk, Dusky Tegula, Fingered Limpet, Hooded Puncturella, Veiled Chiton, Bat Star, By-the-Wind Sailor, Crumb-of-Bread Sponge, Eye Fringed Worm, Sugar Wrack, Frilled Anemone, Bull Kelp, Ghost Shrimp, Sanderling, Walleye Surfperch, Volcano Barnacle, Stiff-footed Sea Cucumber, Leather Star, Innkeeper Worm, Lug Worm. And I felt the names drawing me into a state of piercing awareness, a state I associate with reading and writing poems. These names—by whom given and agreed on?—these names work as poetry works, enlivening a sensuous reality through recognition or through the play of sounds (the short *i*'s of Fingered Limpet, the open vowels of Bull Kelp, Hooded Puncturella, Bat Star); the poising of heterogeneous images (*volcano* and *barnacle, leather* and *star, sugar* and *wrack*) to evoke other worlds of meaning. Sugar Wrack: a foundered ship in the Triangle Trade? Volcano Barnacle: tiny unnoticed under-growth with explosive potential? Who saw the bird named Sanderling and gave it that caressive, diminutive name? Or was Sanderling the name of one who saw it? These names work as poetry works in another sense as well: they make something unforgettable. You will remember the pictorial names as you won't the Latin, which, however, is more specific as to genus and species. Human eyes gazed at each of all these forms of life and saw resemblance in difference—the core of metaphor, that which lies close to the core of poetry itself, the only hope for a humane civil life. The eye for likeness in the midst of contrast, the appeal to recognition, the association of thing to thing, spiritual fact with embodied form, begins here. And so begins the suggestion of multiple, many-layered, rather than singular, meanings, wherever we look, in the ordinary world.

I began to think about the names, beginning with the sound and image delivered in the name "Great Blue Heron," as tokens of a time when naming was poetry, when connections between things and living beings, or living things and human beings, were instinctively apprehended. By "a time" I don't mean any one historical or linguistic moment or period. I mean *all* the times when people have summoned language into the activity of plotting connections between, and marking distinctions among, the elements presented to our senses.

This impulse to enter, with other humans, through language, into the order and disorder of the world, is poetic at its root as surely as it is political at its root. Poetry and politics both have to do with description and with power. And so, of course, does science. We might hope to find the three activities—poetry, science, politics—triangulated, with extraordinary electrical exchanges moving from each to each and through our lives. Instead, over centuries, they have become separated—poetry from politics, poetic naming from scientific naming, an ostensibly "neutral" science from political questions, "rational" science from lyrical poetry—nowhere more than in the United States over the past fifty years.

———

The Great Blue Heron is not a symbol. Wandered inadvertently or purposefully inland, maybe drought-driven, to a backyard habitat, it is a bird, *Ardea herodias,* whose form, dimensions, and habits have been described by ornithologists, yet whose intangible ways of being and knowing remain beyond my—or anyone's—reach. If I spoke to it, it was because I needed to acknowledge in words the rarity and signifying power of its appearance, not because I thought it had come to me. The tall, foot-poised creature had a life, a place of its own in the manifold, fragile system that is this coastline; a place of its own in the universe. Its place, and mine, I believe, are equal and interdependent. Neither of us—woman or bird—is a symbol, despite efforts to make us that. But I needed to acknowledge the heron with speech, and by confirming its name. To it I brought the kind of thing my kind of creature does.

A Mohawk Indian friend says she began writing "after a motor trip through the Mohawk Valley, when a Bald Eagle flew in front of her car, sat in a tree, and instructed her to write." Very little in my own heritage has suggested to me that a wild living creature might come to bring me a direct personal message. And I know too that a complex humor underlies my friend's statement (I do not mean it is a joke). I am suspicious—first of all, in myself—of adopted mysticisms, of glib spirituality, above all of white people's tendency to sniff and taste, uninvited, and in most cases to vampirize American Indian, or African, or Asian, or other "exotic" ways of understanding. I made no claim upon the heron as my personal instructor. But our trajectories crossed at a time when I was ready to begin something new, the nature of which I did not clearly see. And poetry, too, begins in this way: the crossing of trajectories of two (or more) elements that might not otherwise have known simultaneity. When this happens, a piece of the universe is revealed as if for the first time.

II

Voices from the air

On a bleak December night in 1967, I lay awake in a New York City hospital, in pain from a newly operated knee in traction. It was too soon for the next pain-dulling injection; I was in the depression of spirits that follows anesthesia, unable to sleep or to discover in myself any thread that might lead me back to a place I used to recognize as "I." Turning the dial of my bedside radio for music, I came upon a speaking voice, deep, a woman's.

"Who am I?" it asked.

Thou art a box of worme-seede, at best, but a salvatory of greene mummey: what's this flesh? a little cruded milke, phantastical puff-paste: our bodies are weaker than those paper prisons boys use to keep flies in: more contemptible: since ours is to preserve earthwormes: didst thou ever see a Larke in a cage? such is the soule in the body. . . .

Am not I, thy Duchess?

Thou art some great woman, sure, for riot begins to sit on thy fore-head (clad in gray haires) twenty years sooner, then on a merry milkmaydes. Thou sleepst worse, then if a mouse should be forc'd to take up her lodging in a cats eare: a little infant, that breedes it's teeth, should it lie with thee, would crie out, as if thou wert the more unquiet bedfellow.

I am Duchess of Malfy still.

That makes thy sleepes so broken:
Glories (like glow-wormes) afarre off, shine bright
But look'd to neere, have neither heate, nor light.

It does not seem strange to me now—it did not seem so then—that this dialogue, in which the opposition of flesh and spirit is so brutally vaunted, and which ends in the strangling of the Duchess, could, crystallized out of the airwaves on an icy night, solace my consciousness to the point of relief. For that is one property of poetic language: to engage with states that themselves would deprive us of language and reduce us to passive sufferers.

––––––

Thirteen years later, a different night, another radio. Driving over the mountains from upstate New York into Massachusetts, once more twisting a dial, I brought in not music, but a voice, speaking words I had read many times:

The house was quiet and the world was calm.
The reader became the book; and summer night

Was like the conscious being of the book.
The house was quiet and the world was calm.

The words were spoken as if there was no book,
Except that the reader leaned above the page,

Wanted to lean, wanted much most to be
The scholar to whom his book is true, to whom

The summer night is like perfection of thought.
The house was quiet because it had to be.

The quiet was part of the meaning, part of the mind:
The access of perfection to the page.

And the world was calm. The truth in a calm world,
In which there is no other meaning, itself

Is calm, itself is summer and night, itself
Is the reader leaning late and reading there.

Wallace Stevens, reading his poetry on a recording. And for those moments, on a mountain road on a calm night, for two listeners in a world we knew to be in fracture, the words— Stevens at his plainest and most mantralike—rose in that flat, understated, actuarial voice to bind the actual night, the moving car, the two existences, almost as house, reader, meaning, truth, summer, and night are bound in the poem. For a few moments, we could believe in it all.

But what is a poem like this doing in a world where even the semblance of calm is a privilege few can afford? Another scenario: Your sister, stabbed in the early morning hours by her boyfriend ("lover" is not the word, "domestic partner" is not the word), called you at 1:30 A.M. You were back from the evening shift at the nursing home; your children and your mother, who lives with you, were asleep. You had just looked in at the children, turned to the refrigerator to pack their lunches for morning. As you searched for cold cuts, the phone rang; it was Connie—Can you drive me to the emergency? he's taken my car. You have had to do this before, you are enraged though differently at both of them; but she's your sister, and you scrawl a note to your mother, push the food back in the refrigerator, and run for the car. On the highway you twist the radio dial for late-night music. There are words, coming through suddenly clear: *house . . . quiet . . . calm . . . summer night . . . book . . . quiet . . . truth.* What would make your hand pause on the dial, why would these words hold you? What, of the world the poem constructs, would seem anything more than suburban separatism, the tranquil luxury of a complacent man? If you go on listening, if the words can draw you in, it's surely for their music as much as for meaning—music that calls up the state of which the words are speaking. You are drawn in not because this is a description of your world, but because you begin to be reminded of your own desire and need, because the poem is not about integration and fulfillment, but about the desire *(That makes thy sleepes so broken)* for those conditions. You listen, if you do, not simply to the poem, but to a part of you reawakened by the poem, momentarily made aware, a need both emotional and physical, that can for a moment be affirmed there. And, maybe, because the phrase "summer night" calls up more than a time and a season.

––––––––

A poem can't free us from the struggle for existence, but it can uncover desires and appetites buried under the accumulating emergencies of our lives, the fabricated wants and needs we have had urged on us, have accepted as our own. It's not a philosophical or psychological blueprint; it's an instrument for embodied experience. But we seek that experience, or recognize it when it is offered to us, because it reminds us in some way of our need. After that rearousal of desire, the task of acting on that truth, or making love, or meeting other needs, is ours.

 III

"What would we create?"

it's like being sick all the time, I think, coming home from work,
sick in that low-grade continuous way that makes you forget
what it's like to be well. we have never in our lives known
what it is to be well. what if I were coming home, I think,
from doing work that I loved and that was for us all, what
if I looked at the houses and the air and the streets, knowing
they were in accord, not set against us, what if we knew the powers
of this country moved to provide for us and for all people—
how would that be—how would we feel and think
and what would we create?
                                —Karen Brodine, "June 78"

I imagine this message in Congress on the State of the Union:
situation tragic,
        left underground only 75 years of iron
        50 years of cobalt
        but 55 years worth of sulphur and 20 of bauxite
        in the heart what?
            Nothing, zero,
                mine without ore,
                cavern in which nothing prowls,
                of blood not a drop left.
                                —Aimé Césaire, "On the State
                                            of the Union"

Yet this is still my country
The thug on duty says What would you change
      —W. S. Merwin, "Caesar"

October 1990. Time to say that in this tenuous, still unbirthed democracy, my country, low-grade depressiveness is pandemic and is reversing into violence at an accelerating rate. Families massacred by fathers who then turn the gun on themselves; the deliberate wounding and killing of a schoolyardful of Asian-American children in a small California town; mass or serial murders of university students in Berkeley and Florida. Violence against women of every color and class, young dark-skinned men, perceived lesbians and gay men. More and more violence committed by children—against themselves, each other, adults: suicides, gang warfare, patricide and matricide. And the violences, violations obscured because they happen in places and to people that are out of sight, out of mind. Much violence that doesn't make the evening news, committed against people in prison, or prostitutes, or American Indians, or undocumented immigrants, or in nursing homes and state hospitals, or just part of Saturday night after a few drinks. When we try to think about this, if we're not too tired to think, we're driven to name old sores within the body politic: racism, homophobia, addiction, male and female socialization. You are tired of these lists; I am too. Some say there should be gun control; others call for law and order. We blame television, as if television were anything but another symptom. Who owns the means of communication, the cables, the satellites? who pays for the commercials? dictates the content of "entertainment"?

―――――

January 1991: War is bestowed like electroshock on the depressive nation: thousands of volts jolting the system, an artificial galvanizing, one effect of which is loss of memory. War comes at the end of the twentieth century as absolute failure of imagination, scientific and political. That a war can be represented as helping a people to "feel good" about themselves, their country, is a measure of that failure.

————

Lip service, at least, is now paid to the fragile ecology of the physical world, the endangerment of algae and plankton, scavengers and pollinators, trees and deserts, ozone itself, whose continuance is vaguely understood to be a guarantee of our own. But our expressive and passionate life is equally an endangered—because an exploited and manipulated—sector. We have museums of the passions, waxworks, taxidermy, emotional cram notes, emotional theme parks, emotional tourism. Feelings become instant commodities; at the San Francisco airport, early March 1991, you could buy *A Gulf War Feelings Workbook for Children* in a bright spiral plastic binder. An out-of-date commodity, soon, no doubt, supplanted by yellow ribbons, which, like flags, are safe and static emblems; they leave no question open, they keep at bay doubt, confusion, bitterness, fear, and mourning.

————

It's possible that our national despair is by now too intricate and interwoven for disentangling. We have individual despair, loss of jobs, loss of shelter, loss of community, isolation within community, bewildered resignation, daily, routine fear, and self-blame. We have people who do not name what they are going through as despair, would be offended or dismissive at the thought. But we see despair when social arrogance and indifference exist in the same person with the willingness to live at devastating levels of superficiality and self-trivialization. We see despair in the self-hatred that clogs the lives of so many materially comfortable citizens. We hear despair in the loss of vitality in our spoken language: "No problem," we say, "that was a healing experience," we say, "thank you for sharing that," we say. We see despair in the political activist who doggedly goes on and on, turning in the ashes of the same burnt-out rhetoric, the same gestures, all imagination spent. Despair, when not the response to absolute physical and moral defeat, is, like war, the failure of imagination.

It's also the fruit of massive national denial, of historic national realities. The passage from Aimé Césaire is part of a poem written on the 1956 murder and mutilation of a Black youth, Emmett Till, in Mississippi, at the hands of white men, who were acquitted by an all-white jury. Césaire alludes, in the poem, to the "five centuries" of white violence on this soil, which are the fifteen-year-old Till's real age. A violence that shows no sign of abating as this century closes.

Is it possible that 1992 is to become a watershed, the year when the histories of the Americas begin to be told and listened to—not as the conqueror's narrative, but as the multiplicity of the real stories, the true voices, of two continents? Is it possible that citizens of the United States, including the most recent immigrants, might turn and face the conditions on which this country was founded, the assumptions—often in the form of images and stories—never examined, the legacies we carry from 1492, from 1619, to begin with, that shaped the propertied-class revolt we call our revolution, the national slogans that the great immigrant waves of the nineteenth and early twentieth centuries received along with citizenship? Could we, still, in the name of transforming ourselves as a people, make some national recognition of our past, of the lies we have been told and have told our children—could we then, as a people, break through despair?

————

For a long time I've been trying to write poems as if, within this social order, it was enough to voice public pain, speak memory, set words in a countering order, call up images that were in danger of being forgotten or unconceived. In a country where, even among the arts, poetry is the least quantifiable, least commoditized, of our "national products," where the idea of "political poetry" is often met with contempt and hostility, this seemed task enough. But I've also lived with other voices whispering that poetry might be little more than self-indulgence in a society so howling with unmet human needs—an elite art, finally, even when practiced by those among us who are most materially at risk. It's been possible to consider poetry as a marginal activity, of passionate concern to its practitioners perhaps, but as specialized, having as little to do with common emergency, as fly-fishing.

But there's been a missing term. I saw, or thought I saw, that poetry has been held both indispensable and dangerous, one way or another, in every country but my own. The mistake I was making was to assume that poetry really is unwanted, impotent, in the late twentieth-century United States under the system known as "free" enterprise. I was missing the point that precisely *because* of its recognitive and recollective powers, precisely because in this nation, created in the search for wealth, it eludes capitalist marketing, commoditizing, price-fixing, poetry has simply been set aside, depreciated, denied public space.

This is the difference between the United States and Turkey in the late 1930s, when the revolutionary poet Nazim Hikmet was sentenced to twenty-eight years in prison "on the grounds that the military cadets were reading his poems." This is the difference between the United States and Greece, where, both in the 1930s and after World War II, the socialist poet Yannis Ritsos was interned in concentration camps, exiled, placed under house arrest, his writings burned. This is the difference between the United States and the Stalinized Soviet Union, when the poet Osip Mandelstam (among countless other writers, in Russian and Yiddish, murdered in those years) was persecuted and exiled for an anti-Stalin poem, or, in the 1970s, the poet Natalya Gorbanevskaya sent to a "penal mental institution," or, in the 1980s, the poet Irina Ratushinskaya to a prison for "dangerous state criminals." This is the difference between the United States and Chile in 1973, where the junta who came into power the day of Pablo Neruda's death sacked the poet's house and banned his books.

In the United States, depending on who you are, suppression is qualitatively different. So far, it's not a question of creating human martyrs, since the blacklisted writers of the McCarthy era, although artists denied state and federal funding as "obscene" are under government censorship, and efforts to deport the writer Margaret Randall, based on her writings, were vigorously pursued for five years by the INS. Instead, poetry itself—I mean not words on paper only, but the social recognition and integration of poetry and the imaginative powers it releases— poetry itself is "banned" (in the terminology of the South African apartheid laws: forbidden to speak in public, forbidden to be quoted, to meet with more than one or two persons at the same time). Poetry itself, in our national life, is under house arrest, is officially "disappeared." Like our past, our collective memory, it remains an unfathomed, a devalued, resource. The establishment of a national "Poet Laureateship" notwithstanding, poetry has been set apart from the practical arts, from civic meaning. It is irrelevant to mass "entertainment" and the accumulation of wealth—thus, out of sight, out of mind.

So the ecology of spirit, voice, and passion deteriorates, barely masked by gentrification, smog, and manic speech, while in the mirrors of mass-market literature, film, television, journalism, our lives are reflected back to us as terrible and little lives. We see daily that our lives are terrible and little, without continuity, buyable and salable at any moment, mere blips on a screen, that this is the way we live now. Memory marketed as nostalgia; terror reduced to mere suspense, to melodrama.

We become stoical; we hibernate; we numb ourselves with chemicals; we emigrate internally into fictions of past and future; we thirst for guns; but *as a people* we have rarely, if ever, known what it is to tremble with fear, to lament, to rage, to praise, to solemnize, to say *We have done this, to our sorrow;* to say *Enough,* to say *We will,* to say *We will not.* To lay claim to poetry.

———

Newsletters come in the mail: North Carolinians against Racial and Religious Violence; The Jewish Women's Committee to End the Occupation; The Center for Constitutional Rights; Men of All Colors Together; The United Farm Workers; The National Coalition against Domestic Violence; The Center for Democratic Renewal—facts, appeals for money, responses to crisis. I have written checks to these and other such organizations in the past and continue to do so: this is "checkbook activism," money in lieu of or in addition to time, to actual presence. And without checks the fragile movements for justice in this country could not exist beyond the local level. I call them fragile because, although unbanned (though undoubtedly under surveillance), organizations like these are essentially responses to crisis: more than a force for new initiatives, they are a struggle responding to erosion and violence. Yet, in an interstitial time between selective democracy, shot through with intimidation, and the fever break this country must inevitably undergo as it enters the next century, they provide essential information not available in the mainstream press. For this alone they are invaluable, and I pay the subscription price of such newsletters as the price of admission to information that in a working democracy would be furnished me daily by my local paper, by the *New York Times*, the radio and television news.

Over time, some of the facts circulated by the newsletters enter my poetry. As an image here. A voice there. Muriel Rukeyser spoke of two kinds of poetry: the poetry of "unverifiable fact"—that which emerges from dreams, sexuality, subjectivity—and the poetry of "documentary fact"—literally, accounts of strikes, wars, geographical and geological details, actions of actual persons in history, scientific invention.

Like her, I have tried to combine both kinds of poetry in a single poem, not separating dream from history—but I do not find it easy.

———

From a notebook, March 7, 1974:

The poet today must be twice-born. She must have begun as a poet, she must have understood the suffering of the world as political, and have gone through politics, and on the other side of politics she must be reborn again as a poet.

But today I would rephrase this: it's not a matter of dying as a poet into politics, or of having to be reborn as a poet "on the other side of politics" (where is that?), but of something else—finding the relationship.

IV

Dearest Arturo

Dearest Arturo,

I'm writing you tonight because I feel mired in the frustration of addressing that "someone" to whom I must explain why poetry and politics aren't mutually exclusive. Maybe I can begin if I think of myself as talking to you, who would, at the very least, know what I'm trying for, even if I say it badly.

How to plunge in? We're different generations, cultures, genders; we're both gay, both disabled, both writers; and that has helped in our friendship. And so has laughter, good food, and anger. Yet the very poetics you and I grew up with—the music, the undervoices, the languages—are different, whatever we love in common. Sometimes, in our conversations, I've heard myself asking, *Does this make sense to you?* Not wanting to take anything for granted.

"JEWISH ROOTS IN MISSISSIPPI" says the text on the poster hanging over my desk. Husband and wife, Wolfe and Leah Zigransky, of Meridian, with their two little girls, a nine-teenth-century family group, solid and somber as Victorian mahogany. My own immigrant Sephardic forebears in Vicksburg were, in ways your novels have shown me, not unlike your migrant Mexican-Catholic grandparents. Both our peoples trying to prosper in a foreign culture, to be themselves and yet "American." Family central, home both refuge and locus of pain. Your fiction has helped me know your people and, in some ways, my own. And to see how "middle class" has had different meanings for your family and mine.

Arturo—would you agree?—we're unable to write love, as we so much wish to do, without writing politics. You, as a Chicano/Mexican, gay, not a "man" in your culture's terms. I, as a woman, lesbian, Jew, in my sixties. Like you, I've been a problem within a problem: "the Jewish Question," "the Woman Question"—who the questioner? who is supposed to answer? During the Civil War that found my young great-grandparents, David and Pauline Rice, living in Vicksburg, a reporter for a New Orleans news agency was writing: "The Jews of New Orleans and all the South ought to be exterminated . . . they are always to be found at the bottom of every new villainy." But I've not only Jewish, but white gentile roots in Virginia, North Carolina: middle-class people, poor in their terms after the Civil War, ordinary white and Christian supremacists. Whom I thought I could love, growing up, was dictated by politics, known nowadays as "traditional values."

Yet all this brings me to the brink of another problem—how the word "politics" itself is limited and trivialized. Look at the dictionary definition: *the science and art of political government . . . the conducting of or participation in political affairs, often as a profession . . . political methods, tactics, etc. . . . . political opinions, principles or party connections . . . factional scheming within a group: as, office politics.* Interesting how these definitions exclude not only the "private," domestic sphere, the places where we lie down with our unsanctioned lovers, but all activity not carried on within existing parties, previously institutionalized forms—how the whole question of power, of ends, is left invisible in these definitions. So politics is reduced to government, to contests between the empowered, or to petty in-group squabbles.

I feel as if I've been resisting the limits of these definitions for at least half my life. In 1969 I wrote in a journal:

> The moment when a feeling enters the body—
> is political. This touch is political.

> By which I mean, that *politics* is the effort to find ways of humanely dealing with each other—as groups or as individuals—politics being simply process, the breaking down of barriers of oppression, tradition, culture, ignorance, fear, self-protectiveness.

But, Arturo, you know that those words, that definition (however incomplete), didn't come simply out of one woman's efforts to live and be human, be sexual, in a woman's body. They came as much from a spirit of the times—the late 1960s—that I absorbed through teaching and activism in an institution where the question of white Western supremacism was already being talked about, where students were occupying buildings and teachers either fled the campus or were in constant meetings and teaching "liberation" classes; in a city where parents were demanding community control of the schools; through a certain

kind of openness and searching for transformed relationships in
the New Left, which soon led to thousands of women asking
"the Woman Question" in women's voices; and from reading
Malcolm X, Chekhov's *Sakhalin Journals,* Barbara Deming's
Prison Notes, Frantz Fanon, James Baldwin, and the writings of
my students. I could feel around me—in the city, in the country
at large—the "spontaneity of the masses" (later I would find the
words in Rosa Luxemburg), and this was powerfully akin to the
experience of writing poetry. Politics as expression of the impulse to create, an expanded sense of what's "humanly possible"—this, in the late 1960s and the early women's movement,
was what we tasted, not just the necessities of reactive organizing
and fighting back.

I have never forgotten that taste. In writing a poem, beginning perhaps with a painful dream, an image snatched from riding a bus, a phrase overheard in a bar, this scrap of private vision
suddenly connected—and still connects—with a life greater than
my own, an existence not merely personal, words coming together to reveal what was unknown to me until I wrote them.

———

And you, of course, beginning as we all must with autobiography, with childhood, but out of that—the material of one
life—weaving the fictions of many lives, truest when most imagined. Trying to create a literature not of immigrants, but of
migrants, of the people who were here in this landscape before
the first Europeans crossed the ocean. Writing in English of a
bilingual people whose first language is itself a political question.
Trying to render in fiction, for your own people and for those
who barely know they exist, what "migrant" means on this
continent, how, as you've said, it's a pervasive condition of
Mexicans in this country, citizens or not. A psychological condi-

tion that cannot help but be political. Even when you've written about love in the family, it's with the sense of how men and religion can distort women's lives, how traditional masculinity distorts men, how heterosexuals do violence to gays, how the Chicano family itself, however respectable petty bourgeois, is part of a suspect and marginal group on a literal and cultural borderline. Slowly I'm coming to see what you're up against, the newness of the work you're trying to do. (And, my dear one, I know the brevity of time ticking as you work.) You've talked of feeling you're still learning how to do it, *how best to weave political and historical issues into my narratives so that they do not overwhelm the characters unless I want them to do so. Latin American writers have a gift for being able to incorporate life and death political concerns into their fictions artfully, and I study them with envy and admiration.* But you're not a Latin American, whatever the affinities; you are "on the bridge, at the border," here in this California that is really a lost piece of Mexico, here in this country, itself so lost regarding its art, its soul, its history.

———

You've said, *The great justification for the act of reading and writing fiction is that through it we can be disciplined and seduced into imagining other people's lives with understanding and compassion, even if we do not "identify" with them.* Yes. And, in the act of writing, to feel our own "questions" meeting the world's "questions," to recognize how we are in the world and the world is in us—

———

When I began this letter, Arturo, you were still living, though life was becoming a terrible effort. Well, our conversation goes on, as we promised each other. Tenderly and angrily and with laughter. "There is no death, only dying," you said in your note about one of my poems. And I still need to ask: *Does this make sense to you?*

—Adrienne

V

"Those two shelves, down there"

The lack of the means to distribute is another form of censorship.
—Nadine Gordimer

I've been walking in a largely peach-colored, air-conditioned shopping mall. It's in California, but it could be in Champaign-Urbana, Illinois, or Nashua, New Hampshire, or High Point, North Carolina. Outside in the heat (shopping malls are private property, not public space) one or two people are passing out leaflets on a bill for the protection of the environment, gathering signatures. Inside, in a space the size of a small village, are clothing-chain outlets, fast-food parlors, stores selling computers and camcorders, stuffed animals, papier-mâché cactuses and cow skulls, mugs inscribed with names and mottoes, athletic shoes, real and plastic houseplants, paper plates, cups, napkins for parties (now in the red, white, and blue of the national holiday just past, soon to turn to autumn-leaf motifs, the orange-and-black of Halloween, ancient syncretic carnival now ratified by commerce). I enter this mall rarely, but this time I am on a search. A dull sourness implodes in me when I'm inside; I can slide toward depression or anger, depending on the mind I bring to it. Whatever search you come on must soon dissipate into mental cacophony or restless anomie.

But why? After all, it's a scene—expansive, brightly lit—of human activity, like any street market or city square, with a shoe-repair shop, a bakery, a shop for manicures and facials, even a central fountain from which spokes of wide, banner-hung corridors extend; and around this fountain there are slatted benches where old people sit, where mothers meet with their prams and sodas, though their conversation seems less animated than that on the city park benches I've known. All human enough, isn't it? It serves as a combination of public park and market, surely. But your eyes find it difficult to concentrate on the people in their many colors, shapes, body languages: the sheer overload of objects—highly though flatly colored, or in highly colored packaging—pulls at, distracts, disorients the eye, stifles particularity. The shops are stocked, to the inch, mostly with repetitions of identical merchandise, a plethora of tiny choice-variants on a single model; nothing here is eccentric, nothing bears the imprint of an individual maker. An "antiques" shop displays factory replications of Americana—footstools, end tables, samplers in frames; the bakery turns out row upon row of identical muffins; the ethnic food concessions are chain-tailored. And, of course, I have been using the wrong word throughout this paragraph: these are not shops, they are "franchises."

The terms "commodity" and "mass production" acquire here a queasy-making materiality. Probably a majority of these items—running shoes, T-shirts, tape recorders, three-dimensional cartoon animals, beach towels, plastic sandals, straw and wicker baskets—were manufactured by the hands of women, men, children in the Third World; here they are fingered, priced, rejected, or bought predominantly by women; when the

season changes and the sales are over, are they then shipped to
warehouses in Los Angeles and Canal Street to be wholesaled
back into the Third World?

Here is a chain bookstore, stacked novels lettered in high-
relief luminescence, computer manuals, intimacy manuals, parenting manuals, investment-management manuals, grief-man-
agement   manuals,   college-entrance   manuals,   meditation
manuals, manuals on living with cancer, on channeling, on how
to save the earth. I walk past these gleaming romances, these
secular bibles, and ask the young clerk at the register where the
poetry is. He walks me toward the back of the store: "Those two
shelves, down there." Poetry is underneath, and intermixed
with, the books on rock music, movies, and theater—not a bad
thing, I think, but poetry is awfully low "down there." What I
find down there is: one *1990 Poets' Market,* a publication I didn't
know existed; *One Hundred and One Famous Poems* in a leather-
like binding; the AIDS anthology *Poets for Life;* one copy of
Wallace Stevens's *Collected Poems* in hardcover; a *Selected Poems*
by Robert Bly; *Best Loved Poems of the American People;* a paperback edition of *Final Harvest,* selected poems of Emily Dickinson; Oscar Williams's *Immortal Poems of the English Language;*
James Kavanaugh's *There Are Men Too Gentle to Live among
Wolves;* and several volumes of plays by Shakespeare. Alice
Walker's *In Love and Trouble* (a volume of short stories) is, mis-
shelved, the only book by a person of color or by a living
woman.

Except. Almost the entire bottom shelf is ranged with hardcover and paperback titles by a single female author (or is she a
cottage industry?): *Don't Be Afraid to Love, Don't Ever Give Up
Your Dreams, Marriage Is a Promise of Love, Life Can Be Hard
Sometimes, For a Special Teenager.* There are at least twenty titles;
they seem to cover life crises or, at any rate, life transitions. The
books are uniformly designed and illustrated in a style conform-

ing to everything else in the mall. The verses, each occupying a single page, have short lines, make short declarative statements. There is nothing intrinsically wrong with declarative statements in poetry; but in such quantity the effect is numbing.

But why aren't these books out front like the greeting cards or with the manuals on intimacy, parenting, sex, and grief? Why are they separated from the consumer guides to depression and success? Is it because those come with the stamp of the psychological or technical professional (the author's Ph.D. or M.S.W. displayed on the jacket), implying an authority that "poetry" can't claim? And what are they searching for, who go all the way back and stoop, down there, looking for something labeled "poetry?"

I'm on a search for poetry in the mall. This is not sociology, but the pursuit of an intuition about mass marketing, the so-called free market, and how suppression can take many forms—from outright banning and burning of books, to questions of who owns the presses, to patterns of distribution and availability.

VI

As if your life
depended on it

You must write, and read, as if your life depended on it. That is not generally taught in school. At most, *as if your livelihood depended on it:* the next step, the next job, grant, scholarship, professional advancement, fame; no questions asked as to further meanings. And, let's face it, the lesson of the schools for a vast number of children—hence, of readers—is *This is not for you.*

To read as if your life depended on it would mean to let into your reading your beliefs, the swirl of your dreamlife, the physical sensations of your ordinary carnal life; and, simultaneously, to allow what you're reading to pierce the routines, safe and impermeable, in which ordinary carnal life is tracked, charted, channeled. Then, what of the right answers, the so-called multiple-choice examination sheet with the number 2 pencil to mark one choice and one choice only?

To write as if your life depended on it: to write across the chalkboard, putting up there in public words you have dredged, sieved up from dreams, from behind screen memories, out of silence—words you have dreaded and needed in order to know you exist. No, it's too much; you could be laughed out of school, set upon in the schoolyard, they would wait for you after school, they could expel you. The politics of the schoolyard, the power of the gang.

Or, they could ignore you.

To read as if your life depended on it—but what writing can be believed? Isn't all language just manipulation? Maybe the poet has a hidden program—to recruit you to a cause, send you into the streets, to destabilize, through the sensual powers of language, your tested and tried priorities? Rather than succumb, you can learn to inspect the poem at arm's length, through a long and protective viewing tube, as an interesting object, an example of this style or that period. You can take refuge in the idea of "irony." Or you can demand that artists demonstrate loyalty to that or this moral or political or religious or sexual norm, on pain of having books burned, banned, on pain of censorship or prison, on pain of lost public funding.

Or, you can say: "I don't understand poetry."

 VII

The space for poetry

PABLO CHILE TE RECUERDA
PABLO IN ESTOS DIAS NOS HACES FALTA
    PORQUE
    TE NOS   LUIS Y SONIA 1985
    FUISTE   VENCE
                                        REMOS
    PABLO VIVE Y VIVIRA!   F PMR

After the death of Pablo Neruda, in a time of brutal political
repression in Chile, during which the poet's house was trashed
and sealed up by the military regime, all kinds of people came
surreptitiously to write or scratch, graffiti on the boards of the
fence: messages to the poet, words of resistance, brief phrases,

names. Neruda died on the day that the military junta took power. Even more than in his life, he became a symbol of Chilean resistance. Both in his writings of and for and to his country, and in his countrypeople's response to him, there was a dialogue reaching beyond death. He was internationally famous, of course; of the middle class; a male. It was not the poetry of a dark-skinned mestizo—still less, a mestiza—that so commanded love and respect. Yet he could have betrayed, and did not; could have escaped into the international literary elite, and did not. The fence below his locked and off-limits house became a place for people to continue voicing their hopes and angers, a collective page greater even than the poet's books, a page made possible because of his books, because of the hand that had once crawled over line after line, writing the poems.

What kind of dialogue can exist between poets who are citizens of the United States and their countrypeople? What points of focus or connection exist? What could precipitate such a dialogue?

The answers—good as far as they go—are: Poetry needs to be better taught in the schools. There should be excellent, "exciting" programs about poetry on television, radio. There should be poetry videos, like music videos, to bring poems to a mass audience.

People speak like this about sex education or drug education: How to make their messages popular or at least attention-riveting? How compete with the structures of excitement offered by the passive media—the manic hecticity of human experience represented to us by television and commercial film—the screeching of brakes, the exploding of guns, the strobe-lit blood splashing white limousines of the rich and famous, organ transplants, babies switched at birth, lottery winner dies of stress, paranoid schizophrenic kills children in schoolyard, self and entire family, sixteen women students, girl who refused to date

him, surrogate mother wants visitation, terror on campus, criminal court as theater, everything wrenched from everything else,
from history, from context, the meaninglessness of lives reflected
in a fun-house mirror, a communications system designed to
separate, fragment, disinform mass audiences.

For a mass audience in the United States is not an audience for
a collectively generated idea, welded together by the power of
that idea and by common debates about it. Mass audiences are
created by promotion, by the marketing of excitements that take
the place of ideas, of real collective debate, vision, or catharsis;
excitements that come and go, flash on and off, so fast that they
serve only to isolate us in the littleness of our own lives—we
become incoherent to one another.

So when I speak of the lack of public space for poetry, I don't
mean a mass audience of the kind that exists for commercial
films, top-forty music, MTV, "best-selling" books, network television. What takes up public space is determined by industries
dedicated to mass marketing, by the owners of the means of
communication. Poetry remains an art that can be, and continues to be, produced cheaply, whose material requirements are
modest. On most evenings around the United States, there must
be several thousand poetry readings—in coffeehouses, in gal-
leries, in small basement performance spaces, on campuses, in
synagogues and churches, at outdoor festivals and demonstrations, in public libraries, prisons, and community centers, in
bookstores, at conferences, in theaters, bars, living rooms, barns;
in the amphitheater of an urban teaching hospital. A lectern may
be a collapsible music stand or a pulpit wired for sound; a po-
dium may be the flatbed of a truck or a proscenium stage. The
poet may be reading from pages in a notebook, from a hand-
printed chapbook, from a typescript, from a published volume.
She may be carrying a suitcase full of her books to sell; he may
bring along a mandolin or drum. Or they may be a roster of

poets reading for five minutes apiece (usually going overtime) for the benefit of a magazine, for earthquake relief, for peace, for a battered-women's shelter, for the court case of a writer facing deportation under the McCarran-Walter Act.

———

A late April evening in 1991. At the Nuyorican Poets Café in New York City a play by a Puerto Rican playwright is ending, and the first lesbian and gay poetry reading ever held in this space is about to begin. Down on a scarred and garbage-strewn block on Avenue B, an almost unmarked entrance opens into a narrow space, bar to the right, kitchen audible but not visible, brick walls stretching upward, assorted tables and chairs, and a very small stage, more platform than stage. Coming across the Lower East Side, a fragment from Hart Crane's *The Bridge* has been pursuing me:

> And Rip forgot the office hours,
> and he forgot the pay;
> Van Winkle sweeps a tenement
> way down on Avenue A,— . . .
>
> . . .
>
> And Rip was slowly made aware
> that he, Van Winkle, was not here
> nor there. He woke and swore he'd seen Broadway
> a Catskill daisy chain in May—

The audience for the play, about two homeless men, and the audience for the reading intersect, merge, some leaving, some arriving; but there is an extension of one audience into the other.

The café, founded in 1974 by the writer Miguel Algarín, is in its second Lower East Side location. At first a meeting and performance space for New York Puerto Rican artists, it's become a center for multicultural urban poetry and theater, seeming the more vibrant in a city grown more desolate, singing back to the city furious, satiric, and livid visions from an unextinguished underground soul. This reading, organized by Susan Sherman, poet and editor of the cultural-political feminist journal *I-KON*, includes Korean-born, white-adopted Mi Ok Bruining, Black Latino Bruce L. Burgos, African-Americans Cheryl Clarke, Dorothy Randall Gray, and Donald Woods; the white poets also a class and ethnic brew: Italian-American Rachel Guido de Vries, Catholic Charles Frederick, Portuguese-American David Trinidad, Jewish-Americans Margaret Randall and Susan Sherman. Listening to the poets, you could recognize that some had been working the craft longer, some had not yet stretched themselves to the fullest, some were old hands at reading to an audience, some just beginning. But the mix of the evening created by these different and sometimes conflicting voices was heady, and so was the mix of the audience—in age, sexuality, color—an audience intense in its listening in spite of bangings and clashings from the kitchen area or interference from police walkie-talkies outside.

What the poets had in common, above and beyond poetry itself, or sexuality itself, was each one's stance of claiming a foothold, a platform, a voice among all the voices purporting to speak or sing of North American existence. For none of them could such a foothold be taken for granted; but if certain poetics had excluded them, they were bent on finding others to reveal what it is to be part of the city, part of this republic, as darkskinned, female, half-assimilated Jew, Sicilian, erotically at risk, legally at risk, living in the face of gay bashing, racism, AIDS. There was poetry of mourning, accusation, high erotic comedy, religious heresy, wild fantasy, some banality (almost always mitigated somehow by the poet's own reading style), and several poems of shattering originality, sounding like nothing but themselves. Wide as the social, political, aesthetic differences were among the poets and among us, their hearers, a community arose in that undertaking; under harsh lights, with a sometimes wayward mike, poetry lived, pulling us toward each other.

And perhaps this is the hope: that poetry can keep its mechanical needs simple, its head clear of the fumes of how "success" is concocted in the capitals of promotion, marketing, consumerism, and in particular of the competition—taught in the schools, abetted at home—that pushes the "star" at the expense of the culture as a whole, that makes people want stardom rather than participation, association, exchange, and improvisation with others. Perhaps this is the hope: that poetry, by its nature, will never become leashed to profit, marketing, consumerism.

VIII

How does a poet put
bread on the table?

But how does a poet put bread on the table? Rarely, if ever, by poetry alone. Of the four lesbian poets at the Nuyorican Poets Café about whose lives I know something, one directs an underfunded community arts project, two are untenured college teachers, one an assistant dean of students at a state university. Of other poets I know, most teach, often part time, without security but year round; two are on disability; one does clerical work; one cleans houses; one is a paid organizer; one has a paid editing job. Whatever odd money comes in erratically from readings and workshops, grants, permissions fees, royalties, prizes can be very odd money indeed, never to be counted on and almost always small: checks have to be chased down, grants become fewer and more competitive in a worsening political and eco-

nomic climate. Most poets who teach at universities are untenured, without pension plans or group health insurance, or are
employed at public and community colleges with heavy teaching loads and low salaries. Many give unpaid readings and workshops as part of their political "tithe."

Inherited wealth accounts for the careers of some poets: to
inherit wealth is to inherit time. Most of the poets I know,
hearing of a sum of money, translate it not into possessions, but
into time—that precious immaterial necessity of our lives. It's
true that a poem can be attempted in brief interstitial moments,
pulled out of the pocket and worked on while waiting for a bus
or riding a train or while children nap or while waiting for a new
batch of clerical work or blood samples to come in. But only
certain kinds of poems are amenable to these conditions. Sometimes the very knowledge of coming interruption dampens the
flicker. And there is a difference between the ordinary "free"
moments stolen from exhausting family strains, from alienating
labor, from thought chained by material anxiety, and those other
moments that sometimes arrive in a life being lived at its height
though under extreme tension: perhaps we are waiting to initi-
ate some act we believe will catalyze change but whose outcome
is uncertain; perhaps we are facing personal or communal crisis
in which everything unimportant seems to fall away and we are
left with our naked lives, the brevity of life itself, and words. At
such times we may experience a speeding-up of our imaginative
powers, images and voices rush together in a kind of inevitabil-
ity, what was externally fragmented is internally reorganized,
and the hand can barely keep pace.

But such moments presuppose other times: when we could
simply stare into the wood grain of a door, or the trace of bub-
bles in a glass of water as long as we wanted to, *almost* secure in
the knowledge that there would be no interruption—times of
slowness, of purposelessness.

Often such time feels like a luxury, guiltily seized when it can be had, fearfully taken because it does not seem like work, this abeyance, but like "wasting time" in a society where personal importance—even job security—can hinge on acting busy, where the phrase "keeping busy" is a common idiom, where there is, for activists, so much to be done.

Most, if not all, of the names we know in North American poetry are the names of people who have had some access to freedom in time—that privilege of some which is actually a necessity for all. The struggle to limit the working day is a sacred struggle for the worker's freedom in time. To feel herself or himself, for a few hours or a weekend, as a free being with choices—to plant vegetables and later sit on the porch with a cold beer, to write poetry or build a fence or fish or play cards, to walk without a purpose, to make love in the daytime. To sleep late. Ordinary human pleasures, the self's re-creation. Yet every working generation has to reclaim that freedom in time, and many are brutally thwarted in the effort. Capitalism is based on the abridgment of that freedom.

Poets in the United States have either had some kind of private means, or help from people with private means, have held full-time, consuming jobs, or have chosen to work in low-paying, part-time sectors of the economy, saving their creative energies for poetry, keeping their material wants simple. Interstitial living, where the art itself is not expected to bring in much money, where the artist may move from a clerical job to part-time, temporary teaching to subsistence living on the land to waitressing or doing construction or translating, typesetting, or ghostwriting. In the 1990s this kind of interstitial living is more difficult, risky, and wearing than it has ever been, and this is a loss to all the arts—as much as the shrinkage of arts funding, the censorship-by-clique, the censorship by the Right, the censorship by distribution.

 IX

The muralist

I wish you would write a poem . . . addressed to those who, in
consequence of the complete failure of the French Revolution, have
thrown up all hopes of the amelioration of mankind, and are sinking into
an almost epicurean selfishness, disguising the same under the soft titles of
domestic attachment and contempt for visionary philosophes.
—Samuel Taylor Coleridge
to William Wordsworth (1799)

These were things which I myself saw in my childhood. If, however, I
were to relate what I heard of in those years, it would be a much more
gruesome narrative: stories of men and women torn from their families
and their villages, and sold, or lost in gambling, or exchanged for a couple
of hunting dogs, and then transported to some remote part of Russia for
the sake of creating a new estate; of children taken from their parents and
sold to cruel or dissolute masters; of flogging "in the stables" which
occurred every day with unheard-of cruelty; of a girl who found her only
salvation in drowning herself; of an old man who had grown gray-haired
in his master's service, and at last hanged himself under his master's
window; . . . revolts by serfs . . . suppressed by Nicholas I's generals by
flogging to death each tenth or fifth man taken out of the ranks, and by
laying waste the village, whose inhabitants, after a military execution,
went begging for bread in the neighboring provinces. As to the poverty
which I saw during our journeys in certain villages, especially in those

which belonged to the imperial family, no words would be adequate to describe the misery to readers who have not seen it.

To become free was the constant dream of the serfs.

—Peter Kropotkin, *Memoirs of a Revolutionist* (1899)

Tonight I spoke with my friend the muralist, who, unlike me, makes her art collectively, who says of the work she's currently doing: "We have all the political elements there and agreed-on—I'm still struggling to find a way to make it beautiful." She doesn't mean simply harmonious or attractive, though she makes art that people love to look at as they go through their neighborhoods, art they can recognize their lives in, the difficulty and the beauty. She means that the work shall not be merely logical, of the presently known, but that it shall radiate another dimension, beyond "all the political elements . . . agreed-on."

I tell her, I've been reading Trotsky on revolutionary art. I'll send you some passages.

Right now I see my friend and myself walking out on different, parallel, wooden piers into darkness, star-mixed fog above our heads, in the loneliness and community of our questions. She, whose monumental works, planned out and executed with many others, are visible on walls, inside buildings, from San Francisco to Managua to East Jerusalem and the occupied territories. I, whose words come into permanence in slow solitude, whose poems begin on scraps of paper but whose images, like hers, are mined from dreams, snatches of conversation, street music, headlines, history, love, collective action.

Here are some of the passages from Trotsky I sent her:

The struggle for revolutionary ideas in art must begin once again with the struggle for artistic truth, not in terms of any single

school, but in terms of *the immutable faith of the artist in his* [*sic*] *own inner self.* Without this there is no art. "You shall not lie!"—that is the formula of salvation.

From the point of view of an objective historical process, art is always a social servant and historically utilitarian. It finds the necessary rhythm of words for dark and murky moods, it brings thought and feeling closer or contrasts them with each other, it enriches the spiritual experience of the individual and the community, it refines feeling, makes it more flexible, more responsive, it enlarges the volume of thought in advance and not through the personal method of accumulation of experience, it educates the individual, the social group, the class and the nation. And it does this quite independently of whether it appears in a given case under the flag of a "pure" or of a frankly tendentious art.

The effort to set art free from life, to declare it a craft sufficient unto itself, devitalizes and kills art.

One cannot approach art as one can politics, not because artistic creation is a religious rite or something mystical . . . but because it has its own laws of development, and above all because in artistic creation an enormous role is played by subconscious processes— slower, more idle and less subjected to management and guidance, just because they are subconscious.

Amid all the public cheering over the "death of socialism" I wanted to go back to the revolutionary thinkers of the nineteenth and early twentieth centuries, to refresh my mind as to what they had envisioned, however the visions were betrayed, from within and from without, and whatever crimes had been committed in socialism's name. In particular I wanted to find out how those men and women thought about art and the freedom of art, how they believed it was interwoven with the creation of new relationships between man and man, woman and man, woman and woman. I was suspicious of the cartoons of "socialist realism" floating in my head. The figures of Ding Ling, of Mandelstam, exiled and doing forced labor for their words—were these truly the harvest of socialism? I did not want the current times, with their images of falling walls and slogans about a "new world order," to wash out for me all continuity with revolutions of the past and the hopes they had touched in so many nerves. I knew that for Marx himself, Communism had never meant less than the means for freeing human creativity in all persons to the fullest: he believed that the release of that very creativity would ensure that no revolution turned in on itself, stagnated, and froze; that in "revolution in permanence," "new passions and new forces" would repeatedly arise as the creative currents of each and all found voice. You could say that the passion for human creativity forced Marx into the study of how Capital, by its own internal laws, had suppressed the flow of human activity and passions.

I knew, yet needed to remind myself, that the old theorists of socialism—and the artists of responsiveness and responsibility— had a far more complex sense of the interplay between the artist and society than have either the arts administrators of capitalism or the Central Committees of Moscow or Beijing.

> **It is one thing to understand something and express it logically, and quite another to assimilate it organically, reconstructing the whole system of one's feelings, and to find a new kind of artistic expression for this new entity.**

You could derive from Trotsky's assertion, that an "engaged" or "committed" art, an art critical of society, the kind of art usually labeled "political" in the United States, is bad (when it is bad) not because it is engaged, but because *it is not engaged enough:* when it tries to express what has been logically understood but not yet organically assimilated.

————

There is a kind of political poetry that does not surprise the poet, in which the poet foresees and controls the poem's development according to an ideology of theme and even style—the poem as propaganda for revolt, for a specific revolutionary program, for a new kind of consciousness. Bertolt Brecht, Rubén Darío, Pablo Neruda all wrote such poems, and such poems can be very good indeed: an example would be Thomas McGrath's "Ordonnance":

> During a war the poets turn to war
> In praise of the merit of the death of the ball-turret gunner.
> It is well arranged: each in his best manner
> One bleeds, one blots—as they say, it has happened before.
>
> After a war, who has news for the poet?
> If sunrise is Easter, noon is his winey tree.
> Evening arrives like a postcard from his true country.
> And the seasons shine and sing. Each has its note
>
> In the song of the man in his room in his house remembering
> The ancient airs. It is good. But is it good
> That he should rise once to his song on the fumes of blood
> As a ghost to his meat? Should rise so, once, in anger
>
> And then no more? Now the footsteps ring on the stone—
> The Lost Man of the century is coming home from his work.

"They are fighting, fighting"—Oh, yes. But somewhere else.
In the dark.
The poet reads by firelight as the nations burn.

Poets write against war, then in "peacetime" turn to their personal themes and melodies; the struggle of the working man
(and, in this poem too, the working woman) goes on unsung,
invisible, although this too is a war burning the nations. The
poem is hortatory, addressed to poets: *What is missing from your
poems?* (The poet who actually wrote the poem entitled "The
Death of the Ball-Turret Gunner" was Randall Jarrell, whose
poems about bomber pilots in World War II are powerful evo-
cations of the meaninglessness of war. Jarrell himself both served
in the war and wrote about it.) But it also reaches beyond poets
to the readers who do not grasp what is missing, who accept
conventional definitions of "war" and "peace." It could be read
as a socialist manifesto about the proper themes for poetry. But it
is much more than this thanks to McGrath's changes of tone, the
drama of contrasts he creates, the long run-on lines of the third
stanza, which pour over into the fourth, the different voices
arguing within the poem.

My friend the muralist writes back to me: *I have some thoughts
on the subject of beauty unlocking hate and fear.*

Some days, as I work on this book, I hear voices from within
that tell me this work is not real activism, political though it may
be. On other days, when I also go to a meeting, or write and mail
out a memo responding to other memos from a collective, or
edit another woman's article on coalition building for a grass-
roots journal, or drive to a nearby city to read in a political

benefit, or write to a foundation in support of a grass-roots project, I don't hear such voices. When I'm writing poetry, and often when reading it, the voices fade away as the old integrative powers rush together: it's as if the process of poetry itself temporarily releases me into that realm of human power which Marx said is its own end. By "human power," he meant the opposite of possessive, exploitative power: the power to engender, to create, to bring forth fuller life. Chances and privileges of birth early gave me a foothold in that realm, so that, making poems, even as a child, I came to experience flashes of that kind of power. And finally to thirst for it everywhere.

Working with others to plan a demonstration, draft and distribute a flier, write a collective pamphlet, set up a conference, is a different mode of creation, and its purposes—to dispense information, to dispel disinformation, to create a collective understanding of the meaning of events and facts—require a different mode of language. Yet the same thirst lies underneath, and the same need for a taproot into the imagination. Politics *is* imagination or it is a treadmill—disintegrative, stifling, finally brutalizing—or ineffectual.

———

There is a happiness in creation that is not without its own pain and struggle, a sensation that feels sometimes buoyant and sometimes earthbound, sometimes like lighting fires in snow, sometimes like untying knots in which you have been bound. New questions, new problems—of shape, of strategy, of materials, and, yes, of purpose—unfold even as you unlock present difficulties. There is a happiness in finding *what will work* simultaneously with the discovery of *what it works for,* which has often been reduced to separate issues of "form" and "content." Denise Levertov describes how in organic poetry the form sense or "traffic sense," . . . is ever present along with . . . fidelity to the revelations of meditation. The form sense is a sort of Stanislavsky of the imagination: putting a chair two feet downstage there, thickening a knot of bystanders upstage left, getting this actor to raise his voice a little and that actress to enter more slowly; all in the interest of the total form he intuits. Or it is a sort of helicopter scout flying over the field of the poem, taking aerial photos and reporting on the state of the forest and its creatures—or over the sea to watch for the schools of herring and direct the fishing fleet toward them.

This partnership of unconscious and conscious work can also happen in collectivity. And the happiness I'm speaking of, which knows itself as part of a continually unfolding process, which can never be complacent, is what I imagine true revolution would look like: subjectivity and objectivity, vision and technology, together inventing conditions for the spontaneous imaginative life of all of us.

———

The great sculptor and printmaker Elizabeth Catlett, speaking from the authority of her artistic development:

We work alone but we also work with and for others, and it is expressed by two words: one is "solitarity," in which we create out of what is in us, from our innermost feelings, ideas, emotions, knowledge—all of this combined in other elements also; we also create from "solidarity," which is what we have in our innermost selves that comes from what we have gotten from our solidarity with other people. I always feel that collective thought is better than individual thought. There's the give-and-take and coming together and a separating that are very important in developing ideas.

Among other things, I learned that my sculpture and my prints had to be based on the needs of people. These needs determine what I do. Some artists say they express themselves: they just reflect their environment. We all live in a given moment in history and what we do reflects what level we are on in that moment. You must, as an artist, consciously determine where your own level is.

Consciously [*to*] *determine where your own level is.* By "level" I believe Catlett means at least two things: first, the artist's positioning in society—Is the sculptor an African-American woman who had access to educational privileges along with the assaults of racism? Is the poet a white male heir to one of the great early twentieth-century American fortunes? Where did the poet find her first poem? Did a classically grounded Catholic schooling mitigate his poverty? When did the child ever meet a living artist or poet? Was the art of his people's tradition disparaged or acclaimed? Did she work as a nude model to pay for painting lessons? Did his mother wash other people's floors? And what effect has any of these, or other, contingencies on the practice of eye, ear, perception that is the basis for making art? What can be seen from any of these levels? What is hidden? Does the artist, the poet, know to ask such a question?

But also *your own level* of responsiveness, of responsibility, to what lies around you. To say that a poet is responsive, responsible—what can that mean? To me it means that she or he is free to become artistically most complex, serious, and integrated when most aware of the great questions of her, of his, own time. When the mind of the maker is stretched to the fullest by the demands of the time—not fads, vogues, cliques, chic, propaganda, but the deep messages of crisis, hope, despair, vision, the anonymous voices, that pulse through a human community as signs of imbalance, sickness, regeneration pulse through a human body.

When Catlett says *You must, as an artist, consciously determine where your own level is,* I believe she is speaking on behalf of art. Just as if she said *You must, as a sculptor, consciously become aware of the properties and difficulties of many kinds of wood, of metals, kinds of stone, clay.* You must become responsive, responsible, to the materials.

The painter and poet Michele Gibbs expands still further on Catlett's "levels":

Choosing to be an artist (ie a distiller and creator rather than an imitator, copyist, critic, or technician) is, itself, a level. Then arise questions of:

1) what are you calling attention to?
2) what energy/action does your creation feed?
3) what reach will your creations (voice/images) have; & where are you directing their force?
4) what counts for connection?

The more all-encompassing one's consciousness, needless to say, the greater the burden of intentionality and the more company one seeks. The issue of *connection,* ie, verifying the authenticity of one's vision by the responses and parallel/complementary creation of others, implies the *centrality* of *communality* in the artistic process.

This process of building community, of course, begins from the self outward . . . but culminates in new possibilities for the personality only through intimate bonding (immersion) in the great movements of people in one's time *and* a commitment to respond to the daily needs of those human beings closest to us (ie, not just "the people," but "my sister Edna's son Che,") also caught in those movements.

With specific reference to poetry . . . it seems to me that the most *integrative* social power contained in words is liberated in performance. . . . For me, it is the *activist* & spoken element which follows on the contemplative act of composition which is most capable of vitalizing folk.

Do I envy my friend the muralist? On some days, yes: I imagine she, at least, must feel no division between her art and action. On others, I realize that the social fragmentation of poetry from life has itself been one of the materials that demanded evolution in my poetic methods, continually pushed at me to devise language and images that could refute the falsely framed choices: ivory tower or barricades, intuition or documentary fact, the search for beauty or the search for justice. (Of course a change in poetic methods means other kinds of change as well.)

When I can pull it together, I work in solitude surrounded by community, solitude in dialogue with community, solitude that alternates with collective work. The poetry and the actions of friends and strangers pass through the membranes of that solitude. This kind of worklife means vigilance, for the old definitions of "inner" and "outer" still lurk in me and I still feel the pull of false choices wrenching me sometimes this way, sometimes that. But if we hope to mend the fragmentation of poetry from life, and for the sake of poetry itself, it's not enough to lie awake, in Lillian Smith's words, listening only to the sound of our own heartbeat in the dark.

X

The hermit's scream

He said I had this that I could love,
As one loves visible and responsive peace,
As one loves one's own being,
As one loves that which is the end
And must be loved, as one loves that
Of which one is a part as in a unity,
A unity that is the life one loves,
So that one lives all the lives that comprise it
As the life of the fatal unity of war.
                          —Wallace Stevens, "Yellow Afternoon"

I am a failure then, as the kind of revolutionary Anne-Marion and her
acquaintances were. (Though in fact she had heard of nothing
revolutionary this group had done, since she left them ten summers ago.
Anne-Marion, she knew, had become a well-known poet whose poems
were about her two children, and the quality of the light that fell across a
lake she owned.)
                          —Alice Walker, *Meridian*

I've been haunted by a poem, apparently as simple as a ballad and
with a ballad's appeal of timelessness. It's by Elizabeth Bishop, a
white North American with middle-class roots. Orphaned and

deracinated as a child, she grew up as a lesbian, a traveler-exile, living a significant part of her life in Brazil. She's not thought of as a political poet by most people who admire her; she's most often praised as a poet of minute observation and description. The poem is called "Chemin de Fer":

> Alone on the railroad track
>   I walked with pounding heart.
> The ties were too close together
>   or maybe too far apart.
>
> The scenery was impoverished:
>   scrub-pine and oak; beyond
> its mingled gray-green foliage
>   I saw the little pond
>
> where the dirty hermit lives,
>   lie like an old tear
> holding onto its injuries
>   lucidly year after year.
>
> The hermit shot off his shot-gun
>   and the tree by his cabin shook.
> Over the pond went a ripple.
>   The pet hen went chook-chook.
>
> "Love should be put into action!"
>   screamed the old hermit.
> Across the pond an echo
>   tried and tried to confirm it.

Love might be put into action by firing a gun, yes—at whom? In what extremity?

The gun in this poem, like a real gun, might be fired out of despair at love's inaction, passivity, inertness, abuses, neglect. It's a "dirty hermit" who fires the shotgun at nothing in particular, who screams at no one in particular the ethical imperative "Love *should* be put into action!" Someone long isolate, outside community, who like the pond has been "holding onto [his] injuries/ *lucidly* year after year." And who is the other character in the poem, the narrator of all this? Someone alone, whose heart is pounding, walking the road of iron, the railroad track, the hobo track—a child trying to run away from home? turned out from home?—someone, in any case, who still hasn't gotten far from home, who has known this landscape—the pond, the hermit's cabin—*year after year*. Someone needing to get far away, someone whose eyes have seen, perhaps, destruction of community, preventable disintegration, a child of loss, emigration, passive neglect, intrafamilial violations; someone not yet, but potentially, a hobo or a dirty hermit. A someone who is legion across the globe. For whom the hermit's scream, the shout of the shotgun, might be relief in a scene of enormous, unnameable tension and impoverishment. But there is nothing lonelier-sounding or more futile than an echo, and the poem ends with this.*

What does it take for the walker on the railroad track to become not a hobo or a hermit, but an artist and/or an activist? What would it mean to put love into action in the face of lovelessness, abandonment, or violation? Where do we find, in or around us, love—the imagination that can subvert despair or the futile firing of a gun? What teaches us to convert lethal anger into steady, serious attention to our own lives and those of others? What, in North America in the 1990s, are we given to help us ask these questions—the language of therapy groups, of

---

*James Merrill comments that "to anyone who has known love the merest hint of ties grown unmanageable will suffice." I agree.

twelve-step programs, of bleached speech? I continue to hear the dirty hermit's scream and to want it to become a general cry.

———

What is political activism, anyway? I've been asking myself.

It's something both prepared for and spontaneous—like making poetry.

When we do and think and feel certain things privately and in secret, even when thousands of people are doing, thinking, whispering these things privately and in secret, there is still no general, collective understanding from which to move. Each takes her or his risks in isolation. We may think of ourselves as individual rebels, and individual rebels can easily be shot down. The relationship among so many feelings remains unclear. But these thoughts and feelings, suppressed and stored-up and whispered, have an incendiary component. You cannot tell where or how they will connect, spreading underground from rootlet to rootlet till every grass blade is afire from every other. This is that "spontaneity" which party "leaders," secret governments, and closed systems dread. Poetry, in its own way, is a carrier of the sparks, because it too comes out of silence, seeking connection with unseen others.

———

I think at this point of my friend Barbara Deming, her life of commitment to nonviolent political action, her active claiming of her untimely death from cancer. Who walked "for peace," no doubt with pounding heart, on an interracial march through the segregated South in 1964 and found herself in jail—not about peace, but about racism. Who walked with women from the Seneca Peace Encampment in 1983, finding herself and the others confronted by a hostile mob—jeered not on grounds of peace or nuclear arms, but as Jews/Communists/lesbians. Who spoke and wrote about nonviolence, named the repressed murderous anger within the nonviolence movement, made room for the revolutionary possibility of killing without hating, out of tragic necessity, though she felt it "blurred the vision" of a world in which all had the right to live. Who had an income that permitted her to devote her life to activism, though many might have used that freedom differently. Who for years felt constrained, like so many others, to hide her love for women, her desire, in the very movements calling for fundamental change in human relationships, whose anger at those years of self-denial was great, who tried to distinguish between anger as "affliction" and anger as "the concentration of one's whole being in the determination: This must change." I think of her because, though the peace movement as she knew it could be simplistic, she herself was not simplistic. I want to keep her lanky, earthy, elegant, erotic, amused, keenly attentive presence in mind even as I know that if alive today she would perforce be stretching the limits of her imagination, her definitions of peace, war, violence.

Because I know that for Barbara, as for many others then committed to nonviolent direct action, it was all about the connections between love and action. The marches and sit-ins were, have been, not—as some propaganda of later decades would have it—mere eruptions of youthful excitement. As Barbara herself wrote of nonviolent direct action, it was a way of living the future in the present, treating hostile adversaries as human beings like yourself, respecting them even as you tried to change their minds. Each nonviolent demonstrator, as she propounded it, had to embody in her or his own person the respect of one being for another that "after the revolution" would become the basis for human society. This was literally one-on-one communication, the demonstrator gone limp, being dragged by police, trying to keep eye contact, trying to hold on to a distinction between the role of the police enforcer or National Guardsman or prison guard, and the person inside the uniform. Between the hostile mob and the individuals within it, their fears and unmet needs. But the preparation for this was the creation of a group in which the like-minded were bound with ties of love and of attention to one another. The hope was that action informed by the love of justice and of the actual human being could change the perceptions of those at whom the actions were directed— could teach by example.

I wrote "hope" but I should say more accurately "faith." Not in the sense of religious faith, though some who practice nonviolence in action do so as members of religious groups. And not in the dictionary's other sense—of "unquestioning belief." Barbara herself was always questioning; she was one of the leading critics of the peace movement from within, as a feminist, as a lesbian, as a white person who learned much from Black activists. An activist's faith can never be unquestioning, can never stop responding to "new passions and new forces," can never oversimplify, as believers and activists are often tempted or pressured to do.

The Gulf War, which Barbara did not live to see, brought into high relief certain realities that had been long in the making. It revealed the invasions of Grenada in 1983, of Panama in 1989, as rehearsals, war games, dressed in a rhetorical language of rescue and the deposition of a monster. Manipulative images—a crusade against a new monster, a "butcher" (recently our client in the arms trade)—were used to camouflage in 1991 the fact that the invention, manufacture, and sale, not of nuclear arms but of the most dazzlingly refined "conventional" weapons, have become the lifeblood of global capitalism. The "arms race" is really the ancient race for the gold for which men have always killed each other: a false economy based on arms production and arms selling. Arsenal building for profit, legal and illegal, plays off old and new nationalisms and ideologies, while a more and more sophisticated weaponry allows both for the closing down of old military bases and the reduction of nuclear arms. These new "conventional" weapons, after all, have the cumulative power of a nuclear bomb to paralyze a city or a country without apparently laying it waste. A "third way" has been found between long-drawn-out ground war and instant nuclear devastation—or so it would seem. Cleaner, quicker, safer, more surgical wars? *A unity that is the life one loves?*

———

Less than a decade before the bombing of Baghdad, the Swedish feminist and social reformer Alva Myrdal, accepting her Nobel Peace Prize, had connected the arms race and "its needless excesses of armaments and its aggressive rhetoric" with "an ominous cult of violence in contemporary societies," which were "in the process of being both militarized and brutalized. Because of the tremendous and needless proliferation of arms through production and export, sophisticated weapons were now freely available on the domestic market as well, right down to handguns and stilettoes. . . . And she singled out the powerful role of the mass media in promoting violence, most of all among the young," while "Western exporting of films and TV programs worked in tandem with the arms trade to saturate the Third World in patterns of brutality."*

Barbara Deming sought to effect change by the most grass-

*She might have traced these "patterns of brutality," exported by the West back to the slave trade and colonialism, and the films and TV programs promoting violence, to earlier Western cultural texts depicting people of color as apes, monsters, subhuman, needing subjugation.

roots and personal means: a walk for disarmament through small towns, dialogues with people met along the way, or in prison cells, handing out leaflets, arguing with comrades in the North American peace and women's movements, civil disobedience. Alva Myrdal tried to use institutions like the International Labor Organization and UNESCO, her position as Sweden's ambassador to India, her contacts in the worlds of diplomacy and international politics, to achieve a rechanneling of global resources from war into social and economic development. Her allies were men of power: Dag Hammarskjöld, Nehru, and, in some ways, her husband, Gunnar Myrdal.

Both Deming and Myrdal were feminists and saw along a spectrum of social violence that had nuclear annihilation as its extreme. Barbara Deming chose toward the end of her life to focus on a women's peace movement that connected militarism with transnational violence by men against women. Alva Myrdal wanted to use her Nobel prize—both the visibility and the money it provided—to create a high-powered international "antiviolence" movement that would hold to account the "propagandizers and profiteers of violence" and the use of violence for power and profit throughout social institutions, including the family.

"Nonviolence," "antiviolence." The feebleness of the language, however passionate the determination, tells us something. *Violence* is what looks out at us from those phrases: its expressionless or grinning face is what we see, not what it displaces. War goes on demanding its "fatal unity." What face has "visible and responsive peace"? What does it mean, to put love into action? Why do I go on as if poetry has any answers to that question?

Peace I have feared you hated you scuffed dirt
on what little of you I could bear near me

scorned you called you vicious names Every time
you have settled over an afternoon
a friendship a night walk my brow my sleep
I have lashed free of your desolate island
back to the familiar continent
Coward I have watched you buckle under
nightsticks and fire hoses You have
disgusted me slipping flowers into guns
holding hands with yourself singing to bullets
and dogs Who can speak your language but
animals and saints What history records
your triumphs Over what centuries
have you reigned Miasma Where are the stone
lists of those who have died in your name
In the land where you are loved what becomes
of the veterans of all against all How
will I clothe myself How will I eat How
will I teach my children whom to respect
how to find themselves on a map of the world
when I have so seldom seen your face
Tell me Bloodless Outlaw Phantom what is
the work of the belligerent in
your anarchic kingdom Where is my place
     —Suzanne Gardinier, "To Peace"

"There is not a real poet alive today, or for some time past, who would do what Homer did even if he/she could, or Virgil or the author of the Chanson de Roland or the Shakespeare of the chronicles—the glorification of war and conquest. The refusal to do so is precisely at the heart of poetic (and existential) heroism as we have come to understand it," writes the poet Hayden Carruth. For centuries, people reading Homer's *Iliad* took it, along with the Hebrew Bible (also filled with poetry and scenes of battle) as a poetic starting gate, a point of origins for Western civilization. In the poem just quoted, Suzanne Gardinier speaks through the spirit of violence as it has thrashed its way through history, not the violence of the powerful so much as the violence of those who have fought and bled in the service of power, "the veterans of all against all," "the belligerent" hating peace because unable to see how it can ever include them; or those who have grown up knowing that violent resistance is the only way to stay alive. The questions of the poem need concern all those who condemn violence, who place themselves beyond its seductions.

About the *Iliad* as a kind of cultural ancestry for citizens of the United States, Gardinier has written:

> By content, the *Iliad* is not the epic of slaves, nor of those who hold the earth sacred, nor of those who deeply value words at all, as sacred vessels, as anything more than the ritual preludes to battle. It is the epic of soldiers, and of the cultures whose sense of connection to a universe that is whole has been broken, whose peace is the interval between wars. As such, it is clearly one of our ancestors, whether we hold this country's sword of power or live at its point. Whether or not it is this one among all the others to whom we will pledge allegiance remains to be seen.

She suggests other possible ancestors:

> As residents of the Western Hemisphere, we might claim the Mayan *Popol Vuh,* or some yet un-knit Nahuatl sequence—or the Delaware Big House Ceremony set down, or the Mohawk Ritual of Condolence, or the story of the peace made among the Five Nations of the Iroquois. As residents of the United States, we might claim *Leaves of Grass*—or sew together and claim the folk tales and songs with the story of the survival of slavery in them, as

the Finns made their Kalevala in the last century from what peasants remember.

In the nineteenth century some people attended military battles as spectators, watching live war through telescopes and field glasses. Today we view airbrushed images of war's technological beauty on our television screens. And at Revolutionary or Civil War battle sites, becalmed on the landscape as national monuments, amateurs of history annually reenact old charges and routs in full period military costume. Perhaps these theatrics can distract from, or console for, the knowledge that at the end of the twentieth century there is no demilitarized zone, no line dividing war from peace, that the ghettos and barrios of peacetime live under paramilitary occupation, that prisoners are being taken and incarcerated at an accelerating rate, that the purchase of guns has become an overwhelming civilian response to perceived fractures in the social compact.

Almost twenty years ago I was teaching in a public college in Harlem where many of my colleagues and students were poets. Walking up to Convent Avenue from Broadway, and in the classroom, I saw much that became part of my own education, having to do with the daily struggle of poor African-Americans and Puerto Ricans to live and, if possible, to love and, where possible, to put love into action. Somewhere in that time, in response to the turning-away by a Brooklyn hospital of a Black youth struck by a city bus, my colleague June Jordan wrote a grief-stricken, bitter, and lyrical poem:

FOR MICHAEL ANGELO THOMPSON
(October 25, 1959–March 23, 1973)

So Brooklyn has become a holy place

the streets have turned to meadowland
where
wild
free
ponies
eat among the wild
free
flowers
growing there
                              Please do not forget.
A tiger does not fall or stumble
broken by an accident.
A tiger does not lose his stride or
clumsy
slip and slide to tragedy
that buzzards feast upon.
                              Do not forget.
The Black prince Michael Black boy
our younger brother
has not "died"
he
has not "passed away"
the Black prince Michael Black boy
our younger brother
                              He was killed.
                              He did not die.
It was the city took him off
(that city bus)

and smashed him suddenly

to death
deliberate.

It was the city took him off
the hospital
that turned him down the hospital
that turned away from so much beauty
bleeding
bleeding
in Black struggle
                    just to live.
It was the city took him off
the casket names and faces
of the hatred spirit
stripped the force the
laughter and the agile power
of the child
                                He did not die.
                                A tiger does not fall.
                                Do not forget.

The streets have turned to meadowland
where
wild
free
ponies
eat among the wild
free
flowers
growing there

and Brooklyn
has become a holy place.

It took me years to hear the double-edge, the double-voiced-
ness, of this poem, which sounded to me so apparently musical,
sorrowful, and courteous an admonition: *Please do not forget.* I
read that admonition as being for me, for white readers, rather
than for the community to which the poet and the dead child
belonged. *So Brooklyn has become a holy place:* I heard this in the
same tone at the beginning and end of the poem. Only after
years of experience, politics, conversations, listening, I heard the
caustic engrained anger of the first question, *So Brooklyn has
become a holy place?* the question mark omitted but the subtext
clear: You're telling me? these things just happen naturally? that
wild free ponies of Black urban youth just *pass away?* Race came
between me and full reading of the poem: I wanted to believe
the poet was elegaic, not furious; she sets the "Please" in the
midst of the poem, which plays into my reading. But it isn't that
kind of "Please" at all, rather the "Please" of the member of the
community who strides into the church service where perhaps
the facts are about to be buried with the victim.

By the end of the poem the same lines become a requiem.
Having parsed the realities of Michael Angelo Thompson's
death, the poet's voice allows him his transcendence: his death
sacramentalizes the city that "took him off"; Brooklyn is made
holy by and to *him.* The poem becomes both documentation
and ritual whereby the first lines translate into the last lines,
bitterness and fury into recommitment.

"Peace" is not the issue here, but the violent structures of
urban class and racial power. The poem is a skin—luminous and
resonant—stretched across a repetitive history of Black children's deaths in the cities, in a country that offers them neither

hope nor respite. In the face of this violence, apparently so acceptable and ordinary, poets are forced to remind us not to forget. And Jordan herself went on to become one of the most lyrical of activist poets.

———

The difference between poetry and rhetoric
is being
ready to kill
yourself
instead of your children.

I am trapped on a desert of raw gunshot wounds
and a dead child dragging his shattered black
face off the edge of my sleep
blood from his punctured cheeks and shoulders
is the only liquid for miles and my stomach
churns at the imagined taste while
my mouth splits into dry lips
without loyalty or reason
thirsting for the wetness of his blood
as it sings into the whiteness
of the desert where I am lost
without imagery or magic
trying to make power out of hatred and destruction
trying to heal my dying son with kisses
only the sun will bleach his bones quicker.

The policeman who shot down a 10-year-old in Queens
stood over the boy with his cop shoes in childish blood
and a voice said "Die you little motherfucker" and
there are tapes to prove that. At his trial

this policeman said in his own defense
"I didn't notice the size or nothing else
only the color." and
there are tapes to prove that, too.

Today that 37-year-old white man with 13 years of police forcing
has been set free
by 11 white men who said they were satisfied
justice had been done
and one black woman who said
"They convinced me" meaning
they had dragged her 4'10" black woman's frame
over the hot coals of four centuries of white male approval
until she let go the first real power she ever had
and lined her own womb with cement
to make a graveyard for our children.

I have not been able to touch the destruction within me.
But unless I learn to use
the difference between poetry and rhetoric
my power too will run corrupt as poisonous mold
or lie limp and useless as an unconnected wire
and one day I will take my teenaged plug
and connect it to the nearest socket
raping an 85-year-old white woman
who is somebody's mother
and as I beat her senseless and set a torch to her bed
a greek chorus will be singing in 3/4 time
"Poor thing. She never hurt a soul. What beasts they are."

Audre Lorde's "Power" is a poem of documentation, of police records, tapes, a jury verdict. It's also a poem about creative
and destructive rage. An artist *lost/without imagery or magic* in a

desert of whiteness, of "an articulated power that is not on your terms," is an artist driven against the wall. Lorde has said that she heard of the acquittal of the policeman while driving,

and I decided to pull over and just jot some things down in my notebook to enable me to cross town without an accident because I was so sick and so enraged. . . . I was just writing, and that poem came out without craft. . . . I was thinking that the killer had been a student at John Jay [College of Criminal Justice, where Lorde was then teaching] and that I might have seen him in the hall, that I might see him again. What was retribution? What could have been done? There was one Black woman on the jury. It could have been me. . . . Do I kill him? What is my effective role? Would I kill her. . . . —the Black woman on the jury. What kind of strength did she, would I, have at the point of deciding to take a position. . . . There is the jury—white male power, white male structures—how do you take a position against them? How do you deal with things you believe, live them not as theory, not even as emotion, but right on the line of action and effect and change? All of those things were riding on that poem. But I had no sense, no understanding at the time, of the connections, just that I was that woman. And that to put myself on the line to do what had to be done at any place and time was so difficult, and not to do so was the most awful death. And putting yourself on the line is like killing a piece of yourself, in the sense that you have to kill, end, destroy something familiar and dependable, so that something new can come in ourselves, in our world. And that sense of writing at the edge, out of urgency, not because you choose it but because you have to—that sense of survival—that's what the poem is out of, as well as the pain of my spiritual son's death over and over. Once you live any piece of your vision it opens you to a constant onslaught. Of necessities, of horrors, but

of wonders too, of possibilities . . . like meteor showers all the
time, bombardment, constant connections.

———————

An event may ignite a poem (which may then be labeled a
"protest" poem) but not because the poet has "decided" to
address that event. What's clear from Lorde's memory of the first
draft of "Power" is that the event encapsulated great reaches of
her experience, open questions of her life. Hearing a news report
on the radio, she pulls over and reaches for her notebook as a
recourse from harming herself or others—and it is in life-and-
death terms that the poem begins to speak. A so-called "political" poem comes—if it comes as poetry at all—from fearful and
raging, deep and tangled questions within: in Lorde's case—*How
do you deal with the things you believe? How do I put myself on the
line? How can I destroy what needs to die in me without destroying
others at random?* I think again of Bishop's hermit's cry. Two
poems more different than "Chemin de Fer" and "Power" are
hard to imagine. Until you start to listen back and forth between
them.

XI

A leak in history

I'm staying in a house in the Vermont countryside, shaded in front by three big sugar maples. Behind it lies a grove of the same trees, and on a hillside far away I can see another grove, glowing green in rich late-afternoon light. In autumn the leaves turn scarlet; in late winter thaw the pale aqueous sap starts rising and is gathered and laboriously evaporated, in little steamy shacks and cabins, down to its essence, a syrup fine as honey. The Abnaki Indians knew this process before the Yankees came to clear scattered pools of land for grazing, leaving old forest lands in between. Taught by the Abnaki, the first white men made maple sugar in Vermont in 1752.

Under snow, the sap shrinks back. In early thaw, farmers

trudge and horse-sledge through the woods to drill little taps into the rough-barked trunks. The sap used to be collected in wooden firkins, then in tin pails hung over the taps; more recently, where terrain and weather allow, plastic tubing is used. A culture formed around this labor-intensive harvesting, first ritual of the northern spring, the culture of the sugarhouse with its ancient sprung castoff chairs, steaming evaporation trays, wet snow and mud trodden inside on heavy boots, doughnuts and coffee, pickles, frankfurters, and beer brought down by women from farm kitchens, eaten and drunk by men lugging and pouring sap and stoking the wood fires. Hard manual labor—about forty gallons of sap being collected and boiled down to obtain one gallon of syrup—and adept, sensitive calculation of the cycles of thaw and freeze that make for the best sugaring-off; testing for the moment when the thin, faintly sweet sap has reached the density of amber syrup. The sour crispness of pickle on the tongue amid all that sweaty sweetness. There is a summer culture too, at church suppers and county fairs, where "sugar on snow" still competes with cotton-candy machines and barbecue—pans of last winter's snow from icehouse, cemetery vault, or freezer, sticky arabesques of hot syrup poured on, served on paper plates with the necessary pickle and doughnut on the side.

Maple trees reproduce with energy: under any big tree you will find dozens of seedlings crowding each other; in spring the seeds, or keys, blow far afield on little brown wings soon after the new leaves uncurl. The root system of a full-grown maple is many times the circumference of the great crown. In their early-summer-evening green, in the hectic flare of their October changing, in the strong, stripped upreaching of their winter bareness, they are presences of enormous vitality and generosity, trees that yield much to the eye, to the tongue, to the modest cash assets of farm families.

It's said that acid rain and road salt are slowly dooming the sugar maples. Studying and testing the rings of mature trees, scientists have found that up until 1955 they show no evidence of chemical stress; since 1955 acidity has been wearing into the trees and will eventually destroy them. I look out at the grove on the hill, the old trees just outside the window; all seems as it has always been, without smirch or taint.

I remember other trees that stood in this landscape when I first knew it: the wineglass elms. Every village common, every roadside, had them. *Ulmus americanus,* outspreading limbs sweeping up from a straight and slender trunk in the form of a true wineglass, green in summer, golden in autumn, architecturally elegant in nakedness. An old pamphlet from the State Agricultural Service, found in a drawer, implores cooperation in destroying infested bark and wood and protecting still-healthy trees. But the fungus-carrying elm bark beetle won out. Throughout New England, elms fell barren in summer, sick to death, easily splintered by winds. Soon a living elm in leaf was something rare and precious. Now it's hard to remember where they stood.

The poorer we become, the less we remember what we had. Whenever I walk into this house after an absence, I drink, slowly and deliberately, a glass of pure cold water from the spring-fed tap. I don't drink from most taps because I don't like their ill flavor. And the taste of bottled water from the supermarket has no savor; it reminds me of nothing. The spring water flowing into this house does—in its transparency, its lucidity, its original cold. Of course it tastes of this place, sharp with memories, but also of water I drank as a child in the 1930s, from an iron pipe set in the side of a ravine where I used to play. It seemed like the saving, merciful drink of water in legends or poetry; through it I sensuously understood the beautiful, lip-smacking words "to quench a thirst." This was not in the country, but in a wooded park in Baltimore. There was a stream there too, where we waded, and plunged our hands in to the wrists, and never got sick.

Three thousand miles to the west, where I live now, on a much-traveled hill road winding eastward from the coast, there is a standing pipe called the Lombardi Spring. A few cars and trucks are almost always parked on the shoulder, people lined up with jugs and bottles, because that water is held to be particularly delicious and good. And it is free.

Sensual vitality is essential to the struggle for life. It's as simple—and as threatened—as that. To have no love for the taste of the water you drink is a loss of vitality. If your appetite is embalmed in prescriptives, you are weakened for the struggle. Under the most crushing conditions of deprivation, people have to fill their stomachs, eat earth, eat plain starch, force down watery and rancid soup, drink urine for survival. Yet there's another story. In the newsletter produced by inmates in a women's facility, among columns on law, religion, politics, current prison issues, there is the "Konvict Kitchen," with recipes for special microwaved dishes to be created by combining items from the prison store:

1 can Mixin' Chicken
1 Shrimp Noodle Cup
Jalapeño Peppers (optional)
Onions (optional)
Bell Peppers (optional)
2 Packages Margarine

Crush noodles and put in large micro-wave bowl with enough water to cover them. Let sit for three minutes. Take bell peppers, onions, and hot peppers and saute in micro-wave for two minutes. Take mixture out, add noodles, stir thoroughly and cook in micro-wave for approximately 20–25 minutes, until noodles are crisp. Stir every five minutes. Keep lid lightly on mixture but not tightly closed. Serves 2.

—Gloria Bolden

Poetry being a major form of prison literature, it goes without saying that there are poems in the newsletter. Like the recipe above, they work within the prison context but refuse to be subdued:

This is prison not the Hilton
Heard we got it made in here?
This is livin' at its finest?
Country clubs with kegs of beer?
Say—listen up my friend
let me tell you what it's like
to be livin' in the sewer
flushed further down the pipe . . .

This is prison not the Hilton
Election time is on its way
you'll hear it on the T.V.
we should suffer every day
days of torture
nights of terror—
feel your heart's been torn in shreds?
Say you're showered with asbestos,
drinking nitrate in your bed? . . .

This is prison not the Hilton
care to change your place for mine?
Think that 20 out of 60
isn't doing enough time?
Care to try this life of leisure?

Care to leave your folks behind?
This is prison not the Hilton
and its hell here all the time.
    —composed by Jacqueline Dixon-Bey and Mary Glover,
        inside Florence Crane Women's Prison, Coldwater,
    Michigan, Spring 1990; recipe and poem from *INSIGHT:*
        Serving the Women of Florence Crane Women's Facility
                        2d quarter ed. (1990)

———

Sensual vitality is essential to the struggle for life. Many people drink as if filling themselves with dirt or starch: the filling of an emptiness. But what comes after is a greater emptiness. In the reputations of poets like Hart Crane, Dylan Thomas, Kenneth Rexroth, James Wright, Richard Hugo, Delmore Schwartz, Robert Lowell, Elizabeth Bishop, John Berryman, Anne Sexton, drinking has been romanticized as part of the "poetic fate," the "despondency and madness" of the poet—as if bricklayers, surgeons, housewives, miners, generals, salesmen haven't also poured down liquids to fire up or numb interior spaces of dread. A politician's wife confesses to having drunk aftershave, nail-polish remover, in desperate substitute for confiscated bottles. Whether done with nail-polish remover or antique liqueur of pear, this is self-poisoning.

But there's a sensual vitality in drinking wine and "spirits" as in drinking pure water. Both belong to ancient human rites and memories. People have fermented the apple, the grape, the palm, hops and barley, rice, berries, the potato, the dandelion, the plum. Along with the rising of the yeast in bread was the fermentation of the grain, the fruit. Blessed be the Spirit of the Universe, who created the fruit of the vine. For us to use it as we may.

That so many of us use, or have used, the fruit of the vine in an attempt to fill our terrifying voids may point to the failure of a general communal vitality more than to some inherent poisoning in the fermentation process. I don't minimize the ultimate transaction between the individual and the bottle. But the individual's sense of emptiness reflects—and helps perpetuate—a public emptiness.

When a vast, stifling denial in the public realm is felt by every individual yet there is no language, no depiction, of what is being denied, it becomes for each his or her own anxious predicament, a daily struggle to act "as if" everything were normal. Alcohol, drugs offer a reprieve—not ceremony or celebration, but a substitute for vital bonds of community and friendship, for collective memory and responsibility. Where there is no public face of interdependence, of justice and mercy, where there is no social language for "picking up the pieces when we don't know what/where they are," anomie and amnesia, alcohol and drug abuse can work as social controls and, because they appear "normal," can be more effective—in a very large country—than terrorization by a secret police.

The danger lies in forgetting what we had. The flow between generations becomes a trickle, grandchildren tape-recording grandparents' memories on special occasions perhaps—no casual storytelling jogged by daily life, there being no shared daily life what with migrations, exiles, diasporas, rendings, the search for work. Or there is a shared daily life riddled with holes of silence. In 1979 Helen Epstein published her book of interviews, *Children of the Holocaust*. In 1985 Judy Kaplan and Linn Shapiro edited *Red Diaper Babies: Children of the Left,* a compilation of transcripts of taped sessions at two conferences held in 1982 and 1983 by children of leftist and Communist families, then in their thirties and forties. There are haunting resonances between the two groups of testimony: the children's experience of knowing that there was something of major weight at the center of their parents' lives, something secret, unspoken, unspeakable. (Epstein refers to "that quiet, invisible community, that peer group without a sign.") Both groups of children knowing about things that could not be discussed on the playground or with "strangers," that were to a greater or lesser degree unmentionable even at home. A tattoo on an aunt's wrist. A neighbor's withdrawal. A mother's nightmares; a parent's terror when a child left the house or came home late. A father in jail or underground. Close friends who suddenly could not be mentioned. Certain newspapers having to be hidden; jobs inexplicably lost; children trained that "the walls have ears"; a car parked across the street for hours, one day every week, two men sitting inside. There can be no question of equalizing the events that catalyzed these two silences. Yet the passing on of living history is an essential ingredient of individual and communal self-knowledge, and in both cases that continuity was breached. Forty years is a wilderness of silence.

The loss can be a leak in history or a shrinking in the vitality of everyday life. Fewer and fewer people in this country entertain each other with verbal games, recitations, charades, singing, playing on instruments, doing anything as amateurs—people who are good at something because they enjoy it. To be good at talk, not pompously eloquent or didactic, but having a vivid tongue, savoring turns of phrase—to sing on key and know many songs by heart—to play fiddle, banjo, mandolin, flute, accordion, harmonica—to write long letters—to draw pictures or whittle wood with some amount of skill—to do moderately and pleasingly well, in short, a variety of things without solemn investment or disenabling awe—these were common talents till recently, crossing class and racial lines. People used their human equipment—memory, image making, narrative, voice, hand, eye—unself-consciously, to engage with other people, and not as specialists or "artistes." My father and his mother both loved to recite poetry learned long ago in school. He had Poe's "The Raven" and "Annabel Lee" from memory, and he had won a school medal for his recitation of a long narrative poem called "Lasca," which began:

> I want free life and I want fresh air,
> And I sigh for the canter after the cattle,
> The crack of whips like shots in a battle,
> The green below, and the blue above,
> And dash, and danger, and life, and love—
> And Lasca.

And my grandmother still remembered a poem she'd learned in Vicksburg, Mississippi—Jewish girl sent to a convent school where there were no secular schools. In her seventies she could recite, black eyes glowing, "Asleep at the Switch":

> It was down in the Lehigh Valley,
> At the bottom of the bottomless ditch,
> I lived alone in a cabin,
> And attended the railway switch.

The reciters of these two poems could not have been in person more unlike the "speaker" of each poem, and that was part of the excitement: to see a known person become someone new and different, change his or her identity but within a framework that allowed each to change back at the end—from Texan desperado to my sedentary, scholarly father; from negligent, solitary

switchman to my sheltered, precise grandmother. And such recitations let a child feel that poetry (verse, really, with its struc-
tured rhymes, meters, and ringingly fulfilled aural expectations)
was not just words on the page, but could live in people's minds
for decades, to be summoned up with relish and verve, and that
poetry was not just literature, but embodied in voices.

For ordinary people to sing or whistle used to be as common
as breathing. I remember men whistling, briskly or hauntingly,
women humming with deep-enclosed chest tones. Where did it
go? A technology of "canned" music available through car ra-
dios, portable "boom boxes," and cassette players, programmed
music piped into the workplace, has left people born in the 1950s
and later largely alien to the experience of hearing or joining in
casual music making. Knowing how to pitch your voice isn't the
privilege of the conservatory; people used to learn it from hearing others casually, unself-consciously sing, as they learned language, accent, inflection in speech. Now singing belongs to pro-
fessionals, is preserved in churches; rap, a spontaneous and
sophisticated expression of Black street youth at first, quickly
became a commodity on videotape, adapted as a new style for
television commercials. (Yet rap goes on around the world,
picking up on local griefs, local insurgencies.)

Part of the experience of casual singing was the undeliberate
soaking up of many songs, many verses. Ballads, hymns, work
songs, opera arias, folk songs, popular songs, labor songs, school-
children's playground songs. And, of course, with the older
songs words changed over time, new generations of singers mis-
remembering or modifying. Tunes changed, too, as songs traveled: from England or Wales to Appalachia, from Africa to the
Sea Islands, France to Québec, and across the continent.

To ears accustomed to high-technology amplification and recording processes, the unamplified human voice, the voice not

professionally trained, may sound acoustically lacking, even perhaps embarrassing. And so we're severed from a physical release
and pleasure, whether in solitude or community—the use of
breath to produce song. But breath is also *Ruach,* spirit, the
human connection to the universe.

XII

Someone is writing a poem

The society whose modernization has reached the stage of integrated spectacle is characterized by the combined effect of five principal factors: incessant technological renewal, integration of state and economy, generalized secrecy, unanswerable lies, and eternal present.

The spectator is simply supposed to know nothing and deserves nothing. Those who are watching to see what happens next will never act and such must be the spectator's condition.

—Guy Debord

In a political culture of managed spectacles and passive spectators, poetry appears as a rift, a peculiar lapse, in the prevailing mode. The reading of a poem, a poetry reading, is not a spectacle, nor can it be passively received. It's an exchange of electrical currents through language—that daily, mundane, abused, and ill-prized medium, that instrument of deception and revelation, that material thing, that knife, rag, boat, spoon/reed become pipe/tree trunk become drum/mud become clay flute/ conch shell become summons to freedom/old trousers and petticoats become iconography in appliqué/rubber bands stretched around a box become lyre. Diane Glancy: *Poetry uses the hub of a torque converter for a jello mold*. I once saw, in a Chautauqua vaudeville, a man who made recognizably tonal music by manipulating a variety of sizes of wooden spoons with his astonishing fingers. Take that old, material utensil, language, found all about you, blank with familiarity, smeared with daily use, and make it into something that means more than it says. What poetry is made of is so old, so familiar, that it's easy to forget that it's not just the words, but polyrhythmic sounds, speech in its first endeavors (every poem breaks a silence that had to be overcome), prismatic meanings lit by each others' light, stained by each others' shadows. In the wash of poetry the old, beaten, worn stones of language take on colors that disappear when you sieve them up out of the streambed and try to sort them out.

———

And all this has to travel from the nervous system of the poet, preverbal, to the nervous system of the one who listens, who reads, the active participant without whom the poem is never finished.

———

I can't write a poem to manipulate you; it will not succeed. Perhaps you have read such poems and decided you don't care for poetry; something turned you away. I can't write a poem from dishonest motives; it will betray its shoddy provenance, like an ill-made tool, a scissors, a drill, it will not serve its purpose, it will come apart in your hands at the point of stress. I can't write a poem simply from good intentions, wanting to set things right, make it all better; the energy will leak out of it, it will end by meaning less than it says.

I can't write a poem that transcends my own limits, though poetry has often pushed me beyond old horizons, and writing a poem has shown me how far out a part of me was walking beyond the rest. I can expect a reader to feel my limits as I cannot, in terms of her or his own landscape, to ask: *But what has this to do with me? Do I exist in this poem?* And this is not a simple or naive question. We go to poetry because we believe it has something to do with us. We also go to poetry to receive the experience of the *not me,* enter a field of vision we could not otherwise apprehend.

Someone writing a poem believes in a reader, in readers, of that poem. The "who" of that reader quivers like a jellyfish. Self-reference is always possible: that my "I" is a universal "we," that the reader is my clone. That sending letters to myself is enough for attention to be paid. That my chip of mirror contains the world.

But most often someone writing a poem believes in, depends on, a delicate, vibrating range of difference, that an "I" can become a "we" without extinguishing others, that a partly common language exists to which strangers can bring their own heartbeat, memories, images. A language that itself has learned from the heartbeat, memories, images of strangers.

———

Spectacles controlled and designed to manipulate mass opinion, mass emotions depend increasingly on the ownership of vast and expensive technologies and on the physical distance of the spectators from the spectacle. (The bombing of Baghdad, the studios where competing camera shots were selected and edited and juxtaposed to project via satellite dazzling images of a clean, nonbloody war.) I'm not claiming any kind of purity for poetry, only its own particular way of being. But it's notable that the making of and participation in poetry is so independent of high technology. A good sound system at a reading is of course a great advantage. Poetry readings can now be heard on tape, radio, recorded on video. But poetry would get lost in an immense technological performance scene. What poetry can give has to be given through language and voice, not through massive effects of lighting, sound, superimposed film images, nor as a mere adjunct to spectacle.

I need to make a crucial distinction here. The means of high technology are, as the poet Luis J. Rodriguez has said of the microchip, "surrounded by social relations and power mechanisms which arose out of another time, another period; . . . [they are] imprisoned by capitalism." The spectacles produced by these means carry the messages of those social relations and power mechanisms: that our conditions are inevitable, that randomness prevails, that the only possible response is passive absorption and identification.

But there is a different kind of performance at the heart of the renascence of poetry as an oral art—the art of the griot, performed in alliance with music and dance, to evoke and catalyze a community or communities against passivity and victimization, to recall people to their spiritual and historic sources. Such art, here and now, does not and cannot depend on huge economic and technical resources, though in a different system of social relations it might well draw upon highly sophisticated technologies for its own ends without becoming dominated by them.

———

Someone is writing a poem. Words are being set down in a force field. It's as if the words themselves have magnetic charges; they veer together or in polarity, they swerve against each other. Part of the force field, the charge, is the working history of the words themselves, how someone has known them, used them, doubted and relied on them in a life. Part of the movement among the words belongs to sound—the guttural, the liquid, the choppy, the drawn-out, the breathy, the visceral, the down-light. The theater of any poem is a collection of decisions about space and time—how are these words to lie on the page, with what pauses, what headlong motion, what phrasing, how can they meet the breath of the someone who comes along to read them? And in part the field is charged by the way images swim into the brain through written language: swan, kettle, icicle, ashes, scab, tamarack, tractor, veil, slime, teeth, freckle.

Lynn Emanuel writes of a nuclear-bomb test watched on television in the Nevada desert by a single mother and daughter living on the edge in a motel:

THE PLANET KRYPTON

Outside the window the McGill smelter
sent a red dust down on the smoking yards of copper,
on the railroad tracks' frayed ends disappeared
into the congestion of the afternoon. Ely lay dull

and scuffed: a miner's boot toe worn away and dim,
while my mother knelt before the Philco to coax
the detonation from the static. From the Las Vegas
Tonapah Artillery and Gunnery Range the sound

of the atom bomb came biting like a swarm
of bees. We sat in the hot Nevada dark, delighted,
when the switch was tripped and the bomb hoisted
up its silky, hooded, glittering, uncoiling length;

it hissed and spit, it sizzled like a poker in a toddy.
The bomb was no mind and all body; it sent a fire

of static down the spine. In the dark it glowed like the coils
of an electric stove. It stripped every leaf from every

branch until a willow by a creek was a bouquet
of switches resinous, naked, flexible, and fine.
Bathed in the light of KDWN, Las Vegas,
my crouched mother looked radioactive, swampy,

glaucous, like something from the Planet Krypton.
In the suave, brilliant wattage of the bomb, we were
not poor. In the atom's fizz and pop we heard possibility
uncorked. Taffeta wraps whispered on davenports.

A new planet bloomed above us; in its light
the stumps of cut pine gleamed like dinner plates.
The world was beginning all over again, fresh and hot;
we could have anything we wanted.

In the suave, brilliant wattage of the bomb, we were/not poor. This,
you could say, is the political core of the poem, the "meaning"
without which it could not exist. All that the bomb was meant to
mean, as spectacle of power promising limitless possibilities to
the powerless, all the falseness of its promise, the original devastation of two cities, the ongoing fallout into local communities,
reservations—all the way to the Pacific Islands—this is the driving impulse of the poem, the energy it rides. Yet all this would
be mere "message" and forgettable without the poem's visual
fury, its extraordinary leaps of sound and image: *Ely lay dull/and
scuffed: a miner's boot toe worn away and dim. . . . Taffeta wraps
whispered on davenports.* The Planet Krypton is Superman's
planet, falling apart, the bits of rubble it flings to earth dangerous
to the hero; Earth has become its own Planet Krypton—auto-
toxic.

At a certain point, a woman, writing this poem, has had to reckon the power of poetry as distinct from the power of the nuclear bomb, of the radioactive lesions of her planet, the power of poverty to reduce people to spectators of distantly conjured events. She can't remain a spectator, hypnotized by the gorgeousness of a destructive force launched far beyond her control. She can feel the old primary appetites for destruction and creation within her; she chooses for creation and for language. But to do this she has to see clearly—and to make visible—how destructive power once seemed to serve her needs, how the bomb's *silky, hooded, glittering, uncoiling length* might enthrall a mother and daughter as they watched, two marginal women, clinging to the edges of a speck in the desert. Her handling of that need, that destructiveness, in language, is how she takes on her true power.

 XIII

Beginners

The two best-known poets of the nineteenth-century United States were a strange uncoupled couple, moving together in a dialectic that the twentieth century has only begun to decipher. Walt Whitman (1819–1892) and Emily Dickinson (1830–1886) were both "beginners" in the sense of Whitman's poem:

How they are provided for upon the earth (appearing at intervals)
How dear and dreadful they are to the earth,
How they inure to themselves as much as to any—what a paradox
    appears their age,
How people respond to them, yet know them not,
How there is something relentless in their fate, all times,
How all times mischoose the objects of their adulation and reward,

And how the same inexorable price must still be paid for the same
  great purchase.

Whitman's "beginners" aren't starters-out on a path others
have traveled. They are openers of new paths, those who take
the first steps, who therefore can seem strange and "dreadful" to
their place and time ("dear" can mean "beloved" but also
"costly," a sense echoed in the final line above). To "inure"
means to "accustom yourself to something difficult and painful."
Whitman also uses "inure" in the sense of "inhere" or "belong," as in:

All this is thenceforth to be thought or done by you whoever you are,
  or by anyone,
These inure, have inured, shall inure, to the identities from which
  they sprang, or shall spring.

These "beginners" cost difficulty and pain to themselves as
well as to others, in whom they arouse strong feelings yet by
whom they remain unknown—their age feels paradoxical because of their presence in it. The appearance of the beginner is a
necessary, even a "relentless," event in human history, yet these
persons appear as misfits, are not what "the times" adulate and
reward. Both the person and the times pay a price for this, yet
the beginner is "provided for"—part of the longer scheme of
things.

Whitman and Dickinson shared this problematic status as
white poets in a century of slavery, wars against the Indians,
westward expansion, the Civil War, and the creation of the
United States as an imperial power. In terms of their social origins and their places in the social order, the two shared little
beyond white skin. The woman—daughter of a lawyer, legisla-
tor, and treasurer of Amherst College, raised in a home with

Puritan roots and Irish servants, briefly attending a female seminary, dropping out to keep house for an ill mother, rarely leaving the village of her birth or even her father's house—might seem the very type and product of the mid-nineteenth-century's diagram for patriarchally protected middle-class femininity, married or not. The man—son of a Puritan farmer-carpenter and a Dutch-Welsh mother, educated in the Brooklyn public schools, turned traveling journalist, journeyman printer, war correspondent and field nurse, rambler from Niagara to New Orleans—might seem one paradigm of "New World" masculinity, the stock of explorers, pioneers, frontiersmen, allowed, as a male of northern European/Anglo origins, the free expression of his personality in an expansive era.

And so they have come down to us, as reclusive, compressed Emily and all-hailing, instinctual Walt, white dress and neckribbon, shaggy beard and wide-brimmed hat. For Dickinson, the private life, intense, domestic, microcosmic; for Whitman, the "kosmos," the "democratic vistas" of the urban panorama, the open road, *the middle range of the Nineteenth century in the New World; a strange, unloosen'd, wondrous time.* For Dickinson, a father's library, letters as link to the world, poem itself as "letter," books as metaphors for and lines into experience, life itself as "Primer" to the "Book" of eternity:

> He ate and drank the precious Words—
> His Spirit grew robust . . .
>
> And this Bequest of Wings
> Was but a book—What Liberty
> A loosened Spirit brings—

For Whitman, a world of newspapers and printshops, city wanderings, casual sexual encounters, Civil War hospitals, and always his suspicion of printed texts, of the failures of the dictionary, the published history or biography. *I cannot divest my appetite of literature, yet I find myself trying it all by Nature; The real war will never get in the books; What is it that you express in your eyes? It seems to me more than all the print I have read in my life.* The poem as *national* product, engendering the heroic identities of a democracy: *Without yielding an inch the working-man and working-woman were to be in my pages from first to last.* For Dickinson, several anonymously anthologized poems, the rest enclosed in letters, stitched into sequences stored in a bedroom chest. For Whitman, the 1855 edition of *Leaves of Grass*, no name on the title page, the poet's open-shirted likeness as frontispiece, his authorship revealed in the text of the poems. Dickinson: *Renunciation is a piercing virtue; No is the wildest word we consign to language.* Whitman: *I celebrate myself . . . one of the roughs, a kosmos/Disorderly fleshly and sensual, eating drinking and breeding.*

For Dickinson:

> On my volcano grows the Grass
> A meditative spot—
> An acre for a Bird to choose
> Would be the General thought—
>
> How red the Fire rocks below—
> How insecure the sod
> Did I disclose
> Would populate with awe my solitude.

For Whitman:

> Through me forbidden voices,
> Voices of sexes and lusts, voices veil'd, and I
>   remove the veil,
> Voices indecent by me clarified and transfigur'd.

Didn't they seem to fit their age, though, these "beginners"? Didn't they seem to act out precisely the chartered roles, the constructions of white, middle-class masculinity and femininity that suited the times? Were they really "beginners," then, or just polar incarnations of a nineteenth-century sexual dualism?

Both took on North America as extremists. She from her vantage point: female, New England, eccentric within her world, not the spinster servicing the community, but a violently ambitious spirit married to the privacy of her art. He from his vantage point: male within a spectrum that required some males to be, like Dickinson's father, stiff-collared wardens of society, while allowing others to hanker, ramble on open roads. Both showed masks to the world: behind her acceptable persona of gingerbread-baking self-effacement, a woman artist remaking poetic language; the metaphysical and sensual adventures of her poems; and what Muriel Rukeyser called "her unappeasable thirst for fame."

> I tie my Hat—I crease my Shawl—
> Life's little duties do—precisely
> As the very least
> Were infinite—to me— . . .
>
> To simulate—is stinging work—
> To cover what we are
> From Science—and from Surgery—
> Too Telescopic Eyes
> To bear on us unshaded—
> For their—sake—not for Ours—
> 'Twould start them—
> We—could tremble—
> But since we got a Bomb—

And held it in our Bosom—
Nay—Hold it—it is calm

He, behind the persona of shape-changing omnipresence and "personal force," socially vulnerable as a poet breaking with Puritanism in a mercantile, materialistic nation less than a century old, sexually vulnerable as a frankly desirous man attracted to men.

At the end of the twentieth century these two poets are still hardly known beyond the masks they created for themselves and those clapped on them by the times and customs. Our categories have compressed the poetic energies of the white nineteenth-century United States into a gendered opposition: a sensual, free-ranging, boastful father and a reluctant, elusive, emotionally closeted mother—poetic progenitors neither of whom had children of the flesh. (Whitman boasted of his but clearly never knew who or if they were; Dickinson remains an ostensible daughter to the end.)

Yet that woman and that man *were* beginners *(we know them not):* the woman choosing her inner life and language over inconvenient domestic, social, and literary claims; the man overriding Puritan strictures against desire and insisting that democracy is of the body, by the body, and for the body, that the body is multiple, diverse, untypic.

They were a wild woman and a wild man, writing their wild carnal and ecstatic thoughts, self-censoring and censored, as the empire of the United States pushed into the Far West, Mexico, the Caribbean. He cannot possibly have heard of her unless he chanced to meet one of her rare sponsors (like the novelist Helen Hunt Jackson, hater of the Empire, who wrote *A Century of Dishonor* about the white destruction of Indian cultures and, in a letter, told Dickinson: "You are a great poet"). *She* allowed only that she'd heard his poems were "immoral." In the United States, on this enormous continent, poetry has been a strange crossroads, where poets often pass each other by dawn or twilight and do not know who they are passing.

But the wild woman and the wild man are Americana now: folded into textbooks, glossed in exhaustive scholarly editions. And the protagonist of Maxine Hong Kingston's extraordinary novel *Tripmaster Monkey* is a young Chinese-American poet named Wittman Ah Sing, who reads poetry aloud to the passengers in the buses of San Francisco.

Twenty-one years after the death of Whitman, twenty-seven years after the death of Dickinson, another poet is born. Her name is Muriel Rukeyser.

———

What happens when, the year before the outbreak of World War I, a girl is born into an urban, tempestuous, upwardly mobile, contradiction-ridden, Jewish family? What happens when, at twenty-one, her first book of poems is published, the year is 1934 around the world, and the title of the book (derived from a piloting manual) is *Theory of Flight*? When the first poem of that book is already big, assured, panoramic, accomplished, drawing on techniques of film, yet unflinchingly personal? What happens when that young woman pushes off the class ambitions she was raised in *(I was expected to grow up and become a golfer)*, breaks with her family, to move deeper into her country, her world, her century? When, neither asexual nor self-diminutizing, she affirms herself as large in body and desire, ambitious, innovative; travels to crucial political scenes, in Spain and the United States, as working journalist and poet; learns to pilot a plane; works in film; feels in her imagination the excitement of the lost connections between science and poetry? When her work as a poet continuously addresses the largest questions of her time—questions of power, technology, gender—in many forms: elegies, odes, lyrics, documentary poems, epigrams, ballads, dramatic monologues, biographical narratives? What happens when a woman, drawing on every political and social breakthrough gained by women since Dickinson's death in 1886, assumes the scope of her own living to be at least as large as Whitman's?

Add to this that she writes three major biographies—a life of the "father of American physics," Willard Gibbs; another of the English Renaissance naturalist, mathematician, navigator, astronomer Thomas Hariot; a book about the 1940 U.S. presidential candidate and compromised visionary Wendell Willkie—screenplays, essays, translations of poetry; a haunting documentary novel about sexuality and ritual, *The Orgy;* and a study of our national imagination, *The Life of Poetry.*

She is our twentieth-century Coleridge, our Neruda, and more.

What happens? She falls between the cracks. Her books do not have to be burnt.

In *The Traces of Thomas Hariot* she wrote of her subject as *a lost man who was great. And if he is great, what is his greatness? If he is great, why is he lost?* She describes Hariot as *caught . . . in all the heresies of his time, scientific, political, philosophical, sexual . . . a rebel who appears to fail at every climax of his life. He can be seen to go deeper at these times.* She was also touching a finger to the pulse of her own reputation, her own development.

In an interview late in her life, Rukeyser said:

> One of the attacks on me for writing that Hariot book spoke of me as a she-poet—that I had no business to be doing this, and I was broken for a while and looked out the window for awhile.

And then I thought, yes, I am a she-poet. Anything I bring to this is because I am a woman. And this is the thing that was left out of the Elizabethan world, the element that did not exist. Maybe, maybe, maybe that is what one can bring to life.

———

It is by a long road of presumption that I come to Willard Gibbs. When one is a woman, when one is writing poems, when one is drawn through a passion to know people today and the web in which they, suffering, find themselves, to learn the people, to dissect the web, one deals with the processes themselves. To know the processes and the machines of process: plane and dynamo, gun and dam. To see and declare the full disaster that the people have brought on themselves by letting these processes slip out of the control of the people. To look for the sources of energy, sources that will enable us to find the strength for the leaps that must be made. To find sources, in our own people, in the living people. And to be able to trace the gifts made to us to two roots: the infinite anonymous bodies of the dead, and the unique few who, out of great wealth of spirit, were able to make their own gifts. Of these few, some have been lost through waste and its carelessness. This carelessness is complicated and specialized. It is a main symptom of the disease of our schools, which let the *kinds* of knowledge fall away from each other, and waste knowledge, and time, and people. All our training plays into this; our arts do; and our government. It is a disease of organization, it makes more waste and war.

Presumption it is to call it a disease, to say that it is one of the reasons Gibbs was lost, and the main reason he has not been found.

Lost, I say, and *found;* but he was never lost. It was that he has

not reached far enough, and that we have not reached far enough
to meet him.

Rukeyser herself was never literally lost. In her lifetime, she
was sometimes the target of extraordinary hostility and ridicule,
based on a critic's failure to read her well or even try to understand her methods: often, during the 1940s and 1950s especially,
because she was too complicated and independent to follow any
political "line" or because she would not trim her sails to a
vogue of poetic irony and wit, an aesthetics of the private middle-class life, an idea of what a woman's poetry should look like.
    Rukeyser lived and worked through a period of general polit-
ical discontent in the 1940s and 1950s—disillusionment with
Stalinism leading to a blind hatred of Marxism for some ex-
Communists, compounded by FBI and McCarthy Committee
persecution of suspected Communists and "fellow travelers." At
the same time, white and male middle-class poets, especially in
the northeastern United States, were being hired into the universities as writing teachers, while university-trained scholar-
critics were replacing poets as the interpreters of poetry. Rukeyser's books were praised by a range of her peers. Through her
mature life she was recognized with those grants and honors that
she called "the toys of fame." But in the history of poetry and
ideas in the United States—always difficult to grasp because of
narrow definitions, cultural ghettos, the politics of canon mak-
ers—she has not been seriously considered in the way that, say,
the group of politically conservative white southern poets
known as the Fugitives or the generation of men thought to
have shaped "modern poetry"—Ezra Pound, T. S. Eliot, William Carlos Williams, Wallace Stevens—have been considered.
Her thought remains unintegrated into our understanding of the
poetic currents, the architectonic shifts of the twentieth century.
Her poetry not only didn't fit the critical labels, she actually

defied the going classifications, declaring them part of the "disease of our schools."

She was a woman who wrote—as a sexual woman and as a Jew—unapologetically. The chartings of modern poetry were the work not just of men, but of Anglo-Saxons and Christians. She never thought of herself as making an academic career, with its fragmentation into periods or "fields" of all she sought to connect. So those who think in such patterns may have had difficulty reading her.

She was never literally lost, but we have still to reach her.

———

How do we reach her? Most of her work is out of print. Poets speak of her, but she is otherwise barely known—least of all for her biographies, which in their visionary scholarship put to shame the genre as it's generally practiced today. Included in a major current college anthology, her poems are preceded by patronizing and ignorant commentary: "To be absolutely contemporaneous was the aim of Muriel Rukeyser. . . . Her first volume, *Theory of Flight* (1935), displayed her knowledge of aviation. . . . Her poems seem to arise from her like natural growths." Well, Whitman and Dickinson have suffered like silliness and cluelessness in popular anthologies, both in terms of commentary and of selection.

Rukeyser was immersed in history, science, art, and the Western poetic tradition. She revised her poems furiously, was a memorable teacher of poets. How should it be necessary to say this here? Had a man of her class and background put forth this kind of lifework in scholarship and theory along with poetry, would it be so difficult to embrace his achievement, to reach him?

We reach her, of course, as we reach all poetic resources

blocked from us by mindless packaging and spiritless scholarship. We reach her by recognizing our need for her, by going to libraries and taking out volume after volume, by going, finally, to the crossroads—of poetry, politics, science, sexuality—and meeting her there, where she waits, reaching toward us.

 XIV

The real,
not the calendar,
twenty-first century

August 1991. The commander in chief for the Persian Gulf War resigns his command. His memoirs have been purchased for over $5 million. Already a paperback, *Norman Schwarzkopf in His Own Words* appears on the bookrack of my local market.

The leading best-seller in "self-help" nonfiction this month, according to the *New York Times,* is a book on suicide for people with terminal illness. In the bookshop where I buy the papers, there's a notice on the counter: "WE HAVE THIS ON ORDER. SIGN UP FOR IT NOW."

I think of Toni Morrison's *Sula,* of Shadrack, the traumatized veteran of World War I, returning to the poor Black community from which he came:

Shadrack began a struggle . . . to order and focus experience. It had to do with making a place for fear as a way of controlling it. He knew the smell of death and was terrified of it, for he could not anticipate it. It was not death or dying that frightened him, but the unexpectedness of both. In sorting it all out, he hit on the notion that if one day a year were devoted to it, everybody could get it out of the way and the rest of the year would be safe and free. In this manner he instituted National Suicide Day.

On the third day of the new year, he walked through the Bottom down Carpenter's Road with a cowbell and a hangman's rope calling the people together. Telling them that this was their only chance to kill themselves or each other.

At the end of the novel, Shadrack, "still energetically mad," is still alive.

But any of us would want to know how to do it. Not just those with terminal illness, dreading the power of the doctors to keep them technically alive, captive, staked like Gulliver to a bed, with wires and tubing. Any of us would want, taken by the enemy, to have the vial of strychnine to crush under the tongue. And who do we mean by the enemy?

After the sex manuals, the relationship manuals, the success manuals—the suicide manuals?

A society in depression with a fascination for violence wants to know how to do it.

At the end of the year 1989, in the tumult and shift of peoples pressing into the streets, across borders, tearing down boundaries and symbols of the State, arguments went back and forth in the United States press as to whether 1990 or 1991 would actually be the first year of the new decade, whether 2000 or 2001 would be the first year of the new century. As if numerical precision could lend reassurance and order to that anarchy of the unexpected, could save us from the mistake of untimely emotions, premature celebrations, or from arriving late and unready at the new era.

Against that breaking up of Cold War frontiers and fixities, I saw a ghost: a woman with white hair and a hooked nose, the extraordinary profile of her youth, once framed in gleaming black, now turned full-face and fleshy. She lived through 1914, 1917, Stalinist terror, the siege of Leningrad, her son's imprisonment, killing and deportation of friends, censorship, banning, exile, provisional rehabilitation, the Cold War; dying of a heart attack at sixty-seven. She appeared to me half-translucent, super-imposed on a black-and-white image of a cart of logs being trundled by an anonymous old woman through snowy streets, speaking from the poem she was writing to the end of her life, her "Poem without a Hero":

> And ever-present in the freezing, prewar,
>   Lecherous, terrible, stifling air
>   Lurked an incomprehensible rumble . . .
> But then it was barely audible,
>   It scarcely reached the ear
>   And it sank into the snowdrifts by the Neva.
> Just as in the mirror of a horrific night
>   A man is possessed and does not want
>   To recognize himself.

Along the legendary embankment
The real—not the calendar—
Twentieth Century draws near.
—Anna Akhmatova,
looking back to 1914

But the Western dream of quantification expresses itself in anxiety about time as if manageable through numerals. Numerals set in months whose names are rife with mythic associations, intimations of weather and seasonal cycles, which are embedded in other numerals signifying years—"calendar" years, "school" years, "fiscal" years, ritual years, decades, and centuries—the grid on which we try to order individual and collective time. *Time is the school in which we learn,* wrote Delmore Schwartz, *that time is the fire in which we burn.* A new engagement calendar can set off feelings of anxiety, anticipation, melancholy, absurdity— that those neat headings and parallel squares can possibly represent the currents of life in which the unforeseeable has so much power. Like Shadrack, we want to fend off that power with calendar time.

But underlying the names and numerals—15 Elul 5740, February 19, 1942—are the phases of the moon and tides, the planet's tilting in its orbit, and the phases of our incommensurable inner life, for which we have no conscious dating and sometimes no conscious memory. Yet the anniversary of a death, a rape, a fire, a miscarriage, a betrayal, a deep humiliation, a mutilation can year after year extrude its splinters, almost to the day, into the scar tissue of the well-annealed self, determined to obliterate, to go on without looking back. Sometimes we can bring the thing forward, recognize why a certain time of year, even a certain light or smell, carries such disturbance or blankness in a life apparently ongoing. We can come to respect the recurrence, meet it halfway, not as interruption, but as the kind of repetition by which *(Time is the school)* we learn.

And, surely, we can assume that episodes of collective, civil loss, shame, betrayal dwell in the national psyche unacknowledged, embedded like shrapnel, leaving a deep, recurrent ache in the body politic? Not only the trauma's victims are held in thrall by the trauma.

When Maya Lin's black granite wall, the Vietnam War memorial, was unveiled during the third year of Reagan's "feel-good" presidency, it aroused bitter hostility, was assailed as "subversive," "perverse," "degrading." Some critics found its very blackness in a city of white monuments, its lack of a graphic chauvinism, especially offensive. Yet the Wall became a magnet for citizens of every generation, class, race, and relationship to the war perhaps because it is the only great public monument that allows the anesthetized holes in the heart to fill with a truly national grief. Somewhat later, the AIDS quilt began to draw thousands of citizens to gaze upon the evidence, to mourn a different kind of collective loss. Two concrete and spiritual statements: one, permanently set in the midst of official Washington, has become the repository of thousands of offerings and personal messages; the other, stitched together in communities across the country, from fragile materials, still having to be stitched as names still must be added, constantly in travel. Both countering the silences of public and private life; both perhaps more powerful than we yet know—as a communal art can be powerful—in changing our conception of ourselves as a people. Neither has been co-optable for commercial ends.

Is it in 1992 that the real, not the calendar, twenty-first century will begin?

XV

"A clearing in the imagination"

Misprision. I first learned that word in a Shakespeare sonnet I memorized in school. An Elizabethan word, rarely used today. It means "mistakenness," "to have taken something wrong"— "misapprehension" or "misperception" we might say today. *So thy great gift, upon misprision growing/Comes home again, on better judgment making. Misprision* comes to me as I listen to early newscasts of the old-line "coup" against reforms in the Soviet Union. Misprision of power; misprision of meanings, effects of this event; misprision of history. The experts, as in the telecasts of the Gulf War, thrashing in the narrow tunnels of their expertise. Misprision of power, misconduct or neglect of duty by a public official. To have taken something wrongly, to have mis-taken, to have ill used what was taken, what ought not to have been taken, to misrepresent, misapply, divert to other means what ought to have its own rhythm and purpose. *Misprise:* to value wrongly.

To value wrongly—the worst misconduct by a public official since upon it all the others grow like molds.

In the same week as the attempted Soviet coup, the president of the United States, signing a bill for the relief of poverty but declining to approve funding to implement the measure, says, in this way, he demonstrates his sympathy for the poor.

In this time, a critic of poetry writes: *The question for an American poet, living in relative personal and national peace and plenty, is how to find the imaginative interest in life without invoking a false theatricality, how to be modest without being dull, how to be moving without being maudlin.*

For an ever-growing spectrum of our people, the word "relative" in this sentence must be heavily underscored. Images of sub-Saharan famine, of fleeing Kurds massed on mud slopes, of disappearances and torture in Chile, Argentina, El Salvador, Serbo-Croatia may lead some of us to count ourselves fortunate and leave it at that, or—perhaps—to begin asking, On whose suffering does our relative peace and plenty depend?

"To find the imaginative interest in life" suggests a vigorous, gray-headed, comfortably retired middle-class citizen considering the choice of a hobby or volunteer work: hardly the work of the poet. For most people, let alone most poets, the problem is not "finding an imaginative interest in life," but sustaining the blows of the material and imaginative challenges of our time. A growing, perhaps predominant, number of poets write—when and as they are able to—out of fields of stress that cannot be evaded, public crises of neglect and violence.

———

The freeway is crisscrossed by overpasses, narrow pavements stretching next to concrete bulwarks or chain link fences. Along the pavements, from my car, I see more and more walkers. They push laundry carts hung with plastic bags stuffed with sleeping bags, clothing, newspapers, and strung around with smaller bags. They wear heavy clothes in the bright midwinter California sun. They are slung with knapsacks, they carry shopping bags. They are noticeable here where few other pedestrians are seen; elsewhere they mingle with the foot traffic on frontage roads and main avenues. They are men and women of all ages, shades of color, some with children, some with dogs. They, who other people try not to notice, have to have keen eyes, have to notice many things I don't, horrible and useful things, truths about this small town lying in apparent peace and plenty by the Pacific Ocean, truths about other people.

Last night I dreamed I was eating in a restaurant alone. At a table near me, bare of food or utensils, sat a woman, middle-aged, with the ruddy-sheened skin of someone who lives outdoors. I had left half a plate of pasta, was asking for my check when the waitress said, "Do you mind if I give it to her?"

I then understood that the woman was homeless, was waiting for leftover food. I said, "No," and the waitress motioned the woman over to the table where I was sitting. I realized that I was going to have to sit there with her while she ate my leftovers.

Relative peace and plenty. I've sat in actual—not dream—restaurants, at windows where I saw poor people pausing, scanning the posted menu, staring in at my or others' plates of fried dumplings, moo shu pork, moving on. I've sat at white-clothed café tables; a few feet beyond the bright doorway, carefully spaced, a figure, elderly, thin, extending an arm: "Some money please," a monotone to save the muscles of the throat, every gesture an economy. I have had to let go of the ignorant, the arrogant idea of my youth and middle age—that I would always be able to manage, somehow, anywhere, under any circumstances—the idea that has also let me take risks, speak truth to power in my own ways, the idea that if you lost everything you'd still have in mind the books you'd read. I see people living on the streets and know they have capacities, powers, learning I lack. A rigorous eye for function and value, for human character, a quick take on what will help get through another night, a scientific judgment for which cast-away sandwich can be safely eaten, which can give you the bad shits, though still smelling good with fried onions on the crispening autumn air.

This isn't my territory yet, I tell myself—perhaps never. But it feels closer to home than it once did; there are more and more older women furiously evaluating the wares of the public dumpsters, more and more younger women for whom this is just how—fangs bared—you can get along.

———

The critic's task is not to try to deflate, shrink, and contain the scope of poetry, but rather, as John Haines has written, to provide "a space in which creation can take place, a clearing in the imagination."

Haines is criticizing North American poetry for its "sporadic and shallow response to things"—for its lack of ideas, its "casual, happenstance character, the same self-limited frame of reference." "What is such an art beyond mere self-entertainment for the few?" This is a poet speaking who wants more of poetry than modesty without dullness.

Haines is himself a poet who has looked beyond North American "relative peace and plenty" to the cramping of human thought and spirit that is both cause and effect of the evisceration of not-human nature:

I
In the forest without leaves:

forest of wires and twisted steel . . .

The seasons are of rust
and renewal,
or there are no seasons at all,

only shadows that lengthen
and grow small—
sunlight on the edge of a blade.

Nothing that thrives, but metal
feeding on itself—

cables for roots,
thickets of knotted iron,
and hard knots of rivets
swelling in the rain.

Not the shadows of leaves,
but shadows where the leaves might be . . .

VII
Say after me:

I believe in the decimal,
it has divided me.

From my tent of hair
and the gut-strings that held it;
from my floor of grass
and my roof of burning cloud.

I have looked back across
the waste of numerals—
each tortured geometry
of township and lot—

to the round and roadless vista,
to the wind-furrow
in the forest track,
when I had myself entire.

Say after me:

That freedom was weight and pain,
I am well-parted from it.

Each was too large
and the sky too great.

I believe in my half-life,
in the cramped joy
of partitions,
and the space they enclose . . .

VIII
Building with matches,
pulling at strings,
what games we had.

Monopolies, cartels,
careers in the wind,
so many tradesmen of dust.

Steam in the kettles,
blades in the cotton—
big wheels went round.

And soon there was nothing
but lots and corners,
the world chopped to pieces.

Each piece had a name
and a number,
thrown in a box:

games given to children,
they too might learn
to play—
grow old and crooked,

fitting the pieces,
pulling at strings.

IX
Those who write sorrow on the earth,
who are they?

Whose erased beginnings still
control us—sentence
by sentence and phrase by phrase,

their cryptic notations vanish,
are written again
by the same elected hand.

Who are they?

Remote under glass, sealed
in their towers
and conference rooms—

Who are they?

Agents and clerks, masters
of sprawl—
playful men who traffic in pain.

Buried in their paragraphs,
hidden in their signatures—

Who are they?

X
Life was not a clock,
why did we always measure
and cramp our days?

Why the chain and why
the lock,
and why the chainman's tread,

marking acres and stony squares
out of the green
that was given?

To see in a forest
so much lumber to mill,
so many ricks to burn;

water into kilowatts,
soil into dust,
and flesh into butcher cuts—

as we ourselves are
numbered, so many factors
filed in a slot.

Say after me:

The key that winds the clock
turns a lock
in the prison of days. . . .

———

I would rephrase the critic's sentence and say: *The question for a North American poet is how to bear witness to a reality from which the public—and maybe part of the poet—wants, or is persuaded it wants, to turn away.* Then and only then, when this is said, can we talk about the necessity of rejecting false theatricality and maudlinity, and about all the other problems of creating an art rooted in language, a social art, an art that is not mere self-entertainment for the few.

———

When the landscape buckles and jerks around, when a dust column of debris rises from the collapse of a block of buildings on bodies that could have been your own, when the staves of history fall awry and the barrel of time bursts apart, some turn to prayer, some to poetry: words in the memory, a stained book

carried close to the body, the notebook scribbled by hand—a
center of gravity.

> When you imagine trumpet-faced musicians
> blowing again inimitable jazz
> no art can accuse or cannonadings hurt,
>
> or coming out of your dreams of dirigibles
> again see the unreasonable cripple
> throwing his crutch headlong as the headlights
>
> streak down the torn street, as the three hammerers
> go One, Two, Three on the stake, triphammer poundings
> and not a sign of new worlds to still the heart;
>
> *then* stare into the lake of sunset as it runs
> boiling, over the west past all control
> rolling and swamps the heartbeat and repeats
> sea beyond sea after unbearable suns;
> *think:* poems fixed this landscape: Blake, Donne, Keats.
> —Muriel Rukeyser

Or you might say: Senghor, Césaire, Brathwaite, Walcott,
Brand. Or Darío, Neruda, Dalton, Paz. Or Tsvetaeva, Akhmatova, Mandelstam. Or Sor Juana de la Cruz, Mistral, Castel-
lanos, Morejón. Or Hart Crane, Jeffers, Rukeyser. Or McKay,
Harper, Jordan, Lorde, Sanchez. Blake, Donne, and Keats are
magnificent, but they are not enough. And Rukeyser knew it.

Or words on a wall, anonymous:

> On a long voyage I travelled across the sea.
> Feeding on wind and sleeping on dew, I tasted hardships.
> Even though Su Wu was detained among the barbarians, he would

one day return home.
When he encountered a snow storm, Wengong sighed, thinking of
bygone years.
In days of old, heroes underwent many ordeals.
I am, in the end, a man whose goal is unfulfilled.
Let this be an expression of the torment which fills my belly.
Leave this as a memento to encourage fellow souls.

Sadly, I listen to the sounds of insects and angry surf.
The harsh laws pile layer upon layer; how can I dissipate my hatred?
Drifting in as a traveller I met with this calamity.
It is more miserable than owning only a flute in the marketplace
of Wu.

Or—on a different wall—

> En el bote del county
> Con toda mi loca pasión
> Puse tu placa en la celda
> Y con ese pensamiento
> Estoy sufriendo mi desgracia
>
> (In the county jail
> With all my crazy passion,
> I place your name on a cell wall
> And with this thought
> I suffer my disgrace.)

 XVI

What is an
American life?

What is an American life? What houses it?

On the Navaho reservation, hogans, trailers, small adobe
houses; on a back road near Window Rock, cardboard huts like
those in photographs of South African shantytowns or those that
cling to rusted fences under the on-ramp of the Brooklyn
Bridge. On the high mesas, Hopi adobes at the cliff's verge,
material poverty poised above transcendent blue space and silence. Back of the tourist roads at the North Rim of the Grand
Canyon, workers' dorms with rusty barbecue grills, plastic toys,
and broken plastic chairs on the beaten dirt outside; the park
rangers' cabins, manicured like a military base, flag flying in front
of the office. Mormon cottages of gingerbread wood, small well-

watered lawns, rosebushes in a Utah town set at the foot of intransigent rock, mountains barren of vegetation. A Quonset hut with a satellite dish, a pen for animals, a water tank. Tepees, real and lived-in; others fabricated as motel units, "trading posts." School buses driven in for migrant workers' shelter, moored behind barbed wire at a ranch's edge. Low-crouched on the desert, colorless prefab houses, some of which move along the road on the flatbeds of trucks bearing them to construction sites. On the one real street of a village nested in a mountain pass, or left untouched by the freeway, a hand-lettered sign for the in-home beauty parlor housed in someone's bungalow or half a duplex: Casa de Beauté, Lila's Unisex Clip and Curl. Around larger towns everywhere, condominium estates of relentless pastel and earth tones, sameness disguised as variation, weekend homes for the well-to-do or domiciles the bottom of the middle-class struggle to afford. Real wealth is invisible, at the ends of long, unmarked private roads; the landing strips of private planes don't identify themselves.

"Theme parks" proliferate, family farms go bankrupt, white urban flight seeks its own artificial peace and plenty, silent spotless streets behind electric gates, suburbs that never knew an *urbs,* never a civic center or heartbeat. And in the stripped and crippled *urbs,* from Harlem to Houston to Los Angeles, new waves of immigrant labor sleep in rented closets; children go forth to half-gutted schools; incinerators, landfills, sewage and toxic-waste plants are crammed next to the ghettos.

Poems fix this landscape. A full moon rises over the young Jimmy Santiago Baca, housed in a New Mexico prison:

> I saw the moon at first one blue twilight,
> standing, blowing drops of breath into cold air,
> standing in my prison jacket, 4:30,

in the compound, circled with high granite walls,
not a stir, but glare of spotlights, the silent
guard towers and stiff-coated guards above them all.

A big bloated desert moon, there,
how held up, such a big moon? Such a passionate tear!
How, against the velvety spaciousness of purple sky,
how does it hold itself up, and so close to me! To me!

Tell me! What should it mean,
that a moon like a wolf's yellow eye
should stare into my eye directly?
My finger, had I raised my arm,
could have punctured it like a peach and on my head
sweet juice drips, I could have pushed my finger in,
retrieved the seed of its soul, the stern hard pupil,
and placed it upon my tongue, sucked its mighty power

of dreams! Dreams, for how I needed them,
how I howled inside, sweeping great portions of thoughts
away with steel blue blades of the hour,
this, the time of my imprisonment.

I split days open with red axes of my heart,
the days falling like trees
I chopped up into each hour
and threw into the soul's fire.

I had not known the desert's power back then.
I had not known the black-footed demons
pecking each lightray as if it were straw.
I had not known my dreams, diamond hard,
could break at the silence of dragging winds;

no, nor that a pebble could come to mean
a world, unlocking fear. . . .

I looked into that moon, amazed, never
having seen a moon so much mine,
gathering my plundered life into its arms.

Moon! Moon! Moon! that twilight morning,
on the way to the kitchen to have some coffee,
thinking of my ten years to do in prison,
bundled up in my jacket, my boots feeling good and firm,
walking on under the guard's eye, blinded and blank-eyed,
to my escape, my freedom just then,
the guard's ears clogged, deaf,
when the moon said, "You are free,
as all that I have, winds, mountains, you are free. . . .

_____

David Mura, third-generation Japanese-American poet:

What does it mean when poets surrender vast realms of experience to journalists, to political scientists, economists? What does
it mean when we allow the "objectivity" of these disciplines to be
the sole voice which speaks on events and topics of relevance to
us all?

It is equal to living in a tragic land, said Wallace Stevens, *to live in
a tragic time.* But time and place are not separable. Time has been
tragic here for five hundred years; before that, the land was not
tragic, it was vast, fertile, generous, dangerous, filling the needs
of many forms of life. From the first invasion, the first arrogant
claiming, it became a tragic land. In all the explicit destructions,

all the particular locations of the tragedy, this is the fatal contra-
diction, the knowledge Whitman couldn't bear or utter (he was
far more explicit and courageous about sex)—the great rip in the
imaginative fabric of the country-to-be: the extraordinary cruelty, greed, and willful obliteration on which the land of the free
was founded. Cruelty, greed, assassination of cultures are part of
all history. But we, here, have been staggering under the weight
of a national fantasy that the history of the conquest of the
Americas, the "westward movement," was different—was a history of bravery, enlightenment, righteous claiming, service to
religious values and civilizing spirit.

What can this mean for poetry? It hardly matters if the poet
has fled into expatriation, emigrated inwardly, looked toward
Europe or Asia for models, written stubbornly of the terrible
labor conditions underpinning wealth, written from the mi-
crocosm of the private existence, written as convict or aristocrat,
as lover or misanthrope: all our work has suffered from the destabilizing national fantasy, the rupture of imagination implicit in
our history.

But turn it around and say it on the other side: in a history of
spiritual rupture, a social compact built on fantasy and collective
secrets, poetry becomes more necessary than ever: it keeps the
underground aquifers flowing; it is the liquid voice that can wear
through stone.

Poets newly arriving here—by boat or plane or bus, on foot or
hidden in the trunks of cars, from Cambodia, from Haiti, from
Central America, from Russia, from Africa, from Pakistan, from
Bosnia-Herzegovina, from wherever people, uprooted, flee to
the land of the free, the *goldene medina,* the tragic promised
land—they too will have to learn all this.

What can it mean to say, in 1993, that we have no "emergency" situation here in North America, that because this is not Eastern Europe, South Africa, the Middle East, a poetry that doesn't assume a matrix of normality is inauthentic, melodramatic? In her memoir of her husband's persecution and exile as an anti-Stalinist poet, Nadezhda Mandelstam charted not only the methods of a particular system of state terrorism, but the public psychology that accompanied it: not only fear, but self-deception, *the progressive loss of a sense of reality,* the need to feel that *everything is going along as it should, and that life continues—but that is only because the trams are running.*

No one who loves life or poetry could envy the conditions faced by any of the Eastern Europeans or Black South Africans (for a few examples in this century) whose writings were actions taken in the face of solitary confinement, torture, exile, at the very least proscription from publishing or reading aloud their work except in secret. To envy their circumstances would be to envy their gifts, their courage, their stubborn belief in the power of the word and that such a belief was shared (even punitively). And it would mean wanting to substitute their specific emergencies for ours, as if poets lacked predicament—and challenge—here in the United States.

 XVII

"Moment of proof"

Nadezhda Mandelstam says that in 1952, when Anna Akhmatova's son was being held hostage, even that proud, uncompromising poet wrote a couple of "positive" poems to Stalin. They were weak poems, she says, and anyway didn't have much effect. A poet in the United States is not under pressure to write poems in praise of the President, a victorious general, or "democracy." A poet can write *as if* everything were "going along as it should," with, perhaps, a touch of ecological melancholy or a vignette of the homeless. But even this is not demanded. The Kremlin officialdom, and the petty literary bureaucrats who hung to its coattails, dimly understood, as our bureaucrats (and even some of our poets) don't, that poetry is where the imagination's contraband physical and emotional imprintings are most

concentrated, most portable—traceable on a scrap of paper, a bar
of soap, able to be committed to memory as a novel or play
cannot—as only a song or a joke is portable; that it's the imagination that must be taken hostage, or terrorized, or sterilized, in
order for a totalizing unitary power to take control of people's
lives. However stupidly and brutally the Soviet hierarchy may
have grasped this, they understood it because of the residual
power of poetry in the Russian and other sovietized cultures, a
power deriving from oral cultures, still very much alive. The
dying, thrashing state corporate power now prevailing in the
United States has been able to rely—without giving it much
thought—on what Muriel Rukeyser called "the fear of poetry"
in a technologically advanced, corporate-driven society.

In a poem wryly entitled "Reading Time: 1 Minute 26 Seconds," she evokes it:

The fear of poetry is the
fear: mystery and fury of a midnight street
of windows whose low voluptuous voice
issues, and after that there is no peace.

That round waiting moment in the
theatre: curtain rises, dies into the ceiling
and here is played the scene with the mother
bandaging a revealed son's head. The bandage is torn off.
Curtain goes down. And here is the moment of proof.

That climax when the brain acknowledges the world,
all values extended into the blood awake.
Moment of proof. And as they say Brancusi did,
building his bird to extend through soaring air,
as Kafka planned stories that draw to eternity
through time extended. And the climax strikes.

Love touches so, that months after the look of
blue stare of love, the footbeat on the heart
is translated into the pure cry of birds
following air-cries, or poems, the new scene.
Moment of proof. That strikes long after act.

They fear it. They turn away, hand up palm out
fending off moment of proof, the straight look, poem.
The prolonged wound-consciousness after the bullet's shot.
The prolonged love after the look is dead,
the yellow joy after the song of the sun.

The first gesture of fending off is the implied question *How much of my time is this going to take up?* The poem's title answers with clocked, numerical precision. But the poem moves against its title, since a poem might "take" a lifetime. Elsewhere Rukeyser writes:

> I remember a psychologist with whom I talked in New Haven. That is a good town to produce an image of the split life: it is a split town, part fierce industrial city, part college, very little reconciled. . . . I spoke to a psychologist, a man who has made his work and his theme the study of fear, and the talk went well enough until poetry was mentioned. Then, with extreme violence, a violence out of any keeping with what had gone before, the psychologist began to raise his voice and cut the air with his hand flat. He said, his voice shaking, that he had cut poetry out of his life, that that was something he had not time for, that was something out of his concern.

There *is* fear of the experience that leaves a mark, the moment when the brain is not split from the blood, the "moment of proof" against which all other experience is to be tested. Of which Audre Lorde has said:

It forms the quality of the light within which we predicate our hopes and dreams toward survival and change, first made into language, then into idea, then into more tangible action. Poetry is the way we help give names to the nameless so it can be thought. The farthest horizons of our hopes and fears are cobbled by our poems, carved from the rock experiences of our daily lives.

Survival and change. Nadezhda Mandelstam, writing in Moscow in the late 1960s:

> Recently I heard someone say: "It is well known that everybody who has ever tried to make people happy only brought total disaster on them." This was said by a young man who does not want to see any changes now, in case they only bring new misfortune on him and others. There are large numbers of people like him nowadays—among the more or less well-off, needless to say. They are mostly young specialists and scientists whose services are needed by the State. They live in inherited apartments of two (or even three or four) rooms, or they can expect to get one from the organization in which they work. They are horrified at what their fathers have wrought, but they are even more horrified by the thought of change. Their ideal is to pass their lives quietly working at their computers, not bothering their heads about the purpose or result, and devoting their free time to whatever gives them pleasure.

I wonder where they are now—in their fifties, sixties—those once-young people who, *not bothering their heads about . . . purpose or result,* fitted so well and so fatalistically as cogs in a brutal and doomed technocracy. But no one then guessed it was doomed; no one then, after the Prague spring of 1968, could have told them how shudderingly it would come apart.

 # XVIII

"History stops
for no one"

It was not natural. And she was the first. . . .
   A poet can read. A poet can write.
   A poet is African in Africa, or Irish in Ireland, or French on the left
bank of Paris, or white in Wisconsin. A poet writes in her own language.
A poet writes of her own people, her own history, her own vision, her
own room, her own house where she sits at her own table quietly placing
one word after another word until she builds a line and a movement and
an image and a meaning that somersaults all of these into the singing, the
absolutely individual voice of the poet: at liberty. A poet is somebody
free. A poet is someone at home.
   How should there be Black poets in America?
                                    —June Jordan, "The Difficult Miracle
                                       of Black Poetry in America"

Zi shemt zikh/She is ashamed

Zi shemt zikh.

           She has forgotten
           alts fargesn

forgotten it all.

Whom can I speak to?
she wonders. . . .

Mit vemen
ken ikh redn?
Whom can I speak to?

di meysim farshteyen
mir afile nit
even the ghosts
do not understand me. . . .

In der femd
among strangers
iz hir heym
is her home.
—Irena Klepfisz, "*Di rayze aheym/*
The Journey Home"

To have as birthright a poetic tradition that everyone around
you recognizes and respects is one kind of privilege. At very
least, it lets you know what you hold in your hands, as person
and artist. Like a strong parent who both teaches and browbeats,
can be learned from, stormed away from, forgiven, but whose
influence can never be denied. Like a family from which, even
in separation, you bring away certain gestures, tones, ways of
looking: something taken for granted, perhaps felt as constric-
tion, nonetheless a source, a point of departure.

Until recently, North American poetry has largely been the
province of people who possessed—or took on through education—a literary family tree beginning with the King James Bible,
the Greek and Latin classics, branching into the Renaissances of
Europe and England, and transported to the colonies by the
colonizers as part of their civilizing mission to the wilderness.
On that mission, they violently disrupted the original poetry of

this continent, inseparable as it was and is from Indian life. In the determination to destroy tribal life, poetry had to be desecrated. Later, the descendants of the desecraters collected, transcribed, and printed surviving Indian songs and chants as artifacts of a "vanishing" people. Only in the late twentieth century, a renaissance of American Indian culture has produced a new, written, poetic literature expressive of indigenous people who, in the words of the poet Chrystos, are emphatically "Not Vanishing."

Africans carried poetry in contraband memory across the Middle Passage to create in slavery the "Sorrow Songs." A young girl in slavery in Boston, Phillis Wheatley, mastered Anglo-American metrics and conventions to become, after Anne Bradstreet, the second woman (and the first Black) poet published in this country. African-American poets have had to invent and synthesize a language in which to be both African and American, to "write . . . towards the personal truth" of being African-American and create a poetics of that experience. They have above all created a musical language, jazz, which has incalculably affected the national poetic language.

Such writers—men and women of color, poets born to a language other than English, lesbian and gay poets, poets writing in the upsurge of the women's poetry movement of the past twenty years—have not started in cultural poverty even though their cultures have been ruptured and misprized. The relationship to more than one culture, nonassimilating in spirit and therefore living amid contradictions, is a constant act of self-creation. I see the life of North American poetry at the end of the century as a pulsing, racing convergence of tributaries— regional, ethnic, racial, social, sexual—that, rising from lost or long-blocked springs, intersect and infuse each other while reaching back to the strengths of their origins. (A metaphor, perhaps, for a future society of which poetry, in its present suspect social condition, is the precursor.)

One paradigm of this poetry of cultural re-creation is the work of Irena Klepfisz. It begins with a devastating exterior event: the destruction of European Jewry in the Nazi period through the genocide known as the Holocaust or, in Yiddish, *der khurbn*. "The Yiddish word was important, for, unlike the term Holocaust, it resonated with *yidishe geshikte,* Jewish history, linking the events of World War II with *der erste und tsveyster khurbn,* the First and Second Destruction (of the Temple)." Born in 1941 in the Warsaw Ghetto, this poet is unequivocally rooted in the matrix of history. Beginning with almost total loss—of family, community, culture, country, and language—she has taken up the task of re-creating herself as Jew, woman, and writer by facing and learning to articulate that destruction. If she had stopped there, had become only the author of her early poems and of *"Bashert,"* her work would have claimed a unique place in the poetry that necessarily, and stubbornly, came after Auschwitz.

But Klepfisz goes further, not by way of leaving behind *der khurbn*—an impossibility for any Jew or any other person who wants to understand living in the twentieth century—but by searching, through her poetry, for what is possible in a world where *this* was possible. Most poets emerge with existence itself as a given (though not always with literacy as a given, literature as a given). This poet cannot:

> during the war
> germans were known
> to pick up infants
> by their feet
> swing them through the air

and smash their heads
against plaster walls

somehow
i managed
to escape that fate.

Lines like graffiti on a wall. The consciousness that, precisely, existence itself is not to be taken for granted will impel her journey.

What does it mean to be a Holocaust survivor or a child of survivors? The question has haunted Jewish life worldwide since 1945—through denial and silence, through amnesia and myth-ologizing, through a search for resonance. Certainly in the United States it has had its own reverberations and failures of resonance. For Klepfisz this is not just a question of present meaning, but of lost, irreplaceable resources, cultural and emo-tional riches destroyed or scattered before she could know them. The question for her is, then, also what it can mean to grow up as a Jew in the United States in the years after *der khurbn;* to grow into a Jewish woman, single, childless, a lesbian, an artist from a community of survivors who see their great hope for meaning in a new generation of Jewish children. What is allowed, what is available, to the poet located in these ways?

Before *der khurbn,* Yiddish poetry—the tradition Klepfisz might, "under other circumstances," have possessed as a contin-uing heritage—was largely written by men yet in the language called *mame-loshen* or "mother tongue": vivid, emotionally vi-brant, vernacular, as opposed to Hebrew, the language of schol-arship and religious study, reserved for men only. Yiddish was a people's language, a women's language, the language of the Ash-kenazic Jewish diaspora. The women poets of this tradition (many of them still untranslated, so that we have but a few names: Celia Dropkin, Anna Margolin, Kadia Molodowsky, Fradel Schtok, Malka Tussman among them) were known as more sexually frank than the men; but even of them the Anglophone reader knows only what's translated. It's a dead end to try to imagine what might have become of Yiddish poetry—or of Klepfisz as a poet—in a different history. The only history is the one we know, however imperfectly—that a great Western cultural movement was exterminated not only under the Nazis, but under Stalinism. Being "Western" didn't save this movement. And, to the present day, many Europeans of both East and West, many Americans of both North and South are unaware of, or indifferent to, this.

The great flowering of Yiddish literature took place in the late nineteenth and early twentieth centuries along with the rise of Jewish secularism and the Jewish labor and socialist movements. Out of these traditions, history uprooted Irena Klepfisz, depositing her into a community of survivors in New York.

————

In a time when speculative biography has been displacing serious writing about poets and poetry, I touch on this poet's personal history with some reluctance and only because it seems to me inseparable from a serious reading of her work. We have seen an obsession with intimate details, scandals, the clinical or trivializing reduction of artists' lives. The biographies of poets are commodities. It is also true that when a poet who is not male (or white) writes from direct experience, this poetry is subsumed as mere documentary or polemicizing. If I speak here, then, of experiences from which Klepfisz's poetry has been precipitated, it's because historical necessity has made her the kind of poet she is: neither a "universal" nor a "private" stance has been her luxury.

The ghettos of the Nazi period were part of a deliberate plan to destroy the Jewish people in their entirety. Throughout Poland, thousands of Jews were forced to retreat into increasingly densely populated areas enclosed by walls and barbed wire. By 1940 nearly half a million Jews were locked, compressed, within the Warsaw Ghetto; by 1941, the year of Klepfisz's birth, the penalty for attempting to escape was death. Of course, they were all under sentence of death: 83,000 Jews died from hunger and disease within twenty months in the Warsaw Ghetto alone. The ghettos were holding pens for Jews destined for forced labor camps and ultimate destruction—bases for selective deportation.

Throughout the ghettos Jews organized armed resistance movements. In Warsaw they constructed tunnels leading to the sewer system for escape and for bringing in arms and explosives. In street-to-street and under-street fighting the Jews held out. In April 1943 the Nazis decided to subdue the ghetto with an air attack. In this battle Michal Klepfisz, the poet's father, was killed. Because her mother had blue eyes and spoke fluent Polish, she and her child were able to pass and were hidden by Polish peasants. Polish became Klepfisz's first language. They emigrated after the war to Sweden, then to the United States when Klepfisz was eight years old, where she learned English in school while living in a world of spoken Yiddish: a world of people who had carried the remains of their culture to another continent—in their memories, in old snapshots and documents, archives rescued from conflagration, reconstituted institutions. And, not least, Klepfisz's mother, as a presence in her poems, embodies continuity, endurance, and the oral tradition's access to the lost.

The shattering of a culture is the shattering not only of artistic and political webs, but of the webs of family and community within which these are first nurtured and transmitted. Two long early poems, unpublished till 1990, delineate the search for what has most intimately been lost: the father-hero-martyr-deserter, whose absence becomes enormous presence:

> These two:
> widow and half-orphan
> survived and now resided
> in a three-room apartment
> with an ivy-covered fire escape
> which at night
> clutched like a skeleton
> at the child's bedroom wall . . .
>
> The missing one
> was surely
> the most
> > important
> link . . .
>
> And when the two crowded
> into the kitchen at night
> he would press himself between them
> pushing, thrusting, forcing them to remember,
> even though he had made his decision,
> had chosen his own way . . .
> he would press himself between them
> hero and betrayer
> legend and deserter—

> so when they sat down to eat
> they could taste his ashes.

But the search is also for all "those whom I would have known/ had circumstances been different. *Had circumstances been different:* a terse, matter-of-fact phrase behind which lies all the unprovable: history reversed or unwinding differently, the possibility of having lived "an ordinary life," the life of "common things, gestures and events" that Klepfisz invokes elsewhere, to have become not the child survivor lighting candles "for all the children/who have perished," but a child playing with other children, in Jewish Warsaw, in the *yidishe svive,* in a home peopled with parents, extended family, worker-intellectuals.

But because "history stops for no one," Klepfisz has gone on to write poetry of uncompromising complexity, clothed in apparently simple, even spare, language—simple and bare as the stage of a theater in which strict economies of means release a powerful concentrate of feeling.

———

There is extraordinary vitality in Klepfisz's early poems on women in the Holocaust. Images and voices rush. They floodlight a neglected dimension of the resistance to genocide: the survival strategies, the visceral responses, of women. They burn and bristle with urgency, contained within a disciplined and crafted poetics.

> when they took us   to the shower   i saw
> the rebitsin   her sagging breasts   sparse
> pubic hairs   i knew   and remembered
> the old rebe   and turned   my eyes away

i could still hear   her advice   a woman
with a husband   a scholar

when they turned   on the gas   i smelled
it   first   coming at me   pressed myself
hard to the wall   crying   rebitsin   rebitsin
i am here with you   and the advice you gave me
i screamed   into the wall   as the blood burst from
my lungs   cracking   her nails in women's flesh   i watched
her capsize   beneath me   my blood in her mouth   i screamed

when they dragged my body   into the oven   i burned
slowly at first   i could smell my own flesh   and could
hear   them grunt   with the weight of the rebitsin
and they flung   her on top   of me   and i could smell
her hair burning   against my stomach

when i pressed through   the chimney
it was sunny   and clear   my smoke
was distinct   i rose quiet   left her
beneath

"death camp" is a poem of death so alive that its smoke remains in our nostrils. As in other Klepfisz poems, control of tone
and image allow the wild and desperate quality of experience to
be heard. In "perspectives on the second world war," a "terror"—the woman hiding with her child, her hallucinating prescience of worse possibilities—is juxtaposed with a point later in
time when to speak of such things would be "too impolite" in
detached "conversations over brandy." These poems engage
physical and moral immediacy in ways that make them continu-
ingly urgent. In them, Klepfisz takes the considerable risk of
trying to bear witness to this part of her history without compro-

mise and without melodrama. She succeeds because she is a poet, not only a witness.

"Bashert" (Yiddish for "fated," "predestined") is a poem unlike any other I can think of in North American, including Jewish-American, poetry. It delineates not only the survivor experience (in the skin of the mother "passing" as gentile with her young daughter), but what happens after survival—the life that seems to go on but cannot persevere; the life that does go on, struggling with a vast alienation, in a state of "equidistance from two continents," trying to fathom her place as a Jew in the larger American gentile world, first as a student

> walking home alone at midnight. The university seems an island ungrounded. Most of its surrounding streets have been emptied. On some, all evidence of previous life removed except for occasional fringes of rubbish that reveal vague outlines that hint at things that were. On others, old buildings still stand, though these are hollow like caves, once of use and then abandoned. . . . Everything is waiting for the emptiness to close in on itself, for the emptiness to be filled in, for the emptiness to be swallowed and forgotten.

A landscape that might be some blasted Jewish ghetto of postwar Europe but is actually the edges of a Black ghetto surrounding an elite American university:

> I see the rubble of this unbombed landscape, see that the city, like the rest of this alien country, is not simply a geographic place, but a time zone, an era in which I, by my very presence in it, am rooted. No one simply passes through. History keeps unfolding and demanding a response. A life obliterated around me, of those I barely noticed. A life unmarked, unrecorded. A silent mass migration. Relocation. Common rubble in the streets.

This is not the mass-marketed immigrant experience. The poem is not about finding safety, freedom, a better life in America. It stares down the American myth that if you are just hardworking, virtuous, motivated, tenacious enough, the dream of freedom, security, and happiness can be realized. In its rhythmic, relentless, almost choral double dedication, it invokes the random and various shapes of death and survival. *"Bashert"* mourns the dead and the survivor alike, defying such ideas as that the fittest survive or that victims "choose" their destiny. Moving between poetry and blocks of prose in a poem where everything is made concrete and there are no cloudy generalities or abstract pronouncements, Klepfisz has written one of the great "borderland" poems—poems that emerge from the consciousness of being of no one geography, time zone, or culture, of moving inwardly as well as outwardly between continents, landmasses, eras of history; or, as Chicana poet Gloria Anzaldúa expresses it, in "a constant state of mental nepantilism, an Aztec word meaning *torn between ways.*" A consciousness that cannot be, and refuses to be, assimilated. A consciousness that tries to claim all its legacies: courage, endurance, vision, fierceness of human will, and also the underside of oppression, the distortions that quarantine and violent deracination inflict on the heart. When I say that *"Bashert"* is a poem unlike any other, I mean this through and through: in its form, in its verse and prose rhythms, in its insistence on memory without nostalgia, its refusal to let go.

And yet, as the poetry of this continent has become increasingly a poetry written by the displaced, by American Indians moving between the cities and the reservations, by African-Americans, Caribbean-Americans, by the children of the internment camps for Japanese-Americans in World War II, by the children of Angel Island and the Chinese Revolution, by Mexican-Americans and Chicanos with roots on both sides of the border, by political exiles from Latin America, *"Bashert"* takes its place (as does Klepfisz's poetry as a whole) in a multicultural literature of discontinuity, migration, and difference. Much of this new literary flowering is also lesbian or gay, feminist, and working class.

———

Displacement invents its poetics out of a mixture of traditions and styles, out of the struggle to name what has been unnameable in the dominant European traditions. (Yiddish itself has been disparaged by the privileging of Hebrew on the one hand and English on the other.) It is often a bilingual poetry, incorporating patois and languages other than English, not in allusion to Western or Asian high culture, as in Modernist poems of the 1920s and after, but because bilingualism is both created by the experience of being migrant, immigrant, displaced, and expressive of the divisions as well as the resources of difference. Klepfisz's bilingual poems do not—and this is significant—drop Yiddish phrases in a cosy evocation of an idealized past, embodied in *bubbe* and *zayde,* or as a kind of Jewish seasoning on an American tongue. Poems such as *"Di rayze aheym/*The Journey Home," *"Etlekhe verter oyf mame-loshen/*A few words in the mother tongue," or "Fradel Schtok" painfully explore the world of a writer located not only between landscapes, but also between languages; the words of the mother tongue are handled and savored with extreme delicacy, as a precious yet also tenuous legacy. In "Fradel Schtok" we enter the mind of a poet trying to change languages, far more internally rupturing than the change of countries. We meet Fradel Schtok at the moment when she feels her native language fading. *"Di rayze aheym,"* in deceptively simple and brief phrases, transposes *How shall I sing the Lord's song in a strange land?*—that ancient Jewish lament—into *How shall I remember, how shall I speak, in the language of an alien* *culture?* There is a paradox here: Klepfisz uses the Anglo-American language with enormous sensitivity, consciousness, and art. But these qualities emerge not from a triumphant linguistic posture, but precisely from her refusal to pretend that it is the language of choice or the supremely expressively language.

In white North America, poetry has been set apart from the practical arts, from political meaning, and also from "entertainment" and the accumulation of wealth—thus, pushed to the margins of life. Klepfisz, inheriting an entwined European-Jewish-Socialist-Bundist political tradition and a Yiddish cultural tradition, naturally refuses such "enclosures." In particular, the refusal to segregate art from daily life and work is a pressing concern for her. And surely the Holocaust itself—as well as the tradition of *yidishkayt*—demands a renewed vision of what art—poetry, in this instance—stands for and against. Theodor Adorno's drastic statement that "after Auschwitz, to write a poem is barbaric" has to be severely parsed. If taken at face value, it would mean a further desolation even than we have already had to face. Adorno, a German Jew who lived for many years as a refugee in the United States, may have forgotten the ancient role of poetry in keeping memory and spiritual community alive. On the other hand, his remark might be pondered by all poets who too fluently find language for what they have not yet absorbed, who see human suffering as "material." Klepfisz's art resists such temptations, both through the force and beauty of her work, and by the ways in which she demands accountability of art.

———

Survivorhood isn't a stasis; the survivor isn't an artifact, despite efforts perhaps to reify or contain her, give her the lines we think she ought to speak. Klepfisz's poems are the work of a woman who feels, acts, and creates in living time: a feminist, a lesbian, an activist in the women's movement for many years, an essayist and editor as well as a poet. She writes sometimes from cities where a window box, a potted plant, a zoo, an arboretum become "mnemonic devices" for the natural world and "water is a rare sight . . . but it can/be reached"; sometimes from a countryside or a shoreline where

> she'd never before been forced to distinguish
> herself from trees   or sand and sea   and it became ob
> vious that when it came to rocks   she could never prove
> her own distinctness.

From the urban plant that sensualizes the apartment where two women make love, or the fiercely generative tangle of narcissus roots in a glass jar, to a garden of wildflowers transplanted with uneven success to the "inhospitable soil" of a former garage, the sudden wildness of a city cat transplanted to the country, living things are charged in these poems by a fresh and totally unsentimental consciousness. There is a tough and searching empathy; the poet is not outside of nature, looking in: she is observant and participant, a different yet kindred being who instinctively responds to growth, deprivation, persistence, wildness, tameness.

Klepfisz is also one of those artists who, within and by means of her art, explores the material conditions by which the imaginative impulse, which belongs to no gender, race, or class, can be realized or obstructed. "Contexts" places the child's passion for words alongside the seamstress-mother's recognition of how bread must be put on the table; the poet-proofreader along with the aging blind scholar for whom she works; the worker going home wearily by subway with the beggar working the car. "Work Sonnets" depict the crushing of dreamlife and imagination in those who, because of class, race, and gender, get written off by capitalism and its need for robots: they are not expected to dream. But the woman clerical worker who finally speaks in the poem has a dreamlife, if a buried one, and has evolved her own strategies for survival, calculating closely her participation in the system—and even, ironically, in the poem. These poems are political to the core without a single hortatory line. Like their author, they do not take their existence for granted.

Later poems examine the pain and necessity of a Jew who identifies with the Palestinians under Israeli occupation. From the Warsaw Ghetto resistance to the *intifada* her trajectory is clear:

> All of us part.   You move off   in a separate
> direction. The rest of us return
> to the other Jerusalem.   It is night.
> I still hear your voice.   It is in the air
> now   with everything else   except sharper
> clearer.   I think of your relatives
> your uncles and aunts   I see the familiar
> battered suitcases   cartons with strings
> stuffed pillowcases
> children sitting on people's shoulders
> children running to keep up . . .
>
> . . . If I forget thee
> Oh Jerusalem   Jerusalem   Hebron
> Ramallah   Nablus   Qattana . . .
> . . . may I forget
> my own past   my pain
> the depth of my sorrows.

Throughout, this poetry asks fundamental questions about the uses of history. That it does so from a rootedness in Jewish history, an unassimilated location, is one part of its strength. But history alone doesn't confer this strength; the poet's continuing labor with Jewish meaning does. The other part, of course, is the integrity of its poetics. A Klepfisz poem lives amid complex tensions even when its texture may appear transparent. There is a voice, sometimes voices, in these poems that can often best be heard by reading aloud. Her sense of phrase, of line, of the shift of tone is almost flawless. But perfection is not what Irena Klepfisz is after. A tension among many forces—language, speechlessness, memory, politics, irony, compassion, hunger for what is lost, hunger for a justice still to be made—makes this poetry crucial to the new unfoldings of history that we begin, in the 1990s, to imagine.

XIX

The transgressor
mother

The other night I watched Costa-Gavras's film *Missing* on the
VCR—a political film about the collaboration of the United
States with right-wing coups in Latin America in the name of
protecting our business interests. But the story, the reason we
watch, is the quest of a father—a conservative Christian Scientist
from upstate New York—who goes to a Latin American country held in terror by a newly installed junta to find his errant son,
"missing" because the young man has asked too many questions,
been too sympathetic with the wrong side. It's the story of a loss
of innocence, of parent-child bonds stronger than ideology, of
the political education to which these lead.

This is a father/son story, in part a father/daughter-in-law story (Jack Lemmon and Sissy Spacek walking off arm in arm in the final shot, united at last in grief and anger). The fundamental motivating force, the impulse transcending life-style and generation, is the father's determination to recover his son, in uneasy alliance with the far less naive daughter-in-law's determination to find her husband. It's made clear early on that the older man can get attention that the young woman cannot, can elicit male acknowledgment and surface deference even while he's being spun about in the webs of official collaboration with the death squads.

The father's passion for the son (tested, as with Isaac and Abraham; mourning, as David for Absalom) has been a validated passion, involving not only love, but the transfer of power and privilege, initiation into male identity and ritual— the hunt, the whorehouse, sports, prayer, the field of war. The mother's passion for the son is an accused passion: accused of weakening, of binding, of castrating. Feminists too have found it problematic, seeing maternal pride and energy diverted from daughters in preference for sons, or the instrumental mother sending her sons to war for the State. Accusations against the mother, whatever her uses of her passions, proliferate in any event, wherever social institutions fall short of human needs and expectations.

———

In 1989, the Academy of American Poets awarded the Lamont Prize for a distinguished second book of poetry to a collection of poems charged by a lesbian mother's passion for her sons. That is not its only impulse. It is charged as much by the poet's passion for life, a woman's life vaguely unfolding until shocked out of innocence into politics, much as Costa-Gavras's straight

American father is shocked out of innocence into politics: the pain of living becomes more than you can explain by your previous interpretations of the world. It addresses also the question of secrets—what can be told in the face of fear and shame, what can get heard, if told: the secret spoken yet unreceived because it is dissonant with the harmonies we like to hear. And, as the title suggests, this is a book about nature—literally, the natural world as spiritual resource and as home-out-of-home, including rivers, creatures, seasons, shells, blood, mud, the mother's body, the son's body, the bodies of same-sex lovers. It unsettles definitions of what is "natural" and definitions of criminality.

Minnie Bruce Pratt's *Crime against Nature* is, for a number of reasons, a work at the poetic crossroads. It extends the subject of love poetry; it extends the subject of feminist and lesbian poetry; it looks in several directions through the lens of a strong, sensuous poetics, through that fusion of experience with imagination that is the core of poetry, and through cadences founded in the music of speech, tightened and drawn to an individual pitch.

Pratt emerged as a poet in the women's liberation movement in the 1970s with a substantial chapbook, *The Sound of One Fork* (1981), and later a first volume, *We Say We Love Each Other* (1985), published by a lesbian-feminist press. From the first her talent has been striking, her poems rooted in the landscape and culture of the southeastern United States, in female thwartedness and anger, in the ferment of a time when the women's movement was being catalyzed out of the African-American, antiwar, and other movements for liberation. *The Sound of One Fork* is a poetry fresh with the release of long-repressed themes:

> I used to drive down the coast to sleep with her,
> past the faded grey fields of sand and houses

closed up for the night. Sometimes there was a glow in the east
like the fires of the paper mill at Riegelwood, but then
I would curve suddenly where the land flattened to swamp
and the moon would flash orange, rise and turn
yellow as her hair, white and cool as her turned back.

All the way down the moon shone through me.
I was transparent with desire and longing,
clear as glass and ready to break under her look.
The moon shone down on my hands curled
right around the steering wheel, shone down
into the ditch beside the road,
into the oiled water drifting there,
reflected black light back into the stars,
poured down again into the throats of the pitcher plants,
onto the white arms of the bracted sedge, shone
down on the teeth and hinged open jaws
of the Venus' fly trap, its oval leaves like eyelids
fringed with green lashes, its leaves curved
together like clasped palms with fingers intertwined.

We Say We Love Each Other takes as a given love and desire
between women and explores the geography within which they
are enacted—a geography in which women begin to speak of
what had formerly gone into diaries, burned; in which rape and
racial violence continue, uprooted rural women, Black and
white, plant urban gardens, and two women lovers struggle
to stay together. Pratt's love poems have never been romantic or utopian (the title of the poem I quote from above—
"Romance"—is ironic). Their power is fused in a conjunction
of achingly erotic images and the facts of a world beyond: helicopter searchlights outside a window, the torn fabric of a

woman's plaid shirt, an ice storm, a smashed bottle, a political meeting, memories of women on a screened porch in the rural South, the invasion of Grenada, or

> . . . the place of the Piscataway
> and the Nanticoke, of fugitives, and runaway slaves: their homes
> built in the low places: corn patches, pigs, rockfish
> in hand's reach, the children raised under no owner,
> maple seeds into wings like green grasshoppers, summer
> fevers, the messages, plans for rebellion and freeing the land,
> the sudden bloody raids . . .
> by fall, the brief grass shelters overrun
> with catbrier, bullbrier, wild grape, and the struggle begun
> somewhere else, a river lowland, the Mobile, the Tombigbee,
> or in the river of grass, Pahokee, Okeefenokee, or north
> along the Savannah, the Altamaha, the Cape Fear, the Mattaponi,
> the Potomac.

Is this lesbian poetry? Yes—and most potently—because it is grounded in and insistent to grasp the poet's own white southern Christian culture with its segregated history and legacy of contradictions, the beauty and sorrow of its landscape, its sexual codes and nightmares. She knows the region's living creatures, how they move and unfold, how wild country and gardens coexist; she pays attention to people; she tries to "remember, and failing that, invent" (Monique Wittig) where a white woman can stand in that heritage. Is this "southern poetry?" Yes—in a new way: the white woman turned outsider as lesbian connects differently with the white southern literary tradition, Agrarians and Fugitives, required reading in college, Allen Tate, John Crowe Ransom, their loyalties and affiliations with the Confederate dead. And she connects differently with her own ancestors.

Pratt knows the soil of Alabama as a native, while recognizing where her people's land rights and privileges came from, and at whose cost.

The explicit eroticism of the poems—tangled always in the search for mutual knowledge—has been appreciatively noted. What has received less attention, perhaps, is that the sexual women in these poems are activists whose bedroom is never far removed from what happens in the streets. It should go without saying, but probably doesn't, that no lesbian or gay bedroom—in whatever gentrified neighborhood or tent pitched off the Appalachian trail—is a safe harbor from bigotry (and for some, not only bigotry, but lethal violence). But, of course, we'd like to write our poems of lying before or after love, naked in late morning sun, "Il Pastor Fido" or Nina Simone in the background, door innocently ajar to balcony or meadow or fire escape or tent roof dappled with reflected lake water. And sometimes we do, wishfully evoking a privacy we know is always under siege, an innocence we can't really afford. (I'm not speaking of AIDS now, which has given rise to a remarkable poetry of its own.) But the energy of Pratt's erotic poetry derives not only from a female sensuality only now beginning to find its way into poetry, but from the inseparability of sensuality from politics. To act on a criminalized sensuality demands, in this poet's experience, many kinds of decriminalization—not only of sexual acts, but of poverty, skin, difference.

———

Crime against Nature goes to the heart of that experience: the lesbian losing custody of her two young sons because of her sexual "crime" and her refusal to hide it—her rationed visitations with them, their long-distance relationship, her self-accusations, the accusations of others, her struggle to maintain both her integrity and her bonds with her children. Yet the mother's passion holds with her sons; they are bound together by affinities beyond gender or sexuality. Their attachment has to find its way past the terms of accusation, the scenarios of guilt,

> I could do nothing.   Nothing.   Do you
> understand?   Women ask: *Why didn't you—?*
> like they do of women who've been raped.
> And I ask myself: Why didn't I? Why
> didn't I run away with them? Or face
> him in court? Or—
> Ten years ago I
> answered myself: No way for children to live.
> Or: The chance of absolute loss.   Or:
>
> I did the best I could.   It was not
> enough.
> —"The Child Taken from the Mother"

> The first question is: *What do your children*
> *think of you?*   No interest in the kudzu-green
> burial of the first house I lived in,
>
> nor in the whiskey, the heat, or the people sweating
> in church under huge rotate hands in the ceiling.
> The question is never the Selma march, and me
>
> breathing within thirty miles, or the sequence
> of Dante . . .
> —"The First Question"

and through memories of visitations, trips to the water, long car
drives in the dark,

> live heat
>> changed at midnight speed to wind,
>> our mouths singing, drinking the humid
>> cool breath of trees, and yelling swift
>>
>> blackness to come home with us, reckless
>> in the deep night, carrying everything with us,
>> all life and even death without a pause before us,
>>
>> the sudden red-eyed possum, live eyes
>> dead, impossible but gone, our cries,
>> grief, and them questioning me, miles,
>>
>> or perhaps this happened after the curve
>> we hurtled and the moon, huger than a world
>> directly in the road, moved our moves,
>>
>> low orange eye, high hot-white when we got home.
>> —"The First Question"

This, one can say, is the "plot" of the book; but to say it is only a
beginning.

Crime against Nature is in fact a long poem, a form toward
which Pratt has been working since "The Segregated Heart" in
The Sound of One Fork or the "Waulking Songs" and "Reading
Maps" sequences in *We Say We Love Each Other*. We can read it
as a narrative poem, along the lines of the "plot" sketched above.
Or we can read it as a sequence of love poems, of a kind we
haven't seen before. The agonist, the lover, is lesbian; her sexual
hungers are for women. The love in these poems, being love for

her sons, is cross-gender but forbidden—not only because, legally and patriarchally, "lesbian" is equated with "unfit mother," but because, as the poems reveal, this is a subversive maternality, hardly of the cookies-and-milk or "with your shield or on it" variety. Moreover, the mother speaks not only from her love for her sons, but from her need to be, and for them to see her, as she is. This is the poetry of an undomesticated passion.

The dedicatory poem "For My Sons" places itself against a tradition of paternal poetry:

> ... Coleridge at midnight,
> Yeats' prayer that his daughter lack opinions,
> his son be high and mighty, think and act ...
>
> When you were born, my first, what I thought was
> milk ... With you, my youngest, I did not
> think ...
>
> Your father was then
> the poet I'd ceased to be ...
> It's taken me years to write this to you.
>
> ... I can only pray:
> That you'll never ask for the weather, earth,
> angels, women, or other lives to obey you;
>
> that you'll remember me, who crossed, recrossed
> you,
>   as a woman making slowly toward
> an unknown place where you could be with me,
> like a woman on foot, in a long stepping out.

The poems are dug out of long silence—

> A huge sound waits, bound in the ice,
> in the icicle roots, in the buds of snow

on fir branches, in the falling silence
of snow, glittering in the sun . . .
—"Justice, Come Down"

—a silence not only the poet's, but created by lack of resonance.
I think of Käthe Kollwitz's images: *Begging Woman and Child,
Mother Pressing Infant to Her Face, Peasant Woman Holding Child,
Woman with Dead Child, Sleeping Woman with Child*. But we lack
the concept of a mother whose children are living yet absent—
the apparently childless mother. (Photographs of the Madres de
Plaza de Mayo come to mind, women testifying to the disap-
pearance of their children.) Pratt conjures such images: women
in a lesbian bar—

. . . to go in

here is to enter where my own suffering exists
as an almost unheard low note in the music,
amplified, almost unbearable, by the presence
of us all, reverberant pain, circular, endless,
which we speak of hardly at all, unless a woman
in the dim privacy tells me a story of her child
lost, now or twenty years ago, her words sliding
like a snapshot out of her billfold, faded outline
glanced at and away from, the story elliptic, oblique
to avoid the dangers of grief.   The flashes of story
brilliant and grim as strobe lights in the dark,
the dance shown as grimace, head thrown back in pain . . .

All the women caught in flaring light, glimpsed
in mystery: The red-lipped, red-fingertipped woman
who dances by, sparkling like fire, is she here on the sly,
four girls and a husband she'll never leave from fear?

The butch in black denim, elegant as ashes, her son
perhaps sent back, a winter of no heat, a woman's salary.
The quiet woman drinking gin, thinking of being sixteen,
the baby wrinkled as wet clothes, seen once, never again.

Loud music, hard to talk, and we're careful what we say.
A few words, some gesture of our hands, some bit of story
cryptic as the mark gleaming on our hands, the ink
tattoo, the sign that admits us to this room, iridescent
in certain kinds of light, then vanishing, invisible.
       —"All the Women Caught in Flaring Light"

And:

A darkened room. Color film stutters
on the screen. We watch a crowd falter

and surge at crossroads, demanding water.
A dark woman talks about her children. We hear

the parched land, the deaths, the miles.
She sits locked in barracks, steel,

not prison, off-hours from a company job.
No children allowed, just hotplates, cots.

A friend brings the children to her. At the gate
no one in or out. Guards see to that.

She reaches her hands to them through the fence,
through an iron grill, to the heads of her children.
       —"Seven Times Going,
       Seven Times Coming Back"

Crime against Nature might be read as a woman's testimony—her statement to the court, facing the judgment not only of family, law, society, but of the internal prosecutor—in brief, as a defense. But to read it so is to sell its emotional range and values short. This is the narrative of a woman self-described as

> wilful, voluble,
> lascivious, a thinker, a long walker,
> unstruck transgressor, furious, shouting,
> voluptuous, a lover, smeller of blood,
> milk, a woman mean as she can be some nights
> —"Poem for My Sons"

—insistent on her poetry, on her sexuality, but equally insistent on her bonds with her children. Just as, in her erotic poems, Pratt breaks the silence of sexual taboo, so here she breaks the silence that would stifle that other part of her: a mother. Against a system of thinking where women are either mothers full time and "fit" or "nonmothers" (by default or because ruled "unfit"), she reveals another possibility: a motherhood whose meaning has to be constructed, invented, by the forbidden mother in collusion with her children. And, because the mother is a poet, this invention must be made not only in life, but in poetry.

This, then, is the narrative of the transgressor mother. And, of necessity, the voice ranges from lyrical mourning to explosive anger, rasping pain:

> The faint streak of little fish, the dim bottom
> rocks heavy with quartz. Our fingers grope,
> sift sand, brittle mussel shells. We can drift
> close to the place where air, land, water meet,
> edge of the creek, and see on the damp margin

a squiggled trail, infinite small snail tracks,
no beginning or end, wrinkled, undeciphered,
a message left for us, mysterious words seen
through the huge eye of the creek.
—"Dreaming a Few Minutes
in a Different Element"

The long sweating calls to the twelve-year-
old, saying, *Hold on* against the pain,
how I knew it from when I left, the blame
inside, the splintered self, saying to him, *Walk
out*, remind the body you are alive, even if
rain is freezing in the thickets to clatter
like icy seeds, even if you are the only one
plodding through the drifts of grainy snow.
—"Shame"

There is no sentimental haze, no delusion that children as well as mother do not suffer. These are not fluent, mellifluous poems. They are laden with mud, flint, asphalt, blood, their field of energy is restless and impatient of resolutions, they traverse switchbacks between past and present, the mother's childhood, her children's emerging manhood:

There it is: the indelible mark, sketched
on his belly, tattoo of manhood, swirled line
of hair, soft animal pelt, archaic design,
navel to hidden groin.   He squints, reaches
for a shirt, stretches in the tender morning
light high over me.   My shock is his belly
like my young body, abdomen swollen pregnant
and luxuriant with hair, a thick line of fur,

navel to cunt. A secret message written on me
by him before his birth, faded, yet now surfaced
there with his body's heat, a physical thought,
a remark on my strict ideas about men and women.
—"At Fifteen, the Oldest Son
Comes to Visit"

The poet Pratt most makes me think of—or maybe it's the other way around since I've been reading Pratt longer—is Sharon Olds, whose erotic heterosexual poems, like Pratt's lesbian erotic poems, seem to me to have only recently begun to be possible and whose poems to her children—not severed from her by force—are of a comparable passion, the undomesticated passion of the erotically alive mother.

Muriel Rukeyser once said of her own work, "It isn't that one brings life together—it's that one will not allow it to be torn apart." When an undomesticated woman refuses to hide her sexuality, abnegate her maternity, silence her hungers and angers in her poetry, she creates—as Rukeyser did, as Audre Lorde has done, as Pratt and Olds are doing—a force field of extraordinary energy.

———

In *Crime against Nature*—as in Rukeyser's work overall—there is unevenness, patches where the struggle to explain submerges the poetry. Sometimes Pratt deliberately breaks into colloquial prose, as if in despair with poetry. In part, this need for explanation derives from the very nature of her undertaking: the desire, having ruptured a social web, broken a silence, to be heard, to *communicate*. But the communication of poetry takes place beyond frameworks of explanation. I want Pratt to trust the power of her most intense rhythms, her most inspired images, to "slide stone from the cave's mouth" (her words).

In an important essay, "Identity: Skin Blood Heart," Pratt has written about the white southern woman (herself, Confederate diarist Mary Boykin Chestnut) who has listened to Black church music "as if using Black people to weep for me." She says:

> Finally I understood that I could feel sorrow during their music, and yet not confuse their sorrows with mine, nor use their resistance for mine. *I needed to do my own work:* express my sorrow and responsibility myself, in my own words, by my own actions. I could hear their songs as a trumpet to me: a startling, an awakening, a reminder, a challenge: as were the struggles and resistance of other folk: but not take them as replacement for my own work.

So, too, on the other side: we've railed, women poets, at the dead poets' society, the men's bull pen, its extraordinary blinders and self-centeredness, and we've been right. But, without accepting the misogyny, the racism, the sentimentalism, the patriotic gore, the passive aestheticism, the clique-spirit, I believe the new women poets can learn to use what they've sieved up from the old river, combining it anew; it doesn't have to be a dead hand in the boat, and, certainly, it is no replacement for women poets' own new work. Pratt is a classically schooled poet who knows Ovid, Cato, Coleridge, Yeats. I want to say to her: *Use everything—use it all.*

Like African-American, colonized, and working-class writers, feminists (who may be any or all of the above) have paid attention to the processes by which imposed silence, muteness, speechlessness have broken into language. This is only natural, since literacy and education have not been women's historical prerogative, even in classes and cultures where they were open to men. And the privilege of literacy and education doesn't begin to open the doors of taboo against lesbian and feminist authorship and authority. It's no coincidence that the women's liberation movement of the 1970s and 1980s generated not only an astonishing literary renaissance, but presses, periodicals, criticism, a context to nourish it.

———

Pratt's *Crime against Nature,* like her first book, was accepted for publication by a small lesbian-feminist press, Nancy Bereano's Firebrand Books. It then received the Lamont Prize. At the award ceremonies in May 1989, under the auspices of the Academy of American Poets, I found myself, as often when I used to live in New York during the 1960s and 1970s, at the Guggenheim Museum waiting for a poetry reading to begin. But never before had I seen there the convergence of two worlds: the official poetry establishment and the feminist and lesbian poetry and publishing community, laced with activist friends. Clashes of style there were from the first: the clash between what Ira Sadoff, in the *American Poetry Review,* calls "neo-formalism," on the one hand, and "dynamic, unsettling poetry," on the other; between white North American literary culture's discomfiture with politics, on the one hand, and the sense of politics and culture as fused in the women's movement or in the "second culture" or "parallel *polis,*" as Vaclav Havel identified it in Communist Eastern Europe, on the other. Reading Havel's essay "The Power of the Powerless," I was indirectly reminded of the scene at the Guggenheim that evening: two different cultural realities in one society where new social forces are at work. What I observed, in the fidgety-nervous or elaborately condescending behaviors of the two Chancellors of the Academy on the stage, faced with an undomesticated woman poet from the other culture, was the reaction to having a purlieu invaded, a ritual space violated, the rules of decorum broken. Establishment good manners began to fray into irritable gestures (watch-consulting, note-passing during Pratt's reading). Self-control was running thin. Minnie Bruce Pratt, raised as a polite southerner, accepted her award graciously, seriously—hardly an unleashed Fury. Perhaps, by the other culture's etiquette, she accepted it too seriously, in the sense of affirming the context of her work: she paid tribute to the women's and gay liberation movements; she used the word—"lesbian." The transgressor mother, the transgressor poet (in that she wrote of this at all) was evidently an unsettling presence altogether.

I want to say that the Academy of American Poets is not the enemy, despite hostile twitchings on the stage of the Guggenheim that night. The Academy of American Poets hardly possesses the power of the Czechoslovak Communist party of 1975. I want to say that the real enemy is Jesse Helms and the lily-livered legislators, curators, and cohorts of arts foundations who have marched to his words. I want to say this, but I have to qualify it. Institutions like the Academy of American Poets, the Poetry Society of America, the American Academy and Institute of Arts and Letters have a heightened responsibility today. They can be cautious, acquiescent, play it safe in a climate of political instability and riskiness, throw away what power they have, and make the work of repression much easier. Or they can become radicalized—in their vision of what a truly American poetry might be and is becoming, and in their understanding of the political meanings of art, and of how to use the resources they control. As a society in turmoil, we are going to see more—and more various—attempts to simulate order through repression;

and art is a historical target for such efforts. A distaste for the
political dimensions of art, in this time and place, is a dangerous
luxury.

Havel writes:

> The profound crisis of human identity brought on by living within
> a lie, a crisis which in turn makes such a life possible, certainly
> possesses a moral dimension as well; it appears, among other
> things, as *a deep moral crisis* in society. A person who has been
> seduced by the consumer value system . . . and who has no roots
> in the order of being, no sense of responsibility for anything
> higher than his or her own personal survival, is a *demoralized* per-
> son. The system depends on this demoralization, deepens it, it is
> in fact a projection of it into society.

Elsewhere he names the "secret streamlet [that] trickles on beneath the heavy lid of inertia and pseudo-events, slowly and
inconspicuously undercutting it. It may be a long process, but
one day it must happen: the lid will no longer hold and will start
to crack."

These passages were written in 1978 and 1975, respectively.
The lid, here in capitalist North America, is a different lid, constructed of a different amalgam of lies, and we are deep in our
own moral crisis, beyond the crisis of civic infrastructure, economic rifts, the alienation of government from the people. That
secret streamlet to which Havel alludes flows here as well, beneath the toxic dumps of disinformation, and poets and artists are
far from being the only people who try to keep its channel clear.
But certainly we who make any kind of claims for art—that it is a
vital way of perceiving and knowing, that it deserves support in
a system that supports so few human needs, that it is more than a
commodity—need to be thinking seriously now about the lies
within which we are asked to live. That *Crime against Nature*

received a Lamont Prize, that Pratt, Chrystos, and Lorde were awarded NEA writers' grants are signs of the power not only of their work, but of the current of resistance running beneath the inertia and pseudo events that have constituted public life in the United States for two decades. That the NEA grants in 1990 also came with a directive that they are not to be used for the making of art that "in the judgment of the NEA . . . may be considered obscene, including, but not limited to, homoeroticism," is a reminder that art is still guilty until proven innocent, in these United States.

 X X

A communal poetry

One day in New York in the late 1980s, I had lunch with a poet
I'd known for more than twenty years. Many of his poems
were—are—embedded in my life. We had read together at the
antiwar events of the Vietnam years. Then, for a long time, we
hardly met. As a friend, he had seemed to me withheld, de-
fended in a certain way I defined as masculine and with which I
was becoming in general impatient; yet often, in their painful
beauty, his poems told another story. On this day, he was as I had
remembered him: distant, stiff, shy perhaps. The conversation
stumbled along as we talked about our experiences with teaching poetry, which seemed a safe ground. I made some remark
about how long it was since last we'd talked. Suddenly, his
whole manner changed: *You disappeared! You simply disappeared.* I

realized he meant not so much from his life as from a landscape of poetry to which he thought we both belonged and were in some sense loyal.

If anything, those intervening years had made me feel more apparent, more visible—to myself and to others—as a poet. The powerful magnet of the women's liberation movement—and the women's poetry movement it released—had drawn me to coffeehouses where women were reading new kinds of poems; to emerging "journals of liberation" that published women's poems, often in a context of political articles and the beginnings of feminist criticism; to bookstores selling chapbooks and pamphlets from the new women's presses; to a woman poet's workshops with women in prison; to meetings with other women poets in Chinese restaurants, coffee shops, apartments, where we talked not only of poetry, but of the conditions that make it possible or impossible. It had never occurred to me that I was disappearing—rather, that I was, along with other women poets, beginning to appear. In fact, we were taking part in an immense shift in human consciousness.

My old friend had, I believe, not much awareness of any of this. It was, for him, so off-to-the-edge, so out-of-the-way; perhaps so dangerous, it seemed I had sunk, or dived, into a black hole. Only later, in a less constrained and happier meeting, were we able to speak of the different ways we had perceived that time.

He thought there had been a known, defined poetic landscape and that as poetic contemporaries we simply shared it. But whatever poetic "generation" I belonged to, in the 1950s I was a mother, under thirty, raising three small children. Notwithstanding the prize and the fellowship to Europe that my first book of poems had won me, there was little or no "appearance" I then felt able to claim as a poet, against that other profound and as yet unworded reality.

One rainy day in the spring of 1960, the San Francisco poet Robert Duncan arrived at my door, sent to me by our mutual friend Denise Levertov. I had a sick child at home, and we sat in the kitchen drinking tea. My son played fretfully in his high chair, sometimes needing to sit in my lap. Duncan began speaking almost as soon as he entered the house, he never ceased speaking; the fretful child, my efforts with the tea were in another realm from the one whence he spoke. I listened: I had heard much about him from Denise, had read, with difficulty and interest, the City Lights "Pocket Poets" edition of his poems. But I remember only vaguely what he talked about: poetry, the role of the poet, myth. I knew he was a significant experimental poet (and I still think his poetry truly serious and original though occluded in certain ways). It was clear he inhabited a world where poetry and poetry only took precedence, a world where that was possible. My sharpest memory is of feeling curiously negated between my sick child, for whom I was, simply, comfort, and the continuously speaking poet with the strangely imbalanced eyes, for whom I was, simply, an ear.

Later, driving him back to Boston in the rain, I realized my car was running on empty. Nervously, I eased it out of rush-hour traffic into a filling station. Duncan continued to talk, the monologue, perhaps, of a gifted talker, which can be started up, like a record, when the person doesn't know what to say.

I have thought since then that Duncan's deep attachment to a mythological Feminine and to his own childhood may have made it unlikely for him to meet—in any real sense—so unarchetypal a person as an actual struggling woman poet caring for a sick child. But also, Duncan was then trying to write—against the political and poetic tenor of the times, and through the medieval-nostalgic filter of his own vision—openly gay poetry.

Like Gertrude Stein, I'm sure he needed the veil of language, and of a highly discursive personality, that could at times be switched off but that also could be used as protection. I too was using my poetic language as protection in those years, as a woman, angry, feeling herself evil, other. A conversation between two such poets was not possible, on that rainy afternoon.

And yet, Duncan was the poet who had recently written, or was about to write, "Working in words I am an escapist; as if I could step out of my clothes and move naked as the wind in a world of words. But I want every part of the actual world involved in my escape," and

> For this is the company of the living
> and the poet's voice speaks from no
> crevice in the ground between
> mid-earth and underworld
> breathing fumes of what is deadly to know,
> news larvae in tombs
> and twists of time do feed upon,

> but from the hearth stone, the lamp light,
> the heart of the matter where the

> house is held

———

A poet's education. The San Francisco Renaissance of the 1940s and 1950, with which Duncan was identified, the poetic voices of the Black and antiwar movements of the 1960s had created a strong mix of antiestablishment poetics in the United States. But the poetry of women's liberation in the 1970s was *women's* anti-

establishment poetry, challenging not just conventional puritan-
ical mores, but the hip "counterculture" and the male poetry
culture itself. From muses and girlfriends of poets, from arche-
types of the Feminine, women were transforming themselves
into poetic authors. Heterosexual romanticism was being
probed by the sharp, skillful pens of poets like Marge Piercy and,
in Canada, Margaret Atwood. Black women poets were exploding at the intersection of two movements. Lesbian poets were
refusing to encode either their sexuality or their anger. Suddenly
women's poetry was burgeoning everywhere.

Certain poems are etched on this era in my life. I stand in the
City College bookstore, in my hands a yellow chapbook, *The
First Cities,* Audre Lorde's first collection, published by Diane di
Prima's Poets' Press, and I read:

A FAMILY RESEMBLANCE

My sister has my hair   my mouth   my eyes
and I presume her   trustless.
When she was young   open to any fever
wearing gold like a veil of fortune on her face
she waited through each rain
a dream of light.

But the sun came up
burning our eyes like crystal
bleaching the sky of promise and
my sister stood
Black   unblessed and unbelieving
shivering in the first cold show
of love.

I saw her gold become an arch
where nightmare hunted

the porches of her restless nights.
Through echoes of denial
she walks
a bleached side of reason
secret now
my sister never waits
nor mourns the gold
that wandered from her bed.

My sister has my tongue
and all my flesh
unanswered
and I presume her
trustless
as a stone.

I knew that I had found a remarkable new poet and that she
was also a colleague, someone I might actually talk with. Meeting one day on the South Campus of CCNY, we began a conversation that was to go on for over twenty years, a conversation
between two people of vastly different temperaments and cultural premises, a conversation often balked and jolted by those
differences yet sustained by our common love for poetry and
respect for each others' work. For most of those twenty-odd
years, during fourteen of which she struggled with cancer, we
exchanged drafts of poems, criticizing and encouraging back and
forth, not always taking each others' advice but listening to it
closely. We also debated, sometimes painfully, the politics we
shared and the experiences we didn't share. The women's liberation movement was a different movement for each of us, but our
common passion for its possibilities also held us in dialogue.

Lying in bed with 'flu, opening a new journal, *Amazon Quarterly,* to a long poem by a working-class California poet then
unknown to me, Judy Grahn:

A WOMAN IS TALKING TO DEATH

One

Testimony in trials that never got heard

my lovers teeth are white geese flying above me
my lovers muscles are rope ladders under my hands

we were driving home slow
my lover and I, across the long Bay Bridge,
one February midnight, when midway
over the far left lane, I saw a strange scene:

one small young man standing by the rail,
and in the lane itself, parked straight across
as if it could stop anything, a large young
man upon a stalled motorcycle, perfectly
relaxed as if he'd stopped at a hamburger stand;
he was wearing a peacoat and levis, and
he had his head back, roaring, you
could almost hear the laugh, it
was so real.

"Look at that fool," I said, "in the
middle of the bridge like that," a very
womanly remark.

Then we heard the meaning of the noise
of metal on a concrete bridge at 50
miles an hour, and the far left lane
filled up with a big car that had a
motorcycle jammed on its front bumper, like

the whole thing would explode, the friction
sparks shot up bright orange for many feet
into the air, and the racket still sets
my teeth on edge.

When the car stopped we stopped parallel
and Wendy headed for the callbox while I
ducked across those 6 lanes like a mouse
in the bowling alley. "Are you hurt?" I said,
the middle-aged driver had the greyest black face,
"I couldn't stop, I couldn't stop, what happened?"

Then I remembered. "Somebody," I said, "was *on*
the motorcycle." I ran back,
one block? two blocks? the space for walking
on the bridge is maybe 18 inches, whoever
engineered this arrogance, in the dark
stiff wind it seemed I would
be pushed over the rail, would fall down
screaming onto the hard surface of
the bay, but I did not, I found the tall young man
who thought he owned the bridge, now lying on
his stomach, head cradled in his broken arm.

I read on: a narrative poem of two white, working-class lesbians,
driving without a license, afraid to stay and witness, leaving a
Black man to the mercies of the police. I read on:

Four
A Mock Interrogation

. . .

Have you ever committed any indecent acts with women?

Yes, many. I am guilty of allowing suicidal women to die before my eyes or in my ears or under my hands because I thought I could do nothing, I am guilty of leaving a prostitute who held a knife to my friend's throat to keep us from leaving, because we would not sleep with her, we thought she was old and fat and ugly; I am guilty of not loving her who needed me; I regret all the women I have not slept with or comforted, who pulled themselves away from me for lack of something I had not the courage to fight for, for us, our life, our planet, our city, our meat and potatoes, our love. These are indecent acts, lacking courage, lacking a certain fire behind the eyes, which is the symbol, the raised fist, the sharing of resources, the resistance that tells death he will starve for lack of the fat of us, our extra. Yes I have committed acts of indecency with women and most of them were acts of omission. I regret them bitterly.

A few weeks later Grahn came to New York, and I went to hear her read in the Village. Later I wrote: "She read very quietly. I have never heard a poem encompassing so much violence, grief, anger, compassion, read so quietly. There was absolutely no false performance."

This was in 1974. Something the poem had unlocked in me was the audacity of loving women, the audacity of claiming a stigmatized desire, the audacity to resist the temptations to abandon or betray or deny "all of our lovers"—those of whatever sex, color, class with whom we need to make common cause and who need us. "A Woman Is Talking to Death" was a boundary-breaking poem for me: it exploded both desire and politics.

———

And somewhere in those years, riding a commuter train from Penn Station to New Brunswick, crossing the sulfurous reedy flats, I recall reading Margaret Atwood's "Circe/Mud" poems, especially the one beginning

Men with the heads of eagles
no longer interest me
or pig-men, or those who can fly
with the aid of wax and feathers

or those who take off their clothes
to reveal other clothes
or those with skins of blue leather

or those golden and flat as a coat of arms
or those with claws, the stuffed ones
with glass eyes; or those
hierarchic as greaves and steam-engines.

All these I could create, manufacture,
or find easily: they swoop and thunder
around this island, common as flies,
sparks flashing, bumping into each other,

on hot days you can watch them
as they melt, come apart,
fall into the ocean
like sick gulls, dethronements, plane crashes.

I search instead for the others,
the ones left over,
the ones who have escaped from these

mythologies with barely their lives;
they have real faces and hands, they think
of themselves as
wrong somehow, they would rather be trees.

In the tradition of new poetry movements of every geography and generation, this movement founded little magazines, published photo-offset chapbooks, broadsides, new journals like *Aphra, Amazon Quarterly, Azalea, Heresies, Moving Out, The Second Wave, Women: A Journal of Liberation;* anthologies of past and contemporary women's poetry began to appear: *Amazon Poetry, No More Masks!, The World Split Open, Mountain Moving Day.* The women-owned presses were starting up: Diana Press in Baltimore; Shameless Hussy Press, the Oakland Women's Press Collective, Kelsey Street Press, Effie's Press in the San Francisco Bay Area; Out & Out Books in Brooklyn; Motherroot in Pittsburgh; the Iowa City Women's Press. The proliferating feminist bookstores held poetry readings as regular community events. In 1974, at the University of Massachusetts in Amherst, there was a week-long International Women's Poetry Festival with readings and workshops indoors and out, some planned, others spontaneous. And politics were taken for granted as part of our poetic discussions.

A partial roster of women poets becoming active in the United States by the mid-1970s would include Alice Walker, Alta, Audre Lorde, Cherríe Moraga, Enid Dame, Fay Chiang, Honor Moore, Irena Klepfisz, Jan Clausen, Joan Gibbs, Joan Larkin, Judy Grahn, June Jordan, Karen Brodine, Kathleen Fraser, Kitty Tsui, Linda Hogan, Marge Piercy, Marilyn Hacker, Minnie Bruce Pratt, Nellie Wong, Pat Parker, Patricia Jones, Rikki Lights, Robin Morgan, Sara Miles, Sharon Olds, Sonia Sanchez, Stephanie Byrd, Susan Griffin, Susan Sherman, Teru

Kanazawa, Toi Derricotte, Wendy Rose, Willyce Kim. (I drew these names from my own archive of little magazines, anthologies, chapbooks published by women in the 1970s. The list is not definitive.) Here was a new spiraling out of American poetry, a new poetic movement.

Just as the women's liberation movement was a new force released from within the African-American struggle for justice and the New Left, this women's poetry movement was a necessary unfolding, both from the earlier poetic revolution and from the politics of the women's movement. That the origins and nature of poetry are not just personal but communal was an important legacy from the poetics that Kenneth Rexroth, Lawrence Ferlinghetti, Allen Ginsberg, among others, had brought to huge audiences in the 1950s and 1960s and from the Black Arts movement. The women's poetry movement had, thus, both social and poetic roots, and the fact is that they cannot be separated. Significantly, it was this movement that began to re-read and recognize (as in "know again") that great poet of inseparables, Muriel Rukeyser.

———

In 1978 four young New York City women poets (African-American Patricia Jones, Asian-American Fay Chiang, Euro-American Sara Miles, and Latina Sandra Maria Esteves) edited and published *Ordinary Women: An Anthology of Poetry by New York City Women*. The editors wrote: "This is . . . the first book of its kind . . . a woman's anthology that is not predominantly by white women, that is not a showcase for well-known writers. The poems here are by city women in their 20's and 30's, . . . of many races and backgrounds, of diverse styles and aesthetics, who come together to speak the truth about their own lives."

The reality of being women touches all racial and class structures: our intention was to unite on the basis of womanhood . . . voices in an urban reality, riding subways, working in factories, restaurants, offices, theatres, driving cabs, buying groceries, changing diapers.

—Sandra Maria Esteves

I want this book, through the multiracial, muti-ethnic range of works in it, to have an openness that we are beginning to feel: Black, white, Asian, Latin women moving through this city, everyday moving like all other women, tough and mad.

—Patricia Jones

I write poems, songs, otherwise I would be crazy, rationalizing away the feelings and spirits which embody my identity. . . . I hold it and taste it, but it is given form and shared like a meal with other, ordinary women living in the city.

—Fay Chiang

This is not a dream, and it's not easy. But the reality of what we're doing is at once more difficult and more interesting than any dream. It is day-to-day, ordinary, complicated: the links we make here are the bonds that women speaking together have always made, are ambivalent, fragile, hard.

—Sara Miles

As I was a child
hearing timber fall
in forests of anarchy,
faltering spots of
sunshine and injury,
spacing the beat
of time as I wished,

chasing lightning bugs,
as I was a child,
magic as
now
a thin cry
as I lie here,
feet in silver stirrups,
breasts perched on the side
of a precipice,
my cunt favoring
then your kiss,
now arid as Badlands,
torpor of an empress.

my tears are only mine.
    —Teru Kanazawa, "Aborting"

and when the center opened
I saw myself
and I saw my mother
the Moon
walking to the white man's factory
so she could catch sunsets
on the 18th floor
of the projects
    —Sandra Maria Esteves, "Ahora"

a cold place
detention house
not me
i'm glad not me
i said to him
inside not me
i'm glad not me

but you are
said he
you are
—Sandra Maria Esteves, "Visiting"

No backporch   in my mind
but there was beauty: sun
Slow setting on episcopal church
i thought it cathedral, a castle
whose tropical tree peeked
from alley   from back
Gracing the gray sinful concrete
block with relief, recessed
between aging buildings.
Our playcries melted
with fading day
Carhorns, hustlenoise muted
like thin horn players strain
for expression
Strain for expression . . . small store
and efficient. She peered between fronds
of her window jungle. (i would later
wonder: was this like her home?)
calling me, softsmiling, smile   worn
for me alone, deep but small lap
soon outgrown, never outgrown,
large bosom and salt and pepper
hair thickbraided, bound toward a knot.
Al/ways warm, comfort-fragrance
humming smoothe lullabies
Ringing cashregister
giving cookies talking silly
girl little 'n banana brown

oh! the sugarcane mangoes
and bunbread oh! the caresshappiness
funnynames: tutums

Deep times. The nono'African throat-
cluck, guidance gently, greatly indulging.
Growing fierce, steelfaced granite
Strong: for the white bill creature
Cheated but never shortchanged
Old women Sundayscreeching in West Indian church
he arose! he arose! he arose!

Defeated but victorious.
　　　—Akua Lezli-Hope, "To Every Birth Its Pain"

It was in the women's poetry and publishing movement that
I—and, I think, many others—began to perceive something
about the language we were writing in. Because many working-
class women were active in the movement, many women of
color (despite ongoing classism and racism there, as everywhere),
the spoken languages and intonations of diverse communities
were finding their way into poems, which were published in
feminist and lesbian newspapers, magazines and anthologies,
heard aloud at group poetry readings, and thus found their way
across lines that might have separated poets and readers and listeners without the centripetal force of the movement. For the
first time I understood that my poetic language wasn't "English," whatever my inarguable debts to the English poets: it was
American, though I had no full sense of what that might mean
except that my voice belonged here. Later I found, in a letter
from the American Indian writer Leslie Marmon Silko to the
Ohio-born white poet James Wright, her vision of an American
poetic diction:

You are fearless of the language America speaks and you love it. Some I think did not or do not fear it, but they do not love it and so write an English we seldom hear outside the university; and then there are many who love it but are afraid it isn't "poetic" or "literary." . . .

When I say "American" language I mean it in the widest sense—with the expansiveness of spirit which the great land and many peoples allow. No need ever to have limited it to so few sensibilities, so few visions of what there might be in the world. At the English Institute many of the members seemed so reluctant to acknowledge that Jamaican poets are using an English language which at once loves the music of the language so much as it loves the people and life which speak the language. . . . I . . . would like to think that we could see language more flexible and inclusive, that we could begin to look for the passion and the expression instead of language by rote . . . hideous, empty, artificial language television speaks. . . . [T]hat is the result of the past 50 years of working to eradicate regional usages, regional pronunciations, i.e. regional and community expression from American English, always with the melting pot theory in mind. To have a "standardized" language, in a land as big and as geographically diverse as this, certainly seems ridiculous to me.

Ordinary Women was in its own way an embodiment of this vision. And—despite the now surprising absence of identifiably lesbian authorship—it also embodied a sense of the voices of a nonstandardized women's movement that was to emerge more visibly in the Reagan years, even as a hideous, empty, artificial rhetoric seemed to push feminism and other dissident movements back to the wall.

 XXI

The distance between language and violence

She's calling from Hartford: another young dark-skinned man has been killed—shot by police in the head while lying on the ground. Her friend, riding the train up from New York, has seen overpass after overpass spraypainted: "KKK—Kill Niggers." It's Black History Month.

But this is white history.

White hate crimes, white hate speech. I still try to claim I wasn't brought up to hate. But hate isn't the half of it. I grew up in the vast encircling presumption of whiteness—that primary quality of being which knows itself, its passions, only against an otherness that has to be dehumanized. I grew up in white silence that was utterly obsessional. Race was the theme whatever the topic.

In the case of my kin the word sprayed on the overpasses was unspeakable, part of a taboo vocabulary. *That* word was the language of "rednecks." My parents said "colored," "Negro," more often "They," even sometimes, in French, *"les autres."*

Such language could dissociate itself from lynching, from violence, from such a thing as hatred.

A poet's education. A white child growing into her powers of language within white discourse. Every day, when she is about five years old, her father sets her a few lines of poetry to copy into a ruled notebook as a handwriting lesson:

> A thing of beauty is a joy forever;
> Its loveliness increases . . .

> Tyger, Tyger, burning bright,
> In the forests of the night;
> What immortal hand or eye,
> Could frame thy fearful symmetry?

She receives a written word in her notebook as grade: "Excellent," "Very good," "Good," "Fair," "Poor." The power of words is enormous; the rhythmic power of verse, rhythm meshed with language, excites her to imitation. Later, she begins reading in the books of poetry from which she copied her lessons. Blake, especially, she loves. She has no idea whether he, or Keats, or any of the poets is alive or dead, or where they wrote from: poetry, for her, is now and here. The "Songs of Innocence" seem both strange and familiar:

> When the voices of children are heard on the green
> And laughing is heard on the hill,

> My heart is at rest within my breast
> And everything else is still.

And

> My mother bore me in the southern wild,
> And I am black, but O! my soul is white;
> White as an angel is the English child:
> But I am black, as if bereav'd of light.

This poem disturbs her faintly, not because it in any way contradicts the white discourse around her, but because it seems to approach the perilous, forbidden theme of color, the endless undertone of that discourse.

She is not brought up to hate; she is brought up within the circumference of white language and metaphor, a space that looks and feels to her like freedom. Early on, she experiences language, especially poetry, as power: an elemental force that is *with* her, like the wind at her back as she runs across a field.

Only much later she begins to perceive, reluctantly, the relationships of power sketched in her imagination by the language she loves and works in. How hard, against others, that wind can blow.

———

White child growing into her whiteness. Tin shovel flung by my hand at the dark-skinned woman caring for me, summer 1933, soon after my sister's birth, my mother ill and back in the hospital. A half-effaced, shamed memory of a bleeding cut on her forehead. I am reprimanded, made to say I'm sorry. I have "a temper," for which I'm often punished; but this incident remains vivid while others blur. The distance between language and violence has already shortened. Violence becomes a language. If I flung words along with the shovel, I can't remember them. Then, years later, I do remember. *Negro! Negro!* The polite word becomes epithet, stands in for the evil epithet, the taboo word, the curse.

———

A white child's anger at her mother's absence, already translated (some kind of knowledge makes this possible) into a racial language. That *They* are to blame for whatever pain is felt.

———

This is the child we needed and deserved, my mother writes in a notebook when I'm three. My parents require a perfectly developing child, evidence of their intelligence and culture. I'm kept from school, taught at home till the age of nine. My mother, once an aspiring pianist and composer who earned her living as a piano teacher, need not—and must not—work for money after marriage. Within this bubble of class privilege, the child can be educated at home, taught to play Mozart on the piano at four years old. She develops facial tics, eczema in the creases of her elbows and knees, hay fever. She is prohibited confusion: her lessons, accomplishments, must follow a clear trajectory. For her parents she is living proof. A Black woman cleans the apartment, cooks, takes care of the child when the child isn't being "educated."

Mercifully, I had time to imagine, fantasize, play with paper dolls and china figurines, inventing and resolving their fates. The best times were times I was ignored, could talk stories under my breath, loving my improvised world almost as much as I loved reading.

Popular culture entered my life as Shirley Temple, who was exactly my age and wrote a letter in the newspapers telling how her mother fixed spinach for her, with lots of butter. There were paper-doll books of her and of the Dionne Quintuplets—five identical girls born to a French-Canadian family—and of the famous dollhouse of the actress Colleen Moore, which contained every luxury conceivable in perfect miniature, including a tiny phonograph that played Gershwin's *Rhapsody in Blue*. I was impressed by Shirley Temple as a little girl my age who had power: she could write a piece for the newspapers and have it printed in her own handwriting. I must have seen her dancing with Bill "Bojangles" Robinson in *The Littlest Rebel*, but I remember her less as a movie star than as a presence, like President Roosevelt, or Lindbergh, whose baby had been stolen; but she was a little girl whose face was everywhere—on glass mugs and in coloring books as well as in the papers.

Other figures peopling my childhood: the faceless, bonneted woman on the Dutch Cleanser can, Aunt Jemima beaming on the pancake box, "Rastus" the smiling Black chef on the Cream of Wheat box, the "Gold Dust Twins" capering black on orange on soap boxes, also in coloring books given as premiums with the soap powder. (The white obsession wasn't silent where advertising logos were concerned.) The Indian chief and the buffalo, "vanished" but preserved on the nickel. Characters in books read aloud: Little Black Sambo, Uncle Remus—with accompanying illustrations. Hiawatha. The Ten Little Indians, soon reduced to none, in the counting-backward rhyme.

In 1939 came the New York World's Fair. Our family, including my paternal grandmother, took the train from Baltimore and stayed two or three nights at the Hotel Pennsylvania in New York, across the street from Pennsylvania Station. We saw the Rockettes at Radio City Music Hall, spent a day in Flushing Meadows at the Fair, with its Trylon and Perisphere of which we had heard so much. We went to Atlantic City for a day, chewed its saltwater taffy, were pushed in wicker chairs along the boardwalk (a favorite tourist ride in Atlantic City in those days—hard to fathom its appeal to a child). My sister and I had our portraits sketched in pastel by a boardwalk artist. Under her picture he wrote, "Dad's Pride," and under mine, "Miss America, 1949."

It was going to be a long way to 1949. In a month war would be declared in Europe; soon the Atlantic Ocean would be full of convoys, submarines, and torpedoes; in Baltimore we would have blackouts, and air-raid drills at school. I would become part of the first American "teenage" generation, while people my age in Europe were, unbeknownst to me, being transported east in cattle cars, fighting as partisans, living in hiding, sleeping underground in cratered cities. Pearl Harbor would call in the wrath of the United States.

I was keeping a "Line-A-Day" diary and wrote of the World's Fair: "The greatest part was the World of Tomorrow. Men and women of Tomorrow appeared in the sky and sang." Some early version of big-screen vision and sound must have been projected on the dome of the Perisphere, celebrating the World of Tomorrow with its material goods, miracle conveniences, freeways, skyways, aerial transport. No World War II, no Final Solution, no Hiroshima. The men and women of Tomorrow marched with energetic and affirming tread. Whatever they sang, it wasn't the "Internationale"—more like a hymn to

American technology and free enterprise. The Depression was still on, the Nazi invasion of Czechoslovakia only a few weeks away. But the World of Tomorrow—capitalist kitsch—inspired a nine-year-old girl, who, decades later, remembers but one other moment from the New York World's Fair of 1939: a glassblower blew, over live fire, a perfect glass pen and nib in translucent blue-green, and handed it over to her to keep, and she did keep it, for many years.

————

Mercifully, at last, I was sent to school, to discover other, real children, born into other families, other kinds of lives. Not a wide range, at a private school for white girls. Still, a new horizon.

Mercifully, I discovered *Modern Screen, Photoplay,* Jack Benny, "Your Hit Parade," Frank Sinatra, "The Romance of Helen Trent," "Road of Life." The war was under way; I learned to swing my hips to "Don't Sit under the Apple Tree," "Deep in the Heart of Texas," "Mairzy Doats," "Don't Get Around Much Anymore." I loved Water Pidgeon and the singing of the miners in *How Green Was My Valley,* Irene Dunne in *The White Cliffs of Dover.* I learned to pick out chords for "Smoke Gets in Your Eyes" and "As Time Goes By" on the keyboard devoted to Mozart.

————

A poet's education. Most of the poetry she will read for many years, when poetry is both sustenance and doorway, is not only written by white men, but frames an all-white world; its images and metaphors are not "raceless," but rooted in an apartheid of the imagination. In college, for a seminar in modern American poetry that includes no Black (and almost no women) poets, she reads one of Allen Tate's "Sonnets at Christmas":

> Ah, Christ, I love you rings to the wild sky
> And I must think a little of the past:
> When I was ten I told a stinking lie
> That got a black boy whipped; but now at last
> The going years, caught in an accurate glow,
> Reverse like balls englished upon green baize—
> Let them return, let the round trumpets blow
> The ancient crackle of the Christ's deep gaze.
> Deafened and blind, with senses yet unfound,
> Am I, untutored to the after-wit
> Of knowledge, knowing a nightmare has no sound;
> Therefore with idle hands and head I sit
> In late December before the fire's daze
> Punished by crimes of which I would be quit.

This girl, this student, this poet is only barely learning that poetry occurs in "periods" and "movements." She is still trying to read the way she always has: in the here and now, what makes you shudder with delight or trouble, what keeps you reading, what's boring? But she's hearing about a southern poetry (she who grew up in the city of Edgar Allan Poe and Sidney Lanier) that calls itself Fugitive, Agrarian. Nothing helps her to connect these literary movements with southern history, with her own history. Tate's sonnet leaps out at her because it breaks, or seems to break, a silence—at very least it seems to point to something under the surface, the unspeakability of which her pulse is tracking as it flickers through the poem. She is studying in New England, now, joking about her southern heritage, there are a few African-American students (still known as "Negroes") in her classes, she knows now that "segregation" (a name for the laws she grew up under) and "prejudice" (a vaguer notion) are retrograde; the freshman sister assigned to her by the college is the daughter of a famous international diplomat, later a Nobel laureate: a distinguished Negro. She takes her light-skinned, serious "sister" out for lunches and coffee, is supposed to guide her with sisterly advice. How is she equipped for this, in the presumption of whiteness? Some years later, she hears that this young woman, whose unsmiling ivory face and dark, back-strained hair have become a perplexing memory, is a suicide.

Tate's poem teaches her nothing except the possibility that race can be a guilty burden on white people, leading them to Christmas Eve depression, and (more usefully) that a phrase like "stinking lie" can effectively be inserted in an elegant modern sonnet. Only years later will she learn that the writer of the poem, aristocrat of the world of southern letters, was, at the very least, and as part of his literary politics, a segregationist and supporter of the Ku Klux Klan.

 # XXII

Not how to write
poetry, but wherefore

Masters. For all the poetry I grew up with—the Blake, the Keats, the Swinburne and the Shelley, the Elizabeth Barrett Browning, the Whitman, the domesticated versions of Dickinson—in my twenties a greater ocean fell open before me, with its contradictory currents and undertows. Frost, Wylie, Millay seemed like shoreline tidal pools: out beyond lay fogs, reefs, wrecks, floating corpses, kelp forests, sargasso silences, moonlit swells, dolphins, pelicans, icebergs, suckholes, hunting grounds. Young, hungry, I was searching, within the limits of time and place and sex, for words to match and name desire.

Rilke's poem, the antique marble torso of Apollo glinting at the passerby through its pectorals like eyes, saying: *Du musst dein Leben ändern, You have to change your life*. Finding J. B. Leishman and Stephen Spender's translations of Rilke in a bookstore in Harvard Square (at first, thinking this Rainer Maria might be a woman). *Du musst dein Leben ändern.* No poem had ever said it quite so directly. At twenty-two it called me out of a kind of sleepwalking. I knew, even then, that for me poetry wasn't enough as something to be appreciated, finely fingered: it could be a fierce, destabilizing force, a wave pulling you further out than you thought you wanted to be. *You have to change your life.*

In his editor's foreword to my first book of poems, published in 1951, W. H. Auden praised my "talent for versification" and "craftsmanship," while explaining to and of my poetic generation:

> Radical changes and significant novelty in artistic style can only occur when there has been a radical change in human sensibility to require them. The spectacular events of the present time [did he mean the revelations of the Holocaust? the unleashing of nuclear weapons? the dissolution of the old colonial empires?] must not blind us to the fact that we are living not at the beginning but in the middle of a historical epoch; they are not novel but repetitions on a vastly enlarged scale and at a violently accelerated tempo of events which took place long since.
>
> Every poet under fifty-five cherishes, I suspect, a secret grudge against Providence for not getting him [*sic*] born earlier.

If anything, I cherished a secret grudge against Auden—not because he didn't proclaim me a genius, but because he proclaimed so diminished a scope for poetry, including mine. I had little use for his beginnings and middles. Yet he was one of the masters. I had read his much-quoted lines:

... poetry makes nothing happen; it survives
In the valley of its saying where executives
Would never want to tamper; it flows south
From ranches of isolation and the busy griefs,
Raw towns that we believe and die in; it survives,
A way of happening, a mouth.

Auden had written that in January 1939, elegizing W. B. Yeats. He ended it with a charge to living poets (or so I read it; maybe he was still talking to Yeats):

In the nightmare of the dark
All the dogs of Europe bark,
And the living nations wait,
Each sequestered in its hate;

Intellectual disgrace
Stares from every human face,
And the seas of pity lie
Locked and frozen in each eye.

Follow, poet, follow right
To the bottom of the night,
With your unconstraining voice
Still persuade us to rejoice.

With the farming of a verse
Make a vineyard of the curse,
Sing of human unsuccess
In a rapture of distress;

In the deserts of the heart
Let the healing fountain start,

> In the prison of his days
> Teach the free man how to praise.

But I was growing up in a postwar world where executives were increasingly tampering with everything, not least the valleys of saying. And in that world—or in the sector of it I could perceive around me—both women and poetry were being redomesticated.

Masters. In my college years T. S. Eliot was the most talked-of poet. *The Cocktail Party* played on Broadway at that time; his name and work were already part of student conversations, alluded to in courses. I listened to lectures on *The Waste Land,* the *Four Quartets,* earnestly taking notes, trying to grasp the greatness. I came to Eliot's poetry with the zeal of a young neophyte discovering the new and admired.

I came to it also as a young person utterly disaffected from Christianity and from organized religion in general. My experience of the suburban Protestant Church was that it had nothing whatsoever to do with changing one's life. Its images and rituals were wedded to a world I was trying to escape, the world of passionless respectability. I wanted nothing more to do with it. But how could an eighteen-year-old girl from Baltimore critique the fact that the greatest modern poet in English (as everyone seemed to agree) was a High Church Anglican? In my lecture notes, penciled on the endpapers of the copy of *Four Quartets* that I still have, I find: "This = problem of a Christian poem in a secular age—you can't accept it unless you accept Christian religion." The lecturer was F. O. Matthiessen, one of Eliot's earliest interpreters, who one year later, in a suicide note, described himself as a Christian and a socialist. He was also a homosexual.

My Jewish father, calling himself a Deist, my Protestant-born mother, secular by default (as, perhaps, married to a Christian, she'd have been Christian, without strong convictions either way), had sent me to church for several years as a kind of social validation, mainly as protection against anti-Semitism. I learned nothing there about spiritual passion or social ethics. If the liturgy found me, it was through the Book of Common Prayer, mostly the poetry of the King James Bible contained in it. I used to walk home from church feeling that I must be at fault: surely, if I were truly receptive, I would feel "something" when the wafer was given, the chalice touched to my lips. What I felt was that I was acting—we were all in a pageant or a play. Nor was this theater magical. Christianity as thus enacted felt like a theological version of a social world I already knew I had to leave. Sometimes, having to pull away from a world of coldness, you end up feeling you yourself are cold. I wrote this disaffection into an early poem, "Air without Incense."

Christianity aside, there was for me a repulsive quality to Eliot's poetry: an aversion to ordinary life and people. I couldn't have said that then. I tried for some time to admire the structure, the learnedness, the cadences of the poems, but the voice overall sounded dry and sad to me. Eliot was still alive, and I did not know how much his poetry had been a struggle with self-hatred and breakdown; nor was I particularly aware that his form of Christianity, like the religion I had rejected, was aligned with a reactionary politics. He was supposed to be a master, but, as the young woman I was, seeking possibilities—and responsibilities—of existence in poetry, I felt he was useless for me.

————

What I lacked was even the idea of a twentieth-century tradition of radical or revolutionary poetics as a stream into which a young poet could dip her glass. Among elders, William Carlos Williams wrote from the landscape of ordinary urban, contemporary America, of ordinary poor and working people, and in a diction of everyday speech, plainspoken yet astonishingly musical and flexible. But I don't recall being taken out of my skin by any Williams poem, though later I would work with his phrasing and ways of breaking a line as a means of shedding formal metrics. Muriel Rukeyser, the most truly experimental and integratedly political poet of her time, was unknown to me except by her name in a list of former Yale Younger Poets. I don't recall the publication of *The Life of Poetry* in 1949. No one—professor or fellow student—ever said to me that this was a book I needed. And not even the name of Thomas McGrath, the great midwestern working-class poet, was known to me. His chapbooks and small-press editions were not published or discussed by critics in the East; he was himself on the McCarthyite blacklist. Even the Left and Communist journals had trouble with his poetry, finding it "difficult" and unorthodox. In fact, I was to discover Rukeyser only in the late 1960s with the poetry readings against the Vietnam War and, soon after, with the rising women's movement in which she was, late in her life, a powerful voice. I did not read McGrath until the 1980s, when his long historical and autobiographical "Letter to an Imaginary Friend" became available in its entirety. But, in my early twenties, was my life ready for Rukeyser and McGrath? Perhaps not. Yet each of them was asking urgent questions about the place of poetry, questions I had as yet no language for.

———

I was exceptionally well grounded in formal technique, and I loved the craft. What I was groping for was something larger, a sense of vocation, what it means to live as a poet—not how to write poetry, but wherefore. In my early twenties I took as guide a poet of extreme division, an insurance executive possessed by the imagination. But if I was going to have to write myself out of my own divisions, Wallace Stevens wasn't the worst choice I could have made.

 # XXIII

"Rotted names"

A few years ago, in the early California spring, I put my typewriter, suitcase, and a copy of Stevens's *Collected Poems* into the trunk of my car and drove to the town of Twentynine Palms, at the edge of the Joshua Tree National Monument. The town clung along a rough strip, supported largely by a Marine Corps base, now, I believe, shut down. Off the main route, behind a bank of pines and oleanders, I found a little motel built around a courtyard with a swimming pool, banksia rose trees, and palm trees. My room had a kitchenette with a table where I could type and read. Daytimes I drove and walked in the desert among the hairy, mad-hermit shapes of the Joshua trees, sat among gray and gold rocks grizzled with lichen, against whose epochal scale tiny lives played out their dramas—lizards, wasps, butterflies, burrowing bugs, red and gilt flies. I stood at the edge of a lake bed, waterless for centuries, a vast bowl rimmed by mountains, brimming with silence. The Joshua trees were starting to open their creamy, almost shocking blooms. It was still cool in the desert through midday. Late afternoons I went back to the motel and sat on the patio—usually empty—reading Stevens straight through, something I had never done before.

I hadn't been writing poems for a while. I had known I was at the end of a cycle, that were I to write anything it would be a poetry of the past—my own past—that I was unready to write what was still strange and unformed in me, the poetry of the future. It seemed as good a time as any to come to terms with Stevens.

————

"I didn't think much of him when I read him in graduate school," a younger friend of mine, a political activist and passionate reader of poetry, commented recently. I had started reading Stevens in college, but not really as a student. I read all the "modern" poets I encountered (later they would be labeled "modernist") as an apprentice, though a wayward one. I picked and chose with sublime pigheadedness what I thought could help me live and write. Never having been a graduate student, I was never compelled to spend hours and days fettered to the explication of works that felt deadening or alien to me. It was another young poet, David Ferry, who told me I should read a poem called "The Man with the Blue Guitar," and from there I went on, buying the separate volumes as I found them in secondhand bookshops.

From the first I was both attracted and repelled by different Stevens poems, sometimes by different parts of a single poem. I was attracted first by the music, by the intense familiarity yet strangeness of lines like

> She sang beyond the genius of the sea

and

> It was her voice that made
> The sky acutest at its vanishing.
> She measured to the hour its solitude.
> She was the single artificer of the world
> In which she sang . . .
> Then we,
> As we beheld her striding there alone,
> Knew that there never was a world for her
> Except the one she sang and, singing, made.

The metrics and diction were familiar, that "high" tone at the intersection of Victorian and modern poetic English. But "The Idea of Order at Key West" offered me something absolutely new: a conception of a woman maker, singing and striding beside the ocean, creating her own music, separate from yet bestowing its order upon *the meaningless plunges of water and the wind*. This image entered me, in the 1950s, an era of feminist retrenchment and poetic diminishment, as an image of my tongue-tied desire that a woman's life, a poet's work, should amount to more than the measured quantities I saw around me.

> Now grapes are plush upon the vines.
> A soldier walks before my door.
>
> The hives are heavy with the combs.
> Before, before, before my door.

> And seraphs cluster on the domes,
> And saints are brilliant in fresh cloaks.
>
> Before, before, before my door.
> The shadows lessen on the walls.
>
> The bareness of the house returns.
> An acid sunlight fills the halls.
>
> Before, before. Blood smears the oaks.
> A soldier stalks before my door.

If I first loved that poem for its sound, I later loved it for its soundings—its prescience, its concentrated fusion of fulfillment and disaster, autumn and war and death, the stripping down from combs full of honey to acid light, the figure of the soldier, unaccounted for, from the first couplet, so that right away you feel him there, only walking at first, but *stalking* by the end past the blood-smeared oaks. There are many poems of Stevens that have lasted for me in this way.

And there were others that, from the first, I found—and still find—irritating and alienating in tone, mere virtuosity carrying on at great length, like "The Comedian As the Letter C," which begins:

> Nota: man is the intelligence of his soil,
> The sovereign ghost. As such, the Socrates
> Of snails, musician of pears, principium
> And lex. Sed quaeritur: is this same wig
> Of things, this noncompated pedagogue,
> Preceptor to the sea?

I can allow that Stevens—disappointed husband of a beautiful woman, successful insurance lawyer, fugitive in the imagination—was shoring up around him a self-protective, intellectual wit, that his desperation must have needed the excess of virtuosity displayed in many of his poems. But it's a voice of elegance straining against bleakness, renunciation, and truncation much of the time, ending suddenly and bitterly: *So may the relation of each man be clipped.*

Still, as a young woman, impatiently skimming the poem, I found passages that corresponded to my own moments of self-consciousness, of self-questioning: What was *I* really doing as a poet?

> The book of moonlight is not written yet
> Nor half begun, but, when it is, leave room
> For Crispin, fagot in the lunar fire,
> Who, in the hubbub of his pilgrimage
> Through sweating changes, never could forget
> That wakefulness or meditating sleep,
> In which the sulky strophes willingly
> Bore up, in time, the somnolent, deep songs . . .
>
> How many poems he denied himself
> In his observant progress, lesser things
> Than the relentless contact he desired . . .

Of the modern poets I read in my twenties, Stevens was the liberator. Yes: Stevens, whom I found so vexing and perplexing, so given sometimes to cake-decoration, affectations in French, yet also capable of shedding any predictable music to write poems like "Dry Loaf" or "The Dwarf," which force you to hear music of their own, or *The skreak and skritter of evening gone.* It was Stevens who told me, in "Of Modern Poetry":

> It has to be living, to learn the speech of the place.
> It has to face the men of the time and to meet

> The women of the time. It has to think about war
> And it has to find what will suffice.

I took this quite literally. It was he who said to me, *Ourselves in poetry must take their place,* who told me that poetry must change, our ideas of order, of the romantic, of language itself must change:

> Throw away the lights, the definitions
> And say of what you see in the dark
>
> That it is this or it is that,
> But do not use the rotted names.

The last line in the *Collected Poems* is *A new knowledge of reality.* I felt these were messages left along the trail for me. I was going on pure desire; I had no means of fathoming how life and work as a woman poet would force me to rethink ideas of order surrounding me and within me, ideas about scope and destiny, about the place of poetry in a life still so unrealized, so vaguely aware, so conventional. I was to carry Stevens with me into places neither of us could have foreknown, places as dense, implacable, and intricate as the desert at Joshua Tree.

———

In the last days I spent at Twentynine Palms, I thought I was coming down with 'flu. I ached, felt chilled at night; the desert wind seemed to blow across my bed. Mornings, I'd stand a long time in the hot shower, then make my instant coffee and sit on at the kitchenette table staring at the pines across the parking lot, hearing the United States flag whipping in the wind, an arrhythmic, riptide sound. Some days the desert was so dun, so coldly lit

I could hardly bear it. My heart quailed and expanded under influences I couldn't trace.

One evening I drove to an Italian restaurant on the strip to eat dinner, thinking to lift my spirits. I had lasagna, fries and salad, and a glass of ice-cold Chianti in a room otherwise occupied by a table of very young marines, teenagers, heads half-shaved (close over ears and necks, slightly longer on top). They had a bottle of wine, seemed out for a good time, but depressed, ill at ease with each other. I felt their physical strength—a terribly young, uninformed strength—were these kids descendants of European workers on the land, whose forefathers had been foot soldiers in war after war? Generations without education or control over the time and products of their labor?

The young recruits I saw that evening were all apparently white. At the motel, a weekend earlier, an African-American officer and his family had been swimming in the pool, later carried drinks to the patio. Our hosts had seemed to welcome them, but they were soon gone. Almost everyone I had seen hiking or rock climbing in the National Monument appeared to be white except for a Mexican family at one campsite among the rocks. Beyond the strip lay a kind of desert barrio of vaguely marked dirt roads leading to earth-colored shacks.

More than ever in my life I had been taking in the multivarious shadings of human life in the American landscape. Feeling how long whiteness had kept me from seeing that variety—or, in some places, noticing its lack—because whiteness—as a mind-set—is bent only on distinguishing discrete bands of color from itself. That is its obsession—to distinguish, discriminate, categorize, exclude on the basis of clearly defined color. What else is the function of being white? The iris of actual light, the colors seen in a desert shower or rainbow, or in the streets of a great metropolis, speak for continuum, spectrum, inclusion as laws of life.

I have come, through many turnings of life and through many willing and reluctant mentors, to understand that there is no study of race—only of racism. It's a bitter, violent, nauseating study, the study of racism. Race itself is a meaningless category. But people have defined themselves as white, over and against darkness, with disastrous results for human community.

And for poetry?

———

Why, I was asking myself, was that "master" of my youth, that liberatory spokesman for the imagination, that mentor who warned *Do not use the rotted names,* so attracted and compelled by old, racist configurations? How, given the sweep of his claims for the imagination, for poetry as that which gives sanction to life, his claims for modernity, could he accept the stunting of his own imagination by the repetitions of a mass imaginative failure, by nineteenth-century concepts of "civilized" and "savage," by compulsive reiterations of the word "nigger"? Why does the image and rhyming sound of the offensive word "negress" dominate one poem ("The Virgin Carrying a Lantern") and slide, for no apparent reason, into "The Auroras of Autumn"? What impelled him to address the haunting poem "Two at Norfolk" to "darkies" mowing grass in a cemetery? And why should an abstract "black man," a "woollen massa" be summoned up as interlocutors in the two epigrams "Nudity in the Colonies" and "Nudity at the Capitol"? What are these "frozen metaphors," as Aldon Nielsen calls them, doing in his work?

Reading Stevens in other years I had tried to write off that deliberately racial language as a painful but encapsulated lesion on the imagination, a momentary collapse of the poet's intelligence. I treated those figures—not that far removed from Rastus and Aunt Jemima—as happenstance, accidental. There in the high desert I finally understood: *This is a key to the whole. Don't try to extirpate, censor, or defend it.* Stevens's reliance on one-dimensional and abstract images of African-Americans is a watermark in his poetry. To understand how he places himself in relation to these and other dark-skinned figments of his mind—often Latin American and Caribbean lay figures—is to understand more clearly the meanings of North and South in Stevens's poetry, the riven self, the emotionally unhappy white man with a "fairly substantial income," the fugitive in the imagination who is repeatedly turned back by a wall of mirrors, whose immense poetic gift is thus compelled to frustrate itself. It's to grasp the deforming power of racism—or what Toni Morrison has named "Africanism"—over the imagination—not only of this poet, but of the collective poetry of which he was a part, the poetry in which I, as a young woman, had been trying to take my place.

 XXIV

A poet's education

Diane Glancy: "The poet writes as [s]he is written by circumstance and environment." And "I . . . feel I must make use of myself as a found object." Glancy: a woman of the Plains, of Cherokee and poor white "Arkansas backhill culture." Driving hundreds of miles to teach poetry in the public schools of Arkansas and Oklahoma, she keeps a kind of journal, a series of meditations on place, poetry, literacy, oral tradition, words, religion. She has written one of the new sourcebooks brought forth in this country today by poets for whose parents or grandparents literacy or English was not a given. It's a lie that poetry is only read by or "speaks to" people in the universities or elite intellectual circles; in many such places, poetry barely speaks at all.

Poems are written and absorbed, silently and aloud, in prisons, prairie kitchens, urban basement workshops, branch libraries, battered women's shelters, homeless shelters, offices, a public hospital for disabled people, an HIV support group. A poet can be born in a house with empty bookshelves. Sooner or later, s/he will need books. But books are not genes.

———

A poet's education.

Before I was eighteen, I was arrested on suspicion of murder after refusing to explain a deep cut on my forearm. With shocking speed I found myself handcuffed to a chain gang . . . and bussed to a holding facility to await trial. There I met men, prisoners, who read aloud to each other the works of Neruda, Paz, Sabines, Nemerov, and Hemingway. Never had I felt such freedom as in that dormitory. . . . While I listened to the words of the poets, the alligators slumbered powerless in their lairs. Their language was the magic that could liberate me from myself. . . .

And when they closed the books, these Chicanos, and went into their own Chicano language, they made barrio life come alive for me in the fullness of its vitality. I began to learn my own language, the bilingual words and phrases explaining to me my own place in the universe. . . .

Two years passed. I was twenty now, and behind bars again. . . . One night on my third month in the county jail . . . [s]ome detectives had kneed an old drunk and handcuffed him to the booking bars. His shrill screams raked my nerves like hacksaw on bone, the desperate protest of his dignity against their inhumanity. . . . When they went to the bathroom to pee and the desk attendant walked to the file cabinet to pull the arrest record, I shot my arm

through the bars, grabbed one of the attendant's university textbooks, and tucked it in my overalls. It was the only way I had of
protesting.

It was late when I returned to my cell. Under my blanket I
switched on a pen flashlight and opened the thick book at random, scanning the pages. . . . Slowly I enunciated the words . . .
p-o-n-d, ri-pple. It scared me that I had been reduced to this to
find comfort. I always had thought reading a waste of time, that
nothing could be gained by it. Only by action, by moving out into
the world and confronting and challenging the obstacles, could
one learn anything worth knowing.

Even as I tried to convince myself that I was merely curious, I
became so absorbed in how the sounds created music in me, and
happiness, I forgot where I was. . . . For a while, a deep sadness
overcame me, as if I had chanced on a long-lost friend and
mourned the years of separation. But soon the heartache of having missed so much of life, that had numbed me since I was a
child, gave way, as if a grave illness had lifted itself from me and I
was cured, innocently believing in the beauty of life again. I stum-
blingly repeated the author's name as I fell asleep, saying it over
and over in the dark: Words-worth,

Words-worth. . . .

Days later, with a stub pencil I whittled sharp with my teeth, I
propped a Red Chief notebook on my knees and wrote my first
words. From that moment, a hunger for poetry possessed me.

Jimmy Santiago Baca writes of poetry as a birth into the self
out of a disarticulated, violently unworded condition, the
Chicano taught to despise his own speech, the male prisoner *in a
world . . . run by men's rules and maintained by men's anger and
brutish will to survive,* forced to bury his feminine heart save in the
act of opening a letter or in writing poems. *Every poem is an infant*

labored into birth and I am drenched with sweating effort. Tired from the pain and hurt of being a man, in the poem I transform myself into woman. Released from the anguish of speechlessness (*There was nothing so humiliating as being unable to express myself, and my inarticulateness increased my sense of jeopardy, of being endangered*), Baca transforms himself into a woman who has transcended the pain and hurt of being female, who has actually given birth to words, not to a living, crying, shitting child. But how balance the hard labor of bearing a poem against the early depletion of uneducated women bearing children year after year? Or against the effort for speech by a woman whose culture has determined that women shall be silent?

> *En boca cerrada no entran moscas.* "Flies don't enter a closed mouth" is a saying I kept hearing when I was a child. *Ser habladora* was to be a gossip and a liar, to talk too much. *Muchachitas bien criadas,* well-bred girls don't answer back. *Es una falta de respeto* to talk back to one's mother or father. . . . *Hocicona, repelona, chismosa,* having a big mouth, questioning, carrying tales are all signs of being *mal criada.* In my culture they are all words that are derogatory if applied to women—I've never heard them applied to men.

Gloria Anzaldúa, disentangling the heavy hanging strands fringing the cave of mestiza consciousness, finds speechlessness compounded by femaleness, and both by the fact of being alien, "queer," not a woman in her culture's eyes. Her sense of identity is more complicated than Baca's because she's forced to transform many layers of negativity surrounding femaleness itself—images of *Malintzin,* the Indian woman as betrayer, of *la chingada,* the Indian woman as the fucked-one, of *la Llorona,* eternally mourning, long-suffering mother—and to confront the "despot duality" of simplistic masculine/feminine: *I, like other queer people, am two in one body, both male and female. I am the embodiment of the hieros gamos: the coming together of opposite qualities within.*

A poet's education.

In the 1960s, I read my first Chicano novel. It was *City of Night* by John Rechy, a gay Texan, son of a Scottish father and a Mexican mother. For days I walked around in stunned amazement that a Chicano could write and get published. When I read *I Am Joaquín* I was surprised to see a bilingual book by a Chicano in print. When I saw poetry written in Tex-Mex for the first time, a feeling of pure joy flashed through me. . . .

Even before I read books by Chicanos or Mexicans, it was the Mexican movies I saw at the drive-in—the Thursday night special of $1.00 a car—that gave me a sense of belonging. *Vámonos a las vistas,* my mother would call out and we'd all—grandmother, brothers, sister and cousins—squeeze into the car. We'd wolf down cheese and bologna white bread sandwiches while watching Pedro Infante in melodramatic tear-jerkers like *Nosotros los pobres,* the first "real" Mexican movie (that was not an imitation of European movies). . . . I remember the singing type "westerns" of Jorge Negrete and Miguel Aceves Mejía. . . .

The whole time I was growing up, there was *norteño* music, sometimes called North Mexican border music, or Tex Mex music, or Chicano music, or *cantina* (bar) music. I grew up listening to *conjuntos,* three- or four-piece bands made up of folk musicians playing guitar, *bajo sexto,* drums and button accordion, which Chicanos had borrowed from the German immigrants who had come to Central Texas and Mexico to farm and build breweries. . . .

I remember the hot, sultry evenings when *corridos*—songs of love and death on the Texas-Mexican borderlands—reverberated out of cheap amplifiers from the local *cantinas* and wafted in through my bedroom window.

Corridos first became widely used along the South Texas/Mexican border during the early conflict between Chicanos and Anglos. The *corridos* are usually about Mexican heroes who do valiant deeds against the Anglo oppressors. Pancho Villa's song *"La cucaracha,"* is the most famous one. *Corridos* of John F. Kennedy and his death are still very popular in the Valley. Older Chicanos remember Lydia Mendoza, one of the great border *corrido* singers who was called *la Gloria de Tejas.* Her "El tango negro," sung during the Great Depression, made her a singer of the people. The everpresent *corridos* narrated one hundred years of border history, bringing news of events as well as entertainment. These folk musicians and folk songs are our chief cultural mythmakers, and they made our hard lives seem bearable.

A poet's education.

After the divorce, I had new territory, much like the Oklahoma land run when a piece of land was claimed & had to be settled. I had spent years hiding behind my husband, the children & housework. Now the land & sky were open. That's what's frightening about the prairie at first \ its barrenness & lack of shelter. I had always written, but now my sense of place was defined by whatever mattered. I picked up my Indian heritage & began a journey toward ani-yun-wiyu, translated from the Cherokee, 'real people.'

I read journals \ magazines. Poetry \ some fiction. I saw that feelings could be expressed in writing. Feelings of bewilderment

& fear. Especially anger. It was a trend in women's writing \ the pulley I needed out of the separation & isolation I felt without the surroundings of family. I saw women come to grips with themselves. The vulnerability, the struggle, the agonizing choices. I had to find a homestead within myself, or invent one. I dug a potato cellar.

Family had covered the fissures in my life. Now I had fragments \ shards \ whatever the territory offered. My poems & writing were the land I cultivated. I moved toward 'being' in poetry. A struggle for survival. My purpose was to find the truth of what I was \ my voice. What I had to offer. I could not have done it without the other voices \ the sun & rain & soil for myself as a person. The pleasure of being a woman.

I found that I weathered the prairie storms & the limitations that come with the territory. I found acceptance of myself \ the strength to travel prairie roads & talk about poetry in towns where farmers in the cafés stare. I relived the struggle to claim the land \ establish a sod house \ plow the fields \ milk the cow. The rest will come. All this is an internal land, of course. I started late with only a map given to me by other women who said the territory was there. It was a fertile landscape just inside the head. I had only to load the wagon, hitch the horses. A journey which my mother never made before she folded up her camp.

I learned to trust images. I could even experiment with words. Put muffler, glass packs on the wagon. Mud flaps if I wanted. I have what men have had \ liberty to be myself. Maybe women had it too & I just never knew. Wrong \ wright \ whatever. Now I could throw out the ice cubes \ find my severed limbs \ sew them on instead of giving heart & arms & lungs away. I have use for them on the edge of the frontier \ saw-edge after saw-edge.

The glory of the plain self in search of words to say, 'the self' / the delight of it. The birth \ the shedding of invisibility. The pursuit of she-pleasure. SHEDONISM.

The themes \ form \ experimental forms. Words as house & shed & outbuildings on the land. The urgency. The cessation of pounding myself \ hanging my separate parts to dry on low branches & rocks. It's women who influenced my work. Their courage \ their trend toward revelation. I am on the journey to the ani-yun-wiyu.

 XXV

To invent
what we desire

What does a poet need to know?

—That poetry can occur, not just as a
fierce, precarious charge in the imagination, or an almost physical wave of desire, but as something written down,
that remains, so regardless of circumstance you can turn back to that fierce
charge, that desire.

Not everyone who feels
this charge, this desire,
feels licensed to write.

—That you yourself, through recombi-
nations and permutations of the languages you already know, can re-create

Not everyone who is a
poet feels her or his

that fierce charge, for yourself and others, on a page, something written down that remains.

own languages are good enough.

—That this in itself can be a means of saving your life.

"Poetry is not a luxury" (Audre Lorde). Poetry is activity and survival.

—That this in itself can be an activity of keenest joy.

—That no culture, language, caste can claim superiority; across enormous social, national, geographic tracts, poetry lifts its head and looks you in the eye.

Wherever, whenever, you live, this belongs to you.

—That in all ages and cultures, poets have been lost before they could be found and encouraged—lost in childbirth, lost to grinding toil, in massacres, pogroms, genocides, lost to hatred of the messages they bore, that could not be received.

Much that you need has been lost. The poems that we know are merely fragments.

—That to mis-take, to mis-prize, your own life and its landscapes, to imagine that poetry belongs by right to others (of another culture, gender, class, century) and not to you, means falling—if not into silence—into language others found in struggle with their own conditions. Then you become a mouthpiece for the lives of others, you inhabit their rhythms, their vocabularies, you lose

We must use what we have to invent what we desire.

track of your own desire in an adopted style.

—That the poetries of men and women unlike you are a great polyglot city of resources, in whose streets you need to wander, whose sounds you need to listen to, without feeling you must live there.

We cannot work in isolation, or in fear of other voices.

—That to track your own desire, in your own language, is not an isolated task. You yourself are marked by family, gender, caste, landscape, the struggle to make a living, or the absence of such a struggle. The rich and the poor are equally marked. Poetry is never free of these markings even when it appears to be. Look into the images.

Finding "the intimate face of universal struggle" (June Jordan).

 XXVI

Format and form

Long before the invention of the "sound byte," the anarchist poet, essayist, and activist Paul Goodman described the effects of what he called "format" on public language:

> *Format.*—n. 1. the shape and size of a book as determined by the number of times the original sheet has been folded to form the leaves. 2. the general physical appearance of a book, magazine, or newspaper, such as the type face, binding, quality of paper, margins, etc. 3. the organization, plan, style, or type of something: *They tailored their script to a half-hour format. The format of the show allowed for topical and controversial gags.* 4. *Computer Technol.*, the organization of disposition of symbols on a magnetic tape, punch

card, or the like, in accordance with the input requirement of a computer, card-sort machine, etc. . . .

Format has no literary power, and finally it destroys literary power. It is especially disastrous to the common standard style, because it co-opts it and takes the heart out of it.

I wish that Goodman had said "poetic power" instead of "literary power"; I think of poetic power as abroad in the world in many kinds of speech and writing, while "literary power" suggests to me the text on the page merely. But in recognizing the power of format Goodman also recognized one of the terrible powers of the powerful in advanced capitalism. Here he is again:

Format is not like censorship that tries to obliterate speech, and so sometimes empowers it by making it important. And it is not like propaganda that simply tells lies. Rather, authority imposes format on speech because it needs speech, but not autonomous speech. Format is speech colonized, broken-spirited. . . . The government of a complicated modern society cannot lie *much*. But by format, even without trying, it can kill feeling, memory, learning, observation, imagination, logic, grammar, or any other faculty of free writing.

Poetic forms—meters, rhyming patterns, the shaping of poems into symmetrical blocks of lines called couplets or stanzas—have existed since poetry was an oral activity. Such forms can easily become format, of course, where the dynamics of experience and desire are forced to fit a pattern to which they have no organic relationship. People are often taught in school to confuse closed poetic forms (or formulas) with poetry itself, the lifeblood of the poem. Or, that a poem consists merely in a series of sentences broken (formatted) into short lines called "free verse." But a closed form like the sestina, the sonnet, the villanelle remains inert formula or format unless the "triggering subject," as Richard Hugo called it, acts on the imagination to make the form evolve, become responsive, or works almost in resistance to the form. It's a struggle not to let the form take over, lapse into format, assimilate the poetry; and that very struggle can produce a movement, a music, of its own.

I think of Gerard Manley Hopkins's "sprung" sonnets, his wrestling not just with diction and grammar, end rhymes and meters, but with his own rebellious heart:

No worst, there is none. Pitched past pitch of grief,
More pangs will, schooled at forepangs, wilder wring.
Comforter, where, where is your comforting:
Mary, mother of us, where is your relief?
My cries heave, herds-long; huddle in a main, a chief
Woe, world-sorrow; on an age-old anvil wince and sing—
Then lull, then leave off. Fury had shrieked 'No ling-
ering! Let me be fell: force I must be brief'.

O the mind, mind has mountains; cliffs of fall
Frightful, sheer, no-man-fathomed. Hold them cheap
May who ne'er hung there. Nor does long our small
Durance deal with that steep or deep. Here! creep,
Wretch, under a comfort served in a whirlwind: all
Life death does end and each day dies with sleep.

And I think of the Jamaican poet Claude McKay, writing, in more traditional meter and diction, of the 1919 "Red Summer" of Black urban uprisings across the United States:

If we must die, let it not be like hogs
Hunted and penned in an inglorious spot,
While round us bark the mad and hungry dogs,

Making their mock at our accursed lot.
If we must die, O let us nobly die,
So that our precious blood may not be shed
In vain; then even the monsters we defy
Shall be constrained to honor us though dead!
O kinsmen! we must meet the common foe!
Though far outnumbered let us show us brave,
And for their thousand blows deal one deathblow!
What though before us lies the open grave?
Like men we'll face the murderous, cowardly pack,
Pressed to the wall, dying, but fighting back!

McKay's lines hearken back to Shakespeare—not, however, to the sonnets, but to the battle speech from *Henry V* and with a difference: McKay takes the traditional poetic form of the colonizer and turns it into a rebellion cry, takes the poetics of war and turns it into a poetics of resistance.

More than sixty years later, St. Lucian poet Derek Walcott bursts the sonnet while keeping (and adding to) its resonance, breaks it open to his own purposes, a Caribbean poet's confrontation with the contradictions of his middle-class Anglo-Europeanized education, the barbarisms of that civilization as revealed in the slave trade and the Holocaust:

The camps hold their distance—brown chestnuts and gray smoke
that coils like barbed wire. The profit in guilt continues.
Brown pigeons goose-step, squirrels pile up acorns like little shoes,
and moss, voiceless as smoke, hushes the peeled bodies
like abandoned kindling. In the clear pools, fat
trout rising to lures bubble in umlauts.
Forty years gone, in my island childhood, I felt that
the gift of poetry had made me one of the chosen,

that all experience was kindling to the fire of the Muse.
Now I see her in autumn on that pine bench where she sits,
their nut-brown ideal, in gold plaits and *lederhosen,*
the blood drops of poppies embroidered on her white bodice,
the spirit of autumn to every Hans and Fritz
whose gaze raked the stubble fields when the smoky cries
of rooks were nearly human. They placed their cause in
her cornsilk crown, her cornflower iris,
winnower of chaff for whom the swastikas flash
in skeletal harvests. But had I known then
that the fronds of my island were harrows, its sand the ash
of the distant camps, would I have broken my pen
because this century's pastorals were being written
by the chimneys of Dachau, of Auschwitz, of Sachsenhausen?

In the early 1940s, even as the child Walcott was feeling "the fire of the Muse" on his island, the young woman Muriel Rukeyser was writing her own contradictions as an American Jew into a long sequence exploring war, womanhood, and politics: "Letter to the Front." The first draft of one section was written in the open, long-lined form of most of the other sections of "Letter to the Front." It reads like a working through of the poet's ideas—loose and sometimes explanatory *(And in America, we Jews are hostages/in a nation of hostages; we vouch for freedom,/if we are free, all may be free).* The final version is crystallized into fourteen lines, a sonnet that is a kind of prophesying:

> To be a Jew in the twentieth century
> Is to be offered a gift. If you refuse,
> Wishing to be invisible, you choose
> Death of the spirit, the stone insanity.
> Accepting, take full life. Full agonies:

Your evening deep in labyrinthine blood
Of those who resist, fail, and resist; and God
Reduced to a hostage among hostages.

The gift is torment. Not alone the still
Torture, isolation; or torture of the flesh.
That may come also. But the accepting wish,
The whole and fertile spirit as guarantee
For every human freedom, suffering to be free,
Daring to live for the impossible.

———

June Jordan has an essay called "The Difficult Miracle of Black Poetry in America: Something of a Sonnet for Phillis Wheatley." (This is the single most cogent, eloquent, compressed piece of writing about the conditions of North American poetry that I know.) Poetic, not pedantic, it talks about the African cultural world Wheatley lost at the age of seven, and the Western literary tradition to which she was introduced via the auction block, as an African child bought in the whim of pity by a liberal Boston couple on a shopping trip for slaves and early recognized as a precocious, a "special" child.

Jordan talks about a vocabulary and imagery of the poet's situation ("It was written, this white man's literature of England, while someone else did the things that have to be done.") What happens when this is the only poetic language available to a slave? Phillis Wheatley was forcibly turned—and then, in frustrate desire, turned herself—to a formulaic language and poetics in which she acquitted herself so well that she is now known as the first African-American poet. Even in so doing, Jordan shows, she kept alive the subversive pulse in her work.

Jordan then writes a sonnet for Wheatley, a sonnet in ringing

and relentless dactylic meter, a sonnet impeccably end-rhymed,
that says of Wheatley all she could not have said with hope for
publication:

> Girl from the realm of birds florid and fleet
> flying full feather in far or near weather
> Who fell to a dollar lust coffled like meat
> Captured by avarice and hate spit together
> Trembling asthmatic alone on the slave block
> built by a savagery travelling by carriage
> viewed like a species of flaw in the livestock
> A child without safety of mother or marriage

> Chosen by whimsy but born to surprise
> They taught you to read but you learned how to write
> Begging the universe into your eyes:
> They dressed you in light but you dreamed with the night.
> From Africa singing of justice and grace,
> Your early verse sweetens the fame of our Race.

Francisco X. Alarcón writes his political love sonnets *(De Amor
Oscuro/Of Dark Love)* to a young farm worker, using fourteen
lines without end-rhymes though with the inherent internal
rhyming of Spanish, impossible to capture in English translation:

IV	IV
tus manos son dos martillos que clavan	your hands are two hammers that joyfully
y desclavan alegres la mañana,	nail down and pry up the morning,
tiernos puños desdoblados de tierra,	tender fists that unfold from earth,
dulces pencas de plátanos pequeños	sweet bunches of small bananas

tus manos huelen a las
  zarzamoras
que cosechas en los campos que
  roban
tu sudor a dos dólares el bote,
son duras, tibias, jóvenes y sabias

azadones que traen pan a las mesas,
oscuras piedras que al chocar dan
  luz,
gozo, sostén, ancla del mundo
  entero

yo las venero como relicarios
porque como gaviotas anidadas,
me consuelan, me alagran, me
  defienden

your hands smell of the
  blackberries
you harvest in the fields that
  steal
your sweat at two dollars a bucket,
they are hard, warm, young and
  wise

hoes that bring bread to the tables,
dark stones that give light when
  struck,
pleasure, support, anchor of the
  world

I worship them as reliquaries
because like nesting sea gulls,
they console, delight, defend me

XIV

¿cómo consolar al hombre más solo
de la tierra? cómo aliviar su pena?
¿cómo llamar a su puerta
  atrancada
y decirle al oído embocado de
  alma:

"hermano, la guerra ya ha
  terminado:
todos, por fin, salimos
  vencedores:
sal, goza los campos
  liberados:
la explotación es cosa del pasado"?

XIV

how to console the loneliest man
on earth? how to relieve his pain?
how to call through his bolted
  door
and have one's soul speak to his
  ear:

"brother, the war is now
  over:
all of us in the end emerged
  victors:
go forth and enjoy the liberated
  fields:
exploitation is a thing of the past"?

¿qué hacer cuando regrese malherido con alambre de púas entre las piernas? ¿cómo encarar sus ojos que denuncian:	what to do when he returns, wounded with barbed wire between his legs? how to face his eyes accusing:
"hermano, el mundo sigue igual: los pobres todavía somos presa fácil: el amor, si no es de todos, no basta"?	"brother, the world goes on the same: we the poor are still easy prey: love, if it isn't from all, is just not enough"?

Here, too, the "high" European form is turned to the purposes of a new poetry: "dark" in the sense of hidden, forbidden, homosexual; "dark" in the sense of the love between dark people.

In all of these examples, variations on form may be greater or lesser, but what really matters is not line lengths or the way meter is handled, but the poet's voice and concerns refusing to be circumscribed or colonized by the tradition, the tradition being just a point of takeoff. In each case the poet refuses to let form become format, pushes at it, stretches the web, rejects imposed materials, claims a personal space and time and voice. Format remains flat, rigid, its concerns not language, but quantifiable organization, containment, preordained limits: control.

Goodman writes:

> The deliberate response to format is *avant garde*—writing which
> devotes itself, at least in part, to flouting the standard style, to

offending the audience. . . . If a work is felt to be "experimental," it is not that the writer is doing something new but that he [*sic*] is making an effort to be different, to be not traditional.

In any period, powerful artists are likely to go way out and become incomprehensible. They abide by the artistic imperative to make it as clear as possible, but they are not deterred by the fact that the audience doesn't catch on. . . . On hindsight, the incomprehensibility of genius almost always turns out to be in the mainstream of tradition, because the artist took the current style for granted, he [*sic*] worked on the boundary of what he knew, and he did something just more than he knew.

Avant garde artists do not take the current style for granted; it disgusts them. They do not care about the present audience; they want to upset it. . . . *Avant garde* tends to be capricious, impatient, fragmentary, ill-tempered. Yet, except by raging and denying, a writer might not be able to stay alive at all as a writer. As a style, *avant garde* is an hypothesis that something is very wrong in society. . . .

An ultimate step is always Dada, the use of art to deny the existence of meaning. A step after the last is to puff up examples of format itself to giant size, Pop.

But in a confused society, *avant garde* does not flourish very well. What is done in order to be idiotic can easily be co-opted as the idiotic standard.

"Avant-garde" may well be a declaration that "something is very wrong in society." It may be a true "Howl" against a pervasively square, exclusive, dominant art allied with sexual, economic, racial repression. But, as Goodman saw well, in an age of disinformation and co-optation, "avant-garde" may become merely one dish on a buffet table of "entertainment" so arranged that no one item can dominate. It may be drafted into the service of TV commercials, or videos for executives on retreat. Its attempts to shatter structures of meaning may very well be complicit with a system that depends on our viewing our lives as random and meaningless or, at best, unserious.

"Avant-garde," anyway, is a style and movement that depends on the existence of a powerful, if dessicated, and entrenched art world, where grants are awarded, paintings selected for museum purchase, reputations polished. What is its significance in a society of immigrants and survivors of genocide, the meeting place of many colonized cultures, whose emerging artists, far from being disgusted with their peoples' traditions and styles, are trying to repossess and revalue them? "Avant-garde" has historically meant the rebellions of new groups of younger white men (and a few women) against the complacencies and sterilities of older men of their own culture. It was a powerful energy in Western Europe, the United States, and, for a while, in Russia, at the turn of this century. But among poets, at least, many or most of the early twentieth-century avant-garde, the "great modernists," were privileged by gender and class and were defenders of privilege.

The poetry of emerging groups—women, people of color, working-class radicals, lesbians and gay men—poetry that is nonassimilationist, difficult to co-opt, draws on many formal sources (ballad, blues, corrido, reggae, sonnet, chant, cuentos, sestina, sermon, calypso, for a few). But it doesn't pretend to abandon meaning or what Goodman calls "the artistic imperative to make it as clear as possible." *As possible*. Those poetries can be highly complex, layered with tones and allusions, but they are also concerned with making it "as clear as possible" because too much already has been buried, mystified, or written of necessity in code.

 XXVII

Tourism and promised lands

Tourism. Can be a trap for poets, especially poets of North America who may elect to be escapist, breezy, about our empire, the sands we are lying on.

Poems decorated with brilliantly colored flowers, fronds, views from the cabana or through louvered shutters, dark silhouettes gutting fish, bearing mounds of fruit on their heads.

White poetry of the islands: no clue that there are poets, born and living there, who are building literary movements, who are part of an anticolonial resistance. The people of the fabulous realm: abstract figures on a simplified ground.

The exotic—that way of viewing a landscape, people, a culture as escape from our carefully constructed selves, our "real" lives—a trap for poets.

In my twenties, soon after World War II, I viewed Western Europe like that. The dollar was high, and college students from the United States could travel and study abroad with a sense of being on cultural holiday. Coming from our unscorched earth, our unblasted cities, we sought not the European present, traumatized and hectically rebuilding, but the European past of our schoolbooks. Being mostly white, we saw European culture as the ancestor of ours: we romanticized that ancestry, half in awe at its artifacts, half convinced of our own national superiority. In essence, Europe's glorious past had been saved from barbarism by us and for us: a huge outdoor museum.

Many of the poems in my second book were poems of such tourism. It was a difficult, conflicted time in my own life, from which I gladly fled into poems about English or Italian landscape and architecture. Only once, in a poem called "The Tourist and the Town," I tried to place myself as I was, alongside an acknowledgment that life in the foreign town was as "ordinary" as anywhere else.

Poems of tourism: like travel snapshots taken compulsively, a means of capturing, collecting, framing the ruins, the exotic street, the sacred rocks, the half-naked vending child, the woman setting forth under her colorful burden. A means of deflecting the meanings of the place, the meaning of the tourist's presence, in a world economy in which tourism has become a major industry for poor countries and in which a different kind of travel—immigration in search of work—is the only option facing a majority of the inhabitants of those countries.

June Jordan turns this genre inside out in a poem called "Solidarity." She balances the spoken word "terrorist" against the

unspoken word "tourist." But the tourists here are four women
of color visiting Paris:

Even then
in the attenuated light
of the Church of le Sacre Coeur
(early evening and folk songs
on the mausoleum steps)
and armed
only with 2 instamatic cameras
(not a terrorist among us)
even there
in that Parisian downpour
four
Black women (2 of Asian 2
of African descent)
could not catch a taxi
and
I wondered what umbrella
would be big enough to stop
the shivering
of our collective impotence
up
against such negligent
assault
And I wondered
who would build that shelter
who will build and lift it
high and wide
above
such loneliness

Poems of the artists' colony: poems about grass being cut a long way off, poetry of vacation rather than vocation, poems written on retreat, like poems written at court, treating the court as the world.

This is not to deplore the existence of artists' colonies, but rather the way they exist in a society where the general maldistribution of opportunity (basic needs) extends to the opportunity (basic need) to make art. Most of the people who end up at artists' colonies, given this maldistribution, are relatively well educated, have had at least the privilege of thinking that they might create art. Imagine a society in which strong arts programs were integral elements of a free public education. Imagine a society in which, upon leaving school, any worker was eligible, as part of her or his worker's benefits, to attend free arts workshops, classes, retreats, both near the workplace and at weekend or summer camps. The values embodied in existing public policy are oppositional to any such vision. One result is that art produced in an exceptional, rarefied situation like an artists' colony for the few can become rarefied, self-reflecting, complicit with the circumstances of its making, cut off from a larger, richer, and more disturbing life.

Who is to dictate what may be written about and how? Isn't that what everybody fears—the prescriptive, the demand that we write out of certain materials, avoid others?

No one is to dictate. But if many, many poems written and published in this country are shallow, bland, fluent without intensity, timorous, and docile in their undertakings, must we assume that it's only natural? Isn't there something that points a finger in the direction of blandness, of fluency, something that rewards those qualities?

What is it that allows many poets in the United States, their critics and readers, to accept the view of poetry as a luxury (Audre Lorde's term) rather than a food for all, food for the heart and senses, food of memory and hope? Why do poets ever fawn or clown or archly undercut their work when reading before audiences, as if embarrassed by their own claims to be heard, by poetry's function as witness? Why do some adopt a self-conscious snake-oil shamanism, as if the electrical thread from human being through poem to other human beings weren't enough? Why are literary journals full of poems that sound as if written by committee in a department of comparative literature, or by people still rehearsing Ezra Pound's long-ago groan *I cannot make it cohere*—a groan that, after so many repetitions, becomes a whine? Why do so many poems full of liberal or radical hope and outrage fail to lift off the ground, for which "politics" is blamed rather than a failure of poetic nerve? Why have poets in the United States (I include myself) so often accepted that so little was being asked of us? asked so little of each other and ourselves?

The reviewer of a recent anthology of Los Angeles poets comments:

> This book is not a response to public life, although it does share the despair and helplessness of the 1990's, which the riots have helped crystallize. No: The burning here originates in the personal isolation into which these poets have plunged themselves, who appear to choose loneliness and self-pity as guides through their individual pain. . . . [S]uch wounds result not in any explosion, but in uneasy confessions. . . . Predictably, some poems do little more than photograph frustration and numbness. A poetry

of stunned realizations, of therapy, it speaks of art as mere self-disclosure: We tell about our troubles, and we feel better.

Isn't there something that points a finger in the direction of mere self-disclosure, telling our troubles, as an end in itself? From television talk shows to the earnest confessions of political candidates, isn't there a shunting off of any collective vitality and movement that might rise from all these disclosures? *We feel better,* then worse again, we go back to the therapeutic group, the people who understand us, we do not trouble the waters with a language that exceeds the prescribed common vocabulary, we try to "communicate," to "dialogue," to "share," to "heal" in the holding patterns of capitalistic self-help—we pull further and further away from poetry.

The reviewer goes on to criticize the nervelessness of form that accompanies this attitude toward the materials: a "lackadaisical" craft. But even a highly crafted poem may evoke little more than a life of resigned interiority.

Interiority *was* the material for Emily Dickinson, yet she turned her lens both on her personal moment and on eternity. She had to make herself like that, embracing her own authority and linguistic strangeness, or she'd have joined the ranks of sad, fluent female singers of her North American century. She wanted more for poetry than that. More for herself.

———

In a time of great and mostly terrible uprootings, no "promised land" is a land for poetry. For Poetry the Immigrant, surrounded by her hastily crammed bags and baskets, there is no final haven. In its mixture of the ancient and the unthought-of, the well-loved and the unthinkable, its strange tension between conservation and radical excavation, poetry is continually torn between its roots, the bones of the ancestors, and its bent beyond the found, toward the future.

Raya Dunayevskaya wrote of revolution that while "great divides in epochs, in cognition, in personality, are crucial," we need to understand the moment of discontinuity—the break in the pattern—itself as part of a continuity, for it to become a turning point in human history.

Poetry wrenches around our ideas about our lives as it grows alongside other kinds of human endeavor. But it also recalls us to ourselves—to memory, association, forgotten or forbidden languages.

Poetry will not fly across the sea, against the storms, to any "new world," any "promised land," and then fold its wings and sing. Poetry is not a resting on the given, but a questing toward what might otherwise be. It will always pick a quarrel with the found place, the refuge, the sanctuary, the revolution that is losing momentum. Even though the poet, human being with many anxious fears, might want just to rest, acclimate, adjust, become naturalized, learn to write in a new landscape, a new language. Poetry will go on harassing the poet until, and unless, it is driven away.

 XXVIII

What if?

When there is no history
there is no metaphor;
a blind nation in storm
mauls its own harbors
sperm whale, Indian, black,
belted in these ruins.
                    —Michael Harper, "Song: I Want a Witness"

The economy of the nation, the empire of business
within the republic, both include in their basic
premise the concept of perpetual warfare. It is the
history of the idea of war that is beneath our other
histories. . . . But around and under and above it is
another reality; like desert-water kept from the surface
and the seed, like the old desert-answer needing its
channels, the blessings of much work before it arrives
to act and make flower. This history is the history of
possibility.
                    —Muriel Rukeyser, *The Life of Poetry*

We must constantly encourage ourselves and each
other to attempt the heretical actions that our dreams
imply, and so many of our old ideas disparage. In the

forefront of our move toward change, there is only
poetry to hint at possibility made real.
—Audre Lorde, "Poetry Is Not a Luxury"

To be revolutionary is to be original, to know where
we came from, to validate what is ours and help it to
flourish, the best of what is ours, of our beginnings,
our principles, and to leave behind what no longer
serves us.
—Inés Hernández, "An Open Letter
to Chicanas . . ."

Labor Day weekend, 1992. 167,000 jobs lost in the United States in
the month of August. An electoral campaign is being waged
between twentieth-century politicians, while the twenty-first
century starts pushing the hood back from her face and turning
to show herself: an eyebrow, a cheekbone, the line of a mouth
out of shadow.

The country's uniqueness no longer resides in its prosperity.
Among the civilized [*sic*] nations of the world it exists in the
extraordinarily difficult relations between the races and certain
ethnic groups, in the extent and range of the nation's impoverished classes, in the manifestly archaic quality of its criminal justice system, in the inadequacy of its public health and medical
facilities for tens of millions of uninsured, in the burned-out and
deserted slum areas of dozens of cities where public safety is unknown, in the bizarre conditions that exist in too many of the
nation's elementary and secondary schools, that some pretend
will be quickly remedied by something called "privatization."
. . . [T]he prison population of this country is greater than that of
any other civilized democracy in the world. . . . [T]he US criminal
law system is a disgrace, recognized to be that by jurists and law-

yers throughout the world. That situation did not suddenly arise
because of a jury decision in Los Angeles [*sic*] in 1992.

1992 is the five-hundredth year of the white "civilizing" presence in the Americas. There are commemorative stamps, scholarly conferences, reenactments, homages to the invaders, replicas
of Columbus's ships, official theatrics. An enormous grass-roots
countermovement has risen in resistance to these official celebrations. It uses demonstrations, murals, theater, poetry readings,
history, storytelling, banners, postcards, music, and dance; it
publishes collections of essays and poems; it speaks to whomever
will listen, but the primary voices are those of the political, artistic, and intellectual movements of American Indians, Meso-
americans, mestizos and mestizas, Chicana/os, Mexicana/os,
Puerto Riquenos, Puerto Riqueñas, movements building since
the 1960s, through all the years when the Left was being pro-
nounced defunct. This indigenous peoples' response to the
Quincentennial is an educational movement, a movement for
cultural self-definition and for the future. And it's a movement
of peoples who, despite wars of extermination, enslavements,
the theft of their lands, children, and cultures, have never ceased
to recognize poetry as a form of power.

———

The Mexican poet Octavio Paz reads the history of poetry in
the modern age as "nothing but the history of its relations to
[the] myth" of Revolution—revolution thingified with that
capital *R* that usually marks an icon to be shot down. The Revolution of absolute, monolithic State power is dead now, he says,
with the "deaths" of Communism and socialism in Eastern
Europe and the Soviet Union. The statues of Lenin have indeed
been pulled down (and, as one unreconstructed Marxist said to

me recently, even Lenin would have been glad of that); the press has reported former dissident writers as saying they no longer know what to write about. Paz believes that the long association of poetry with revolution (and now I am using the small r that allows for many revolutions, parallel and converging, and for continuing revolution) is at an end. He calls on poetry as the "Other Voice" that speaks of what neither the capitalism now called "market economy" nor the state capitalism known as Communism can address. (Paz does acknowledge that the questions asked by Marx are still unanswered, that the "market economy" cannot answer them, must itself undergo change or self-destruct.) He also states that "for the first time since the Romantic era, no poetic movement of major scope has appeared in thirty years," thus betraying a banal ignorance of the women's and indigenous and mestiza/o poetry movements in all the Americas, the Caribbean, the Pacific Islands, New Zealand, Australia, not to mention Europe and Africa. This ignorance, though banal, is a profound disadvantage for someone trying to pronounce on the present and future relationship of poetry and revolution.

———

Poetry and revolution: poems and changes of consciousness, poems and actions. Invisible, unquantifiable exchanges of energy. On a wall, in an exhibit of paintings ("New World Furrows") by Michele Gibbs, I read two lines from the Irish poet Seamus Heaney:

What looks the strongest has outlived its term;
The future lies with what's affirmed from under.

In Heaney's original poem, these lines are italicized: they appear as the slogan of a revolutionary hope in which his generation has been disappointed. The poem recognizes a new generation rejecting the passivity of disillusionment and ends with a different hope:

> **to know there is one among us who never swerved**
> **from all his instincts told him was right action . . .**
> **whose boat will lift when the cloudburst happens.**

Heaney's poem belongs, in its images, to Ireland and the long, tortuous path of Irish revolutionary politics. It also voices a more general, passive desire for change, easily resigned to what is: the liberal's dead end. The couplet from Heaney's text is, however, transformed in radical juxtaposition with Gibbs's paintings. The iambic pentameter of Shakespeare or Milton or Yeats is here broken up into short phrases, inscribed in blood-red ink, and these Irish words hang in an African-Caribbean system of images—specifically a painting entitled *Homecoming for Mandela* and one called *Phoenix Rising,* the latter an African woman reborn out of a shell or bowl of flames. And they stand along with words from Henry Dumas, Margaret Walker, Aimé Césaire. Whatever irony Heaney means us to hear in these lines is de-ironized, returned to a living principle, in Gibbs's visual meditations on history: it's more than hope or faith; it is a calling-into-being.

As poetry, in that context of words and images, the lines are transmuted. Perhaps they spur me on, by and through the light and shadows of the painting, to move more surely in my contests with the old, dying powers within and outside myself.

Perhaps they have been scribbled into the notebook of a student who may or may not ever read the whole poem but who will always associate them with those images. Judging from the whole of the poem, I don't think Heaney would feel misappropriated.

————

As I've been writing this book, poems and the words of poets have flowed into my hands, onto my table. As often, the work of searching becomes a magnetic field toward which, like iron filings, needed resources fly. At the worst time in this continent's history, when indeed the old, dying forces seem to have pitched us into an irreversible, irremediable disaster spin—air, water, earth, and fire horribly contaminated, the blood pulse in the embryo already marked for sickness, sewage of public verbiage choking the inlets of the mind—an abundance of revolutionary art is still emerging.

> Here is soot Today it is all I have
> to give you My stores of honey and corn
> and fresh water and even sand are empty
> Here With this you can hold the city's
> every corner under your fingernails
> ground into the soles of your shoes riding
> the pulses of your lungs' fragile chambers
> traveling from your eye's edge to the back
> of your hand Here is soot signature
> of the city of fire and its web
> of consequences It has spread its burned
> body over the river filmed the slick
> dark heads of the cormorants as they plunge
> to eat It has settled between pavements
> and the clothes of those who sleep on them
> It testifies to the lost integrity

of forests of the earth's buried black veins
of tenements of poison sealed in drums
against flesh circles of pointed tents
of the bodies of those who would not obey
or who slept on park benches unheeding
It is memory smearing the sunsets
to attract our shattered attention each mote
a crippled survivor voiceless haunting
our eyes and throats trying to find a way in
—Suzanne Gardinier,
"To the City of Fire"

———

A revolutionary poem will not tell you who or when to kill, what and when to burn, or even how to theorize. It reminds you (for you have known, somehow, all along, maybe lost track) where and when and how you are living and might live—it is a wick of desire. It may do its work in the language and images of dreams, lists, love letters, prison letters, chants, filmic jump cuts, meditations, cries of pain, documentary fragments, blues, late-night long-distance calls. It is not programmatic: it searches for words amid the jamming of unfree, free-market idiom, for images that will burn true outside the emotional theme parks. A revolutionary poem is written out of one individual's confrontation with her/his own longings (including all that s/he is expected to deny) in the belief that its readers or hearers (in that old, unending sense of *the people*) deserve an art as complex, as open to contradictions as themselves.

Any truly revolutionary art is an alchemy through which waste, greed, brutality, frozen indifference, "blind sorrow," and anger are transmuted into some drenching recognition of the *What if?*—the possible. *What if—?*—the first revolutionary question, the question the dying forces don't know how to ask. The theme of revolutionary art may of necessity be prevailing conditions, yet the art signals other ways and means. In depicting lives ordinarily downpressed, shredded, erased, this art reveals through fierce attention their innate and latent vitality and beauty. In portraying alienated and exploited labor with delicate, steady concern for the faces and bodies of the laborers, it calls to mind that work is a human blessing, that alienation does not have to be its inseparable companion. In figuring the hunted, whether Indians or slaves or migrants or women, it calls up a landscape where all might be free to travel unmolested. In the ferocious composition of a work by Sue Coe, in the haunting meditative strokes of Michele Gibbs's work on pressed fig-tree bark, in the organic historical vision of a canvas by Jacob Lawrence, there is—thanks to beauty of form and color, anarchic precision of forms and spaces—a conjuring of a possible space where human relationships become as complementary and unenforced as the lines, colors, forms of the pictures themselves. Revolutionary art dwells, by its nature, on edges.

This is its power: the tension between subject and means, between the *is* and what can be. Edges between ruin and celebration. Naming and mourning damage, keeping pain vocal so it cannot become normalized and acceptable. Yet, through that burning gauze in a poem which flickers over words and images, through the energy of desire, summoning a different reality.

Kamau Brathwaite on the assassination of Walter Rodney, Guyanese scholar, activist, and leader:

to be blown into fragments.   your flesh
like the islands that you loved
like the seawall that you wished to heal

bringing equal rights & justice to the brothers
a fearless cumfa mashramani to the sisters whispering their free/zon
that grandee nanny's histories be listened to with all their ancient

flèches of respect

until they are the steps up the poor of the church
up from the floor of the hill/slide
until they become the roar of the nation

that fathers would at last settle into what they own
axe adze if not oil well.   torch
light of mackenzie

that those who have all these generations
bitten us bare to the bone
gnawing our knuckles to their stone

price fix price rise rachman & rat/chet squeeze
how bread is hard to buy how rice is scarcer than the
muddy water where it rides

how bonny baby bellies grow doom-laden dungeon grounded down
to groaning in their hunger
grow wailer voiced & red eyed in their anger . . .

to be blown into fragments.   your death
like the islands that you loved
like the seawall that you wished to heal

bringing equal rights & justice to the bredren
that children above all others would be like the sun.
rise

over the rupununi over the hazy morne de castries over kilimanjaro

any where or word where there is love there is the sky & its blue free
where past means present struggle
towards vlissengens where it may some day end

distant like powis on the essequibo
drifting like miracles or dream
or like that lonely fishing engine slowly losing us its sound

but real like your wrist with its tick of blood around its man
acles of bone
but real like the long marches the court steps of tryall

the sudden sodden night journeys up the the pomeroon
holed up in a different safe house every morning & try
ing to guess from the heat of the hand

shake if the stranger was stranger or cobra or friend
& the urgent steel of the kis
kadee glittering its *qqurl* down the steepest bend in the breeze

& the leaves

ticking & learning to live with the smell of rum on the skull's
breath.   his cigarette ash on the smudge of your fingers
his footsteps into your houses

& having to say it over & over & over again
with your soft ringing patience with your black
lash of wit.   though the edges must have been curling with pain

but the certainty clearer & clearer & clearer again

that it is too simple to hit/too hurt
not to remember

that it must not become an easy slogan or target
too torn too defaced too devalued down in redemption market

that when men gather govern other manner
they should be honest in a world of hornets

that bleed into their heads like lice
corruption that cockroaches like a dirty kitchen sink

that politics should be like understanding of the floor
boards of your house

swept clean each morning.   built by hands that know
the wind & tide & language

from the loops within the ridges of the koker
to the rusty tinnin fences of your yard

so that each man on his cramped restless island
on backdam of his land in forest clearing by the broeken river
where berbice struggles against slushy ground

takes up his bed & walks

in the power & the reggae of his soul/stice
from the crippled brambled pathways of his vision
to the certain limpen knowledge of his nam

this is the message that the dreadren will deliver
groundation of the soul with drift of mustard seed

that when he spoke the world was fluter on his breeze
since it was natural to him like the water.   like the way he listened

like the way he walked.   one a dem ital brothers who had grace

for being all these things & careful of it too
& careless of it too
he was cut down plantation cane

because he dared to grow & growing/green
because he was that slender reed & there were machetes sharp
    enough
to hasten him to bleed.   he was blown down

because his bridge from man to men
meant doom to prisons of a world we never made
meant wracking out the weeds that kill our yampe vine

& so the bomb
fragmenting islands like the land you loved
letting back darkness in

but there are stars that burn that murders do not know
soft diamonds behind the blown to bits
that trackers could not find that bombers could not see

that scavengers will never hide away

the caribbean bleeds near georgetown prison

a widow rushes out & hauls her children free

But the imagining of a different reality requires telling and retelling the terrible true story: a poetry that narrates and witnesses. Muskogee Creek Joy Harjo implants this in her title and in the gloss she provides for her poem:

FOR ANNA MAE PICTOU AQUASH, WHOSE SPIRIT IS PRESENT HERE AND IN THE DAPPLED STARS (FOR WE REMEMBER THE STORY AND MUST TELL IT AGAIN SO WE MAY ALL LIVE)

Beneath a sky blurred with mist and wind,
                                        I am amazed as I watch the violet
heads of crocuses erupt from the stiff earth
                                        after dying for a season,
as I have watched my own dark head
                                        appear each morning after entering
the next world
                    to come back to this one,
                                        amazed.

It is the way in the natural world to understand the place
                              the ghost dancers named
after the heart/breaking destruction.
                    Anna Mae,
                              everything and nothing
                                        changes.
You are the shimmering young woman
                         who found her voice,
when you were warned to be silent, or have your body cut away
from you like an elegant weed.
              You are the one whose spirit is present in the dappled stars.
(They prance and lope like colored horses who stay with us
         through the streets of these steely cities. And I have seen them
         nuzzling the frozen bodies of tattered drunks
                                   on the corner.)
This morning when the last star is dimming
                         and the buses grind toward
the middle of the city, I know it is ten years since they buried you
              the second time in Lakota, a language that could
                                        free you.
I heard about it in Oklahoma, or New Mexico,
                   how the wind howled and pulled everything down
in a righteous anger.
         (It was the women who told me) and we understood wordlessly
the ripe meaning of your murder.
         As I understand ten years later after the slow changing
                         of the seasons
that we have just begun to touch
                   the dazzling whirlwind of our anger,
we have just begun to perceive the amazed world the ghost dancers
         entered
              crazily, beautifully.

In February 1976, an unidentified body of a young woman was found on the Pine Ridge Reservation in South Dakota. The official autopsy attributed death to exposure. The FBI agent present at the autopsy ordered her hands severed and sent to Washington for fingerprinting. John Truedell rightly called this mutilation an act of war. Her unnamed body was buried. When Anna Mae Aquash, a young Micmac woman who was an active American Indian Movement member, was discovered missing by her friends and relatives, a second autopsy was demanded. It was then discovered she had been killed by a bullet fired at close range to the back of her head. Her killer or killers have yet to be identified.

What is represented as intolerable—as crushing—becomes the figure of its own transformation, through the beauty of the medium and through the artist's uncompromised love for that medium, a love as deep as the love of freedom. These loves are not in opposition.

> In another place, not here, a woman might touch
> something between beauty and nowhere, back there
> and here, might pass hand over hand her own
> trembling life, but I have tried to imagine a sea not
> bleeding, a girl's glance full as a verse, a woman
> growing old and never crying to a radio hissing of a
> black boy's murder. I have tried to keep my throat
> gurgling like a bird's. I have listened to the hard
> gossip of race that inhabits this road. Even in this I
> have tried to hum mud and feathers and sit peacefully
> in this foliage of bones and rain. I have chewed a few
> votive leaves here, their taste already disenchanting
> my mothers. I have tried to write this thing calmly
> even as its lines burn to a close. I have come to know
> something simple. Each sentence realised or
> dreamed jumps like a pulse with history and takes a
> side. What I say in any language is told in faultless

knowledge of skin, in drunkenness and weeping,
told as a woman without matches and tinder, not in
words and in words and in words learned by heart,
told in secret and not in secret, and listen, does not
burn out or waste and is plenty and pitiless and loves.
—Dionne Brand, *No Language Is Neutral*

———

Forms, colors, sensuous relationships, rhythms, textures, tones, transmutations of energy, all belong to the natural world. Before humans arrived, their power was there; they were nameless yet not powerless. To touch their power, humans had to name them: whorl, branch, rift, stipple, crust, cone, striation, froth, sponge, flake, fringe, gully, rut, tuft, grain, bunch, slime, scale, spine, streak, globe. Over so many millennia, so many cultures, humans have reached into preexisting nature and made art: to celebrate, to drive off evil, to nourish memory, to conjure the desired visitation.

The revolutionary artist, the relayer of possibility, draws on such powers, in opposition to a technocratic society's hatred of multiformity, hatred of the natural world, hatred of the body, hatred of darkness and women, hatred of disobedience. The revolutionary poet loves people, rivers, other creatures, stones, trees inseparably from art, is not ashamed of any of these loves, and for them conjures a language that is public, intimate, inviting, terrifying, and beloved.

Notes

I. WOMAN AND BIRD

Page 6: "moving from each to each and through our lives." Muriel Rukeyser (1913–1979) is the North American poet who most intuited, explored, and, in her work, embodied this triangulation.

Page 7: "instructed her to write." Beth Brant, *Mohawk Trail* (Ithaca, N.Y.: Firebrand, 1985), p. 96.

II. VOICES FROM THE AIR

Page 9: " 'Who am I?' it asked. . . ." John Webster, *Tragedies* (London: Vision Press, 1946), p. 149.

Page 10: "The house was quiet . . . ." Wallace Stevens, *The Collected Poems of Wallace Stevens* (New York: Knopf, 1954), p. 358.

III. "WHAT WOULD WE CREATE?"

Page 14: "it's like being sick . . . ." Karen Brodine, "June 78," in *Illegal Assembly* (Brooklyn, N.Y.: Hanging Loose Press, 1980), p. 58.

Page 14: "I imagine this message . . . ." Aimé Césaire, "On the State of the Union," in *Aimé Césaire: Collected Poetry,* trans. and ed. Clayton Eshleman and Annette Smith (Berkeley: University of California Press, 1983), pp. 342–43.

Page 15: "Yet this is still my country . . . ." W. S. Merwin, "Caesar," in his *Selected Poems* (New York: Atheneum, 1988), p. 121.

Page 19: "the military cadets were reading his poems." Nazim Hikmet,

Selected Poetry, trans. Randy Blasing and Mutlu Konuk (New York: Persea, 1986), p. 8.

Page 19: "dangerous state criminals." See my *On Lies, Secrets, and Silence: Selected Prose 1966–1978* (New York: Norton, 1979), pp. 116–119, and Irina Ratushinskaya, *Beyond the Limit: Poems,* trans. Frances Padorr Brent and Carol J. Avins (Evanston, Ill.: Northwestern University Press, 1987), p. xiii.

Page 19: "pursued for five years by the INS." See Margaret Randall, *Coming Home: Peace without Complacency* (Albuquerque: West End Press, 1990), for a detailed history of the INS case against Randall.

Page 19: "set apart from the practical arts, from civic meaning." The inclusion of a poet, Maya Angelou, in the 1993 presidential inauguration was a symbolic gesture (augmented by the fact that Angelou is also African-American and a woman). But a captive symbol, like ritual, becomes a true resource only if it can connect with a larger consciousness in everyday life.

IV. Dearest Arturo

Page 23: "bottom of every new villainy." Eli Evans, *The Provincials: A Personal History of Jews in the South* (New York: Athenaeum, 1976), p. 65.

Page 24: "scheming within a group: as, office politics." *Webster's New World Dictionary of the American Language* (Cleveland and New York: World, 1964).

Page 26: "with envy and admiration." Arturo Islas, "On the Bridge, at the Border: Migrants and Immigrants," Fifth Annual Ernesto Galarza Commemorative Lecture, Stanford Center for Chicano Research (Stanford: Stanford University, 1990), p. 3.

Page 26: " 'identify' with them." *Ibid.,* p. 5.

V. "Those two shelves, down there"

Page 29: "The lack of the means to distribute . . . ." Nadine Gordimer is referring to a specific South African context: "the fact that there are virtually no bookshops whatever and very, very few and very, very poor libraries in black townships. The tax on books is high . . . and one of the great problems of local publishers is the fact that there is a monopoly of distribution . . . that hasn't any interest in quality literature, which means that Louis Lamour . . . [is] available while 'commercial' consideration censorship operates against other, quality work." (Personal communication to Stephen Clingman, April 2, 1993.) In the United States, similar conditions obtain in impoverished inner-city areas, while in consumption-driven suburban malls chain bookstores market commodities called books but do not provide accessibility to literature.

Page 31: "patterns of distribution and availability." See Stan Luxenberg, *Books in Chains: Chain Bookstores and Marketplace Censorship.* (1991; National Writers Union, 13 Astor Place, New York, NY 10003). You might also ask why books on community organizing, poor people's empowerment, and strategies for grass-roots movements are not found out front among (or instead of) guides to personal self-improvement.

VII. THE SPACE FOR POETRY

Page 34: "PABLO CHILE TE RECUERDA . . . ." For photographs of the inscriptions on the fence below Neruda's house, see Luis Poirot, ed., *Pablo Neruda: Absence and Presence* (New York: Norton, 1990), pp. 64–75.

Page 37: "McCarran-Walter Act." The McCarran-Walter Immigration and Nationality Act was passed in 1952 by a McCarthyite Congress over President Truman's veto. It listed thirty-three provisions for exclusion or expulsion of aliens from the United States, including polygamy, mental illness, homosexuality, membership in communist, socialist or anarchist organizations or association with members of such groups, and writing, speaking, or disseminating opinions that dissent from official government views. Some 50,000 people have been denied visas to enter the United States under this act. See Margaret Randall, *Coming Home: Peace without Complacency* (Albuquerque: West End Press, 1990).

Page 37: "And Rip forgot the office hours . . . ." Hart Crane, *The Poems of Hart Crane,* ed. Marc Simon (New York and London: Liveright, 1986), pp. 55–56.

Page 39: "profit, marketing, consumerism." *Poetry Flash,* published in the Bay Area, is a monthly tabloid-style calendar of poetry readings and related events chiefly taking place on the West Coast but national in scope; it also offers vivid and eclectic reviews and articles on poetry and poetics. In the January 1993 issue, Richard Silberg, reviewing Dana Gioia's *Can Poetry Matter?,* refutes the notion of the poetry reading as a campus phenomenon, pointing to the increase in nonacademic readings across the country: festivals, open readings, poetry slams (competitions in which poets read before judges), and readings in bars and coffeehouses. He rightly calls the Bay Area "an endemic poetry festival." Like grass-roots politics, grass-roots poetry tends to be ignored by the communications media of corporate interests—hence, the value of a paper like *Poetry Flash* (P.O. Box 4172, Berkeley, CA 94704).

VIII. HOW DOES A POET PUT BREAD ON THE TABLE?

Page 42: "translating, typesetting, or ghostwriting." For a concrete, detailed account of one such life, see Hayden Carruth, "Fragments of Autobiography," in his *Suicides and Jazzers* (Ann Arbor: University of Michigan Press, 1993), pp. 70–75.

IX. THE MURALIST

Page 43: "I wish you would write a poem . . . ." Samuel Taylor Coleridge, *The Letters of Samuel Taylor Coleridge,* ed. E. L. Griggs, 6 vols. (New York: Oxford University Press, 1956), I, p. 527.

Page 43: "These were things which I myself saw . . . ." Peter Kropotkin, *Memoirs of a Revolutionist* (New York: Doubleday/Anchor, 1962), p. 47.

Page 44: "The struggle for revolutionary ideas . . . ." Leon Trotsky, *Art and Revolution,* ed. Paul V. Siegel (New York: Pathfinder Press, 1992), pp. 23–24.

Page 45: "From the point of view of an objective historical process . . . ." *Ibid.,* p. 30.

Page 45: "The effort to set art free . . . ." *Ibid.,* p. 39.

Page 45: "One cannot approach art . . . ." *Ibid.,* pp. 76–77.

Page 46: "It is one thing to understand something . . . ." *Ibid.,* p. 66.

Page 47: "During a war the poets turn to war . . . ." Thomas McGrath, *Selected Poems 1938–1988* (Port Townsend, Wash.: Copper Canyon Press, 1988), p. 105.

Page 48: "unlocking hate and fear." Miranda Bergman, letter, 1991.

Page 50: "in organic poetry the form sense . . . ." Denise Levertov, "Some Notes on Organic Form," in *The Poet in the World* (New York: New Directions, 1973), p. 12.

Page 50: "We work alone . . . ." Samella Lewis, *The Art of Elizabeth Catlett,* published in collaboration with the Museum of African American Art, Los Angeles (Claremont, Calif.: Hancraft Studios, 1984), pp. 93, 94.

Page 52: "Choosing to be an artist . . . ." Michele Gibbs, personal communication, November 17, 1992.

Page 53: "the sound of our own heartbeat in the dark." Lillian Smith, *The Winner Names the Age: A Collection of Writings by Lillian Smith*, ed. Michelle Cliff (New York: Norton, 1978), epigraph. The letters of Lillian Smith, white antiracist writer and activist, edited by Margaret Rose Gladney, have been published by the University of North Carolina Press (Chapel Hill, 1993) under the title *How Am I to Be Heard?*

X. WHAT DOES IT MEAN, TO PUT LOVE INTO ACTION?

Page 54: "He said I had this that I could love . . . ." Wallace Stevens, *The Collected Poems of Wallace Stevens* (New York: Knopf, 1954), p. 236.

Page 54: "I am a failure then, as the kind of revolutionary . . . ." Alice Walker, *Meridian* (New York: Pocket Books, 1976), pp. 200–1.

Page 55: "Alone on the railroad track . . . ." Elizabeth Bishop, *The Complete Poems 1927–1979* (New York: Farrar, Straus & Giroux, 1979), p. 8.

Page 56: "ties grown unmanageable will suffice." James Merrill, Afterword, in David Kalstone, *Becoming a Poet: Elizabeth Bishop with Marianne Moore and Robert Lowell* (New York: Farrar, Straus & Giroux, 1989), p. 253.

Page 58: "a world in which all had the right to live." Barbara Deming, *We Cannot Live without Our Lives* (New York: Viking-Grossman, 1974), pp. 36–52.

Page 58: "This must change." *Ibid.*, p. 45.

Page 60: "saturate the Third World in patterns of brutality." Sissela Bok, *Alva Myrdal: A Daughter's Memoir* (Reading, Mass.: Addison-Wesley, 1991), pp. 345–46.

Page 61: "women's movements, civil disobedience." See Barbara Deming, *Prisons That Could Not Hold: Prison Notes 1964–Seneca 1984* (San Francisco: Spinsters Ink, 1985).

Page 61: "social and economic development." Bok, p. 287.

Page 61: "social institutions, including the family." *Ibid.*, p. 352.

Page 61: "visible and responsive peace." Stevens, p. 236.

Page 61: "Peace I have feared . . . ." Suzanne Gardinier, "To Peace," in her *The New World* (Pittsburgh: University of Pittsburgh Press, 1993).

Page 62: "heroism as we have come to understand it." Hayden Carruth, personal communication, April 6, 1992. Donald Hall tells about Ezra Pound, who in his later years wished to suppress his reading of the poem "Sestina: Altaforte" praising war, on a recording in the Harvard

Poetry Room, on the grounds that "War . . . is no longer—amusing" (Donald Hall, *Their Ancient Glittering Eyes: Remembering Poets and More Poets* [New York: Ticknor & Fields, 1992], p. 207).

Page 63: "By content, the *Iliad* is not the epic . . . ." Suzanne Gardinier, "Two Cities: On 'The Iliad,' " *The Kenyon Review* 14, no. 2 (Spring 1992): 6.

Page 65: "For Michael Angelo Thompson." June Jordan, *Things That I Do in the Dark: Selected Poems* (New York: Random House, 1977), pp. 121–23.

Page 68: "The difference between poetry and rhetoric . . . ." Audre Lorde, "Power," in her *The Black Unicorn* (New York: Norton, 1978), pp. 108–9.

Page 70: "and I decided to pull over and just jot some things down . . . ." Audre Lorde, *Sister Outsider: Essays and Speeches* (Freedom, Calif.: Crossing Press, 1984), pp. 107–8.

XI. A LEAK IN HISTORY

Page 72: "maple sugar in Vermont in 1752." Federal Writers Project, WPA of Vermont, *Vermont: A Guide to the Green Mountain State* (Boston: Houghton Mifflin, 1937), p. 371.

Page 78: "don't know what/where they are." Irena Klepfisz, "Picking up the Pieces When We Don't Know What/Where They Are," speech given for the Jewish Feminist Lecture Series, University of California at Santa Cruz, June 22, 1991.

Page 78: Children of the Holocaust. Helen Epstein, *Children of the Holocaust: Conversations with Sons and Daughters of Survivors* (New York: Bantam, 1979).

Page 78: Red Diaper Babies: Children of the Left. Judy Kaplan and Linn Shapiro, eds., *Red Diaper Babies: Children of the Left* (Somerville, Mass.: Red Diaper Productions, 1985).

Page 79: "peer group without a sign." Epstein, p. 7.

XII. SOMEONE IS WRITING A POEM

Page 83: "The society whose modernization . . . ." Guy Debord, quoted in Thyrza Goodeve, "Watching for What Happens Next," in *War after War,* ed. Nancy J. Peters, City Lights Review no. 5 (San Francisco: City Lights Books, 1992).

Page 84: "torque converter for a jello mold." Diane Glancy, *Claiming Breath* (Lincoln and London: University of Nebraska Press, 1992), p. 75.

Page 86: "imprisoned by capitalism." Ed Oasa, "Speaking the Changes: An Interview with Luis J. Rodriguez," *Poetry Flash* no. 240 (March–April 1993): 4.

Page 87: "The Planet Krypton." Lynn Emanuel, "The Planet Krypton," in her book *The Dig* (Urbana and Chicago: University of Illinois Press, 1992), pp. 4–5.

XIII. BEGINNERS

Page 90: "How they are provided for . . . ." Walt Whitman, *Complete Poetry and Collected Prose* (New York: Library of America, 1982), p. 171.

Page 91: "All this is thenceforth . . . ." *Ibid.,* p. 502.

Page 92: "unloosen'd, wondrous time." *Ibid.,* p. 690n.

Page 92: "He ate and drank the precious Words— . . . ." Emily Dickinson, *The Complete Poems of Emily Dickinson,* ed. Thomas Johnson (Boston and New York: Little Brown, 1960), no. 1587, p. 418.

Page 93: "trying it all by Nature." Whitman, p. 925.

Page 93: "never get in the books." *Ibid.,* p. 778.

Page 93: "all the print I have read in my life." Whitman, *Song of Myself,* no. 13.

Page 93: "my pages from first to last." Whitman, *Complete Poetry,* p. 668.

Page 93: "Renunciation is a piercing virtue." Dickinson, no. 745, p. 365.

Page 93: "we consign to language." Emily Dickinson, *The Collected Letters of Emily Dickinson,* ed. Thomas Johnson (Cambridge, Mass.: Harvard University Press, 1952), no. 562, p. 617.

Page 93: "sensual, eating drinking and breeding." Whitman, *Complete Poetry,* p. 50.

Page 93: "On my volcano grows . . . ." Dickinson, *Poems,* no. 1677, p. 685.

Page 93: "Through me forbidden voices . . . ." Whitman, *Complete Poetry,* p. 211.

Page 94: "her unappeasable thirst for fame." Muriel Rukeyser, *The Life of Poetry* (New York: A. A. Wyn, 1949), p. 93.

Page 94: "I tie my Hat—I crease my Shawl— . . . ." Dickinson, *Poems,* no. 443, p. 212.

Page 96: "become a golfer." Janet Sternburg, ed., *The Writer on Her Work* (New York: Norton, 1980), pp. 219–20.

Page 97: "why is he lost?" Muriel Rukeyser, *The Traces of Thomas Hariot* (New York: Random House, 1970), p. 3.

Page 97: "deeper at these times." *Ibid.,* pp. 3–4.

Page 97: "One of the attacks on me for writing . . . ." William Packard, ed., *The Poet's Craft: Interviews from the "New York Quarterly"* (New York: Paragon, 1987), p. 136.

Page 98: "It is by a long road of presumption . . . ." Muriel Rukeyser, *Willard Gibbs: American Genius* (Garden City, N.Y.: Doubleday, Doran, 1942), p. 12.

Page 99: "what a woman's poetry should look like." See, for example, Randall Jarrell, *Poetry and the Age* (New York: Knopf, 1953), pp. 163–66; R.S.P., "Grandeur and Misery of a Poster Girl," *Partisan Review* 10, no. 5 (September/October 1943): 471–73.

Page 99: "the toys of fame." Rukeyser, *Gibbs,* p. 433.

Page 100: "Anglo-Saxons and Christians." "The Agrarians . . . reaffirmed the history of their inherited European culture. It had a name, but the name had fallen into disuse. It was, of course, Christendom" (Andrew Lytle, Foreword, *The Southern Mandarins: Letters of Caroline Gordon to Sally Wood* [Baton Rouge: Louisiana State University Press, 1984], p. 4).

Page 100: "like natural growths." Richard Ellman and Robert O'Clair, eds., *The Norton Anthology of Modern Poetry,* 2d ed. (New York: Norton, 1988), p. 880. *A Muriel Rukeyser Reader,* edited by Jan Heller Levi, will be published by Norton in 1994.

XIV. THE REAL, NOT THE CALENDAR, TWENTY-FIRST CENTURY

Page 103: "Shadrack began a struggle . . . ." Toni Morrison, *Sula* (New York: Bantam, 1973), p. 12.

Page 104: "And ever-present in the freezing, prewar . . . ." Anna Akhmatova, *The Complete Poems of Anna Akhmatova,* ed. Roberta Reeder, trans. Judith Hemschemeyer, 2 vols. (Somerville, Mass.: Zephyr Press, 1990), II, p. 437.

Page 105: "fire in which we burn." Delmore Schwartz, *Selected Poems* (New York: New Directions, 1967), p. 67.

Page 106: "graphic chauvinism, especially offensive." Reese Williams, ed., *Unwinding the Vietnam War: From War into Peace* (Seattle: Real Comet Press, 1987), pp. 265–66.

XV. "A CLEARING IN THE IMAGINATION"

Page 107: "better judgment making." William Shakespeare, Sonnet 87, in *The Riverside Shakespeare* (Boston: Houghton Mifflin, 1974), p. 1765.

Page 108: "without being maudlin." Helen Vendler, "A Dissonant Triad," *Parnassus: Poetry in Review* 16, no. 2 (1991): 391.

Page 110: "self-entertainment for the few?": John Haines, "The Hole in the Bucket," in *Claims for Poetry*, ed. Donald Hall (Ann Arbor: University of Michigan Press, 1987), pp. 131–40.

Page 111: "In the forest without leaves . . . ." John Haines, "In the Forest without Leaves," in his *New Poems: 1980–1988* (Brownsville, Ore.: Story Line Press, 1990), pp. 79–93.

Page 116: "When you imagine trumpet-faced musicians . . . ." Muriel Rukeyser, "Homage to Literature," in her *The Collected Poems of Muriel Rukeyser* (New York: McGraw-Hill, 1978), p. 109.

Page 116: "On a long voyage . . . ." Poem no. 57, in Him Mark Lai, Genny Lim, and Judy Yung, *Island: Poetry and History of Chinese Immigrants on Angel Island, 1910–1940* (Seattle: University of Washington Press, 1991), p. 122.

Page 117: "Sadly, I listen to the sounds . . . ." Poem no. 18, *ibid.,* p. 56. "Angel Island, now an idyllic state park out in San Francisco Bay not far from Alcatraz, was the point of entry for the majority of approximately 175,000 Chinese immigrants who came to America between 1910–1940. Modelled after New York's Ellis Island, the site was used as the immigration detention headquarters for Chinese awaiting jurisdiction on the outcomes of medical examinations and immigration papers. It was also the holding grounds for deportees awaiting transportation back to the motherland. The ordeal of immigration and detention left an indelible mark in the minds of many Chinese, a number of whom wrote poetry on the barrack walls, recording the impressions of their voyage to America, their longing for families back home, and their outrage and humiliation at the treatment America accorded them" (p. 8).

Page 117: "En el bote del county . . . ." Luis J. Rodriguez, *Always Running: La Vida Loca, Gang Days in L.A.* (Willimantic, Conn.: Curbstone Press, 1993), pp. 189–90. "From the age of 13 on, I ended up in cells like those of the San Gabriel jail house—places like Pomona, Temple City, East L.A., Monterey Park, East Lake's juvenile detention hall and the L.A. county jail system following the [Chicano] Moratorium [against the War in Vietnam, August 29, 1970]. . . . [T]his time, at 17 years old, I faced a serious charge of attempted murder. . . . The cell walls were filled with the warrior's art. . . . Smoked outlines of women's faces were burned onto the painted brick. There were love messages . . . —and poetry."

XVI. WHAT IS AN AMERICAN LIFE?

Page 119: "crammed next to the ghettos." Lester Sloan, "Dumping: A New Form of Genocide?" *Emerge* 3, no. 4 (February 1992): 19–22; Robert F. Kennedy, Jr., and Dennis Rivera, "Pollution's Chief Victims: The Poor," *New York Times* (August 15, 1992), Op-Ed page.

Page 119: "I saw the moon at first . . . ." Jimmy Santiago Baca, "Against," in his *Immigrants in Our Own Land* (New York: New Directions, 1982), pp. 41–42.

Page 121: "What does it mean when poets surrender . . . ." David Mura, "Notes for a New Poem," unpub. essay, quoted by permission of the author.

Page 121: "to live in a tragic time." Wallace Stevens, *The Collected Poems of Wallace Stevens* (New York: Knopf, 1954), p. 199.

Page 122: "fled into expatriation, emigrated inwardly." See Hannah Arendt, *Men in Dark Times* (New York: Harcourt Brace Jovanovich, 1968), p. 19: "During . . . [1933–1938] in Germany there existed the phenomenon known as 'inner emigration' . . . a curiously ambiguous phenomenon. It signified on the one hand that there were persons inside Germany who behaved as if they no longer belonged to the country, who felt like emigrants; and on the other hand it indicated that they had not in reality emigrated, but had withdrawn to an interior realm, into the invisibility of thinking and feeling. . . . [I]n the darkest of times, inside and outside Germany the temptation was particularly strong, to shift from the world and its public space to an interior life, or else simply to ignore that world in favor of an imaginary world 'as it ought to be' or as it once upon a time had been."

One white and working-class poet who refused any kind of "inner emigration" was Richard Hugo. His poetry is almost entirely about what it means to be and feel a failure in the "land of equal opportunity." His poem "What Thou Lovest Well Remains American" is all about the smell of failure and the need to blame it on one's own class or people rather than on the failure of the national fantasy (Richard Hugo, *Making Certain It Goes On: The Collected Poems of Richard Hugo* [New York: Norton, 1984]).

Page 123: "the trams are running." Nadezhda Mandelstam, *Hope against Hope* (New York: Atheneum, 1970), pp. 160–216.

XVII. MOMENT OF PROOF

Page 124: "didn't have much effect." Nadezhda Mandelstam, *Hope against Hope* (New York: Atheneum, 1970), p. 153. In 1937, Osip Mandelstam had forced himself to write an "Ode to Stalin," hoping to save his own life.

Page 125: "The fear of poetry is the . . . ." Muriel Rukeyser, *The Collected Poems of Muriel Rukeyser* (New York: McGraw-Hill, 1978), pp. 160–61.

Page 126: "I remember a psychologist . . . ." Muriel Rukeyser, *The Life of Poetry* (New York: A. A. Wyn, 1949), p. 12.

Page 127: "It forms the quality of the light . . . ." Audre Lorde, "Poetry Is Not a Luxury," in her *Sister Outsider: Essays and Speeches* (Freedom, Calif.: Crossing Press, 1984), p. 37.

Page 127: "Recently I heard someone say . . . ." Mandelstam, p. 253.

XVIII. "HISTORY STOPS FOR NO ONE"

Page 128: "It was not natural. And she was the first . . . ." June Jordan, "The Difficult Miracle of Black Poetry in America," in her *Moving towards Home: Political Essays* (London: Virago, 1989), p. 162.

Page 128: "*Zi shemt zikh*/She is ashamed . . . ." Irena Klepfisz, "*Di rayze aheym*/The Journey Home," in her *A Few Words in the Mother Tongue: Poems Selected and New, 1971–1990* (Portland, Ore.: Eighth Mountain Press, 1990), pp. 216–24.

Page 130: "Not Vanishing." Chrystos, *Not Vanishing* (Vancouver: Press Gang Publishers, 1989).

Page 130: "Sorrow Songs." W. E. B. Du Bois, *The Souls of Black Folk* (1903; rpt. New York: Fawcett, 1969). "These songs are the articulate message of the slave to the world. . . . The ten master songs I have mentioned tell in word and music of trouble and exile, of strife and hiding; they grope toward some unseen power and sigh for rest in the End. . . . Through all the sorrow of the Sorrow Songs there breathes a hope—a faith in the ultimate justice of things. The minor cadences of despair change often to triumph and calm confidence. Sometimes it is faith in life, sometimes a faith in death, sometimes assurance of boundless justice in some fair world beyond. But whichever it is, the meaning is always clear: that sometime, somewhere, men will judge men by their souls and not by their skin. Is such a hope justified? Do the Sorrow Songs sing true?" (pp. 183–89).

Page 131: "Destruction (of the Temple)." Irena Klepfisz, "Secular Jewish Identity: Yidishkayt in America," in her *Dreams of an Insomniac: Jewish Feminist Essays, Speeches and Diatribes* (Portland, Ore.: Eighth Mountain Press, 1990).

Page 131: "during the war . . . ." Klepfisz, *A Few Words*, p. 43.

Page 135: "These two: . . ." *Ibid.*, p. 37.

Page 136: "had circumstances been different." *Ibid.*, p. 30.

Page 136: "common things, gestures and events." Klepfisz, *Dreams*, pp. 132–35.

Page 136: "who have perished." Klepfisz, *A Few Words*, p. 37.

Page 136: "history stops for no one." *Ibid.*, p. 236.

Page 136: "when they took us . . . ." *Ibid.*, p. 47.

Page 137: "conversations over brandy." *Ibid.*, pp. 49–50.

Page 138: "walking home alone . . . ." *Ibid.*, pp. 190–93.

Page 139: "torn between ways." Gloria Anzaldúa, *Borderlands/La Frontera: The New Mestiza* (San Francisco: Spinsters/Aunt Lute Books, 1987), p. 78.

Page 142: "she'd never before been forced . . . ." Klepfisz, *A Few Words*, p. 76.

XIX. THE TRANSGRESSOR MOTHER

Page 147: "*Crime against Nature.*" Minnie Bruce Pratt, *Crime against Nature* (Ithaca, N.Y.: Firebrand, 1990).

Page 147: "I used to drive down the coast . . . ." Minnie Bruce Pratt, "Romance," in her *The Sound of One Fork* (Durham, N.C.: Night Heron Press, 1981), pp. 23–24.

Page 149: ". . . the place of the Piscataway . . . ." Minnie Bruce Pratt, "Reading Maps: Three," in her *We Say We Love Each Other* (San Francisco: Spinsters/Aunt Lute Books, 1985), p. 96.

Page 159: "Finally I understood that I could feel sorrow . . . ." Elly Bulkin, Minnie Bruce Pratt, and Barbara Smith, *Yours in Struggle: Three Feminist Perspectives on Anti-Semitism and Racism* (1984; Ithaca, N.Y.: Firebrand, 1989), p. 41.

Page 160: "a context to nourish it." Oddly enough, if you search through nonfeminist literary journals and periodicals, this groundswell of feminist and lesbian writing would seem to be invisible: it is never mentioned as a literary movement, its writers, save for a few of the most famous, never alluded to. A striking case in point is Ira Sadoff's "Neo-Formalism: A Dangerous Nostalgia," *American Poetry Review* 19, no. 1 (January–February 1990), an essay with much of which I agree but which represents, finally, a truncated version of the state of American poets and poetry today. There are, close to home, among feminist, gay, and lesbian poets, among poets of communities of color, a profusion of what Sadoff is seeking: "poems that make engaged, dramatized, and surprising connections between the self and the social world, the monument and history."

Page 160: "Communist Eastern Europe, on the other." Vaclav Havel, *Vaclav Havel: Living in Truth,* ed. Jan Vladislav (London and Boston: Faber & Faber, 1990), p. 101. Havel attributes the concept of a "second culture" to Ivan Jirous.

Page 161: "an unsettling presence altogether." The prize had been awarded by an independent jury of two men and one woman (Marvin Bell, Alfred Corn, and Sandra McPherson), who described the book as "forceful" and "masterful"—adjectives clearly meant in praise but interesting in terms of the politics of language.

Page 161: "marched to his words." Pratt, along with Black lesbian poet Audre Lorde and American Indian lesbian poet Chrystos, received a $20,000 creative-writing grant from the National Foundation for the Arts in the spring of 1990. Helms sent their names, among others, on an arts blacklist to the comptroller general of the United States.

Page 162: "The profound crisis of human identity . . . ." Havel, p. 62.

Page 162: "start to crack." Ibid., p. 28.

XX. A COMMUNAL POETRY

Page 167: "Working in words 1 am an escapist . . . ." Robert Duncan, *Bending the Bow* (New York: New Directions, 1968), pp. v, 9.

Page 168: "A Family Resemblance." Audre Lorde, "A Family Resemblance," in her *Undersong: Chosen Poems Old and New,* rev. ed. (New York: Norton, 1992), pp. 40–41.

Page 170: "A Woman Is Talking to Death." Judy Grahn, "A Woman Is Talking to Death," in her *The Work of a Common Woman* (Freedom, Calif.: Crossing Press, 1978), pp. 113–31.

Page 173: "Men with the heads of eagles . . . ." Margaret Atwood, *You Are Happy* (New York: Harper & Row, 1974), p. 47.

Page 175: "that great poet of inseparables, Muriel Rukeyser." The poet Enid Dame writes: "You locate the roots of the [women's poetry movement] in the Beat rebel poetry of the '50s and '60s. That's certainly true in my case. Allen Ginsberg's poetry, especially 'Kaddish,' the culture of the East Village, the politics of the New Left, and the emerging women's movement and its encouragement of women artists all affected my own growth and work as a poet. Significantly, like many people in those days, I belonged to several 'small groups'—a women's CR group, a Jewish CR group (men and women) and later best of all, a leaderless, all-women's poetry workshop, the Women's Collage. (We lasted four years and published an anthology.) I was . . . touched by your comment that our movement provided a 'background' for younger women poets—I know they're still out there, writing poems, editing magazines, even, perhaps, 'speaking of revolution' in these increasingly perilous times" (personal communication, February 1, 1992).

Page 176: "The reality of being women . . . ." *Ordinary Women: An Anthology of Poetry by New York City Women,* ed. Sara Miles, Patricia Jones, Sandra Maria Esteves, and Fay Chiang, intro. Adrienne Rich (New York: Ordinary Women Books, 1978), pp. 11–13, 45, 85, 107.

Page 180: "You are fearless of the language . . . ." Leslie Marmon Silko and James Wright, *The Delicacy and Strength of Lace: Letters,* ed. Anne Wright (St. Paul: Graywolf Press, 1985), pp. 81–82.

XXI. THE DISTANCE BETWEEN LANGUAGE AND VIOLENCE

Page 182: "A thing of beauty is a joy forever . . . ." John Keats, "Endymion," in *The Poetical Works of John Keats,* 2 vols. (Boston: Little Brown, 1899), I, p. 85.

Page 182: "Tyger, Tyger, burning bright . . . ." All passages from William Blake are from *The Poetry and Prose of William Blake,* ed. David Erdman (New York: Doubleday/Anchor, 1970).

Page 188: "Ah, Christ, I love . . . ." Allen Tate, "Sonnets at Christmas," in *The Voice That Is Great within Us: American Poetry of the Twentieth Century,* ed. Hayden Carruth (New York: Bantam, 1970), p. 221.

XXII. NOT HOW TO WRITE POETRY BUT WHEREFORE

Page 190: "You have to change your life." Rainer Maria Rilke, *The Selected Poetry of Rainer Maria Rilke,* ed. and trans. Stephen Mitchell (New

York: Random House/Vintage, 1986), pp. 60–61. "You have to change your life" is my American rendering of the line.

Page 191: "Radical changes and significant novelty . . . ." W. H. Auden, Foreword, in Adrienne Rich, *A Change of World* (New Haven: Yale University Press, 1951), p. 8.

Page 192: ". . . poetry makes nothing happen . . . ." W. H. Auden, "In Memory of W. B. Yeats," in his *Collected Poems* (New York: Random House, 1945), p. 50.

Page 192: "In the nightmare of the dark . . . ." *Ibid.,* p. 51.

Page 194: "Air without Incense." Adrienne Rich, *Collected Early Poems 1950–1970* (New York: Norton, 1993), p. 15. Muriel Rukeyser, in an essay on her Jewish identity, wrote of her childhood experience of temple services: "I think that many people brought up in reformed Judaism must go starving for two phases of religion: poetry and politics" (see "Poet . . . Woman . . . American . . . Jew," *Bridges: A Journal for Jewish Feminists and Our Friends* 1, no. 1 (Spring 1990): 23–29.

Page 195: " 'difficult' and unorthodox." Reginald Gibbons and Terrence DesPres, eds., *Thomas McGrath: Life and the Poem* (Urbana and Chicago: University of Illinois Press, 1992), pp. 120–21.

XXIII. "ROTTED NAMES"

Page 199: "She sang beyond the genius of the sea . . . ." Wallace Stevens, *The Collected Poems of Wallace Stevens* (New York: Knopf, 1955), pp. 128–30.

Page 199: "Now grapes are plush upon the vines . . . ." *Ibid.,* p. 266.

Page 200: "Nota: man is the intelligence of his soil . . . ." *Ibid.,* p. 27.

Page 201: "The book of moonlight is not written yet . . . ." *Ibid.,* pp. 33–34.

Page 201: "It has to be living, to learn the speech . . . ." *Ibid.,* pp. 239–40. Stevens's program for modern poetry implies a tradition of poetry that has failed to do these very things.

Page 202: "Throw away the lights, the definitions . . . ." *Ibid.,* p. 183.

Page 204: "frozen metaphors." Aldon Lynn Nielsen, *Reading Race: White American Poets and the Racial Discourse in the Twentieth Century* (Athens and London: University of Georgia Press, 1988), p. 9. Marjorie Perloff notes, in Stevens's letters written during World War II, his dismissive labeling of various literary intellectuals, even those he admired, as "a

Jew and a Communist," a "Jew and an anti-Fascist," "a Catholic," and his attempt, in the long poem "Notes toward a Supreme Fiction," (1941–1942), to construct "an elaborate and daunting rhetoric . . . designed to convince both poet and reader that, despite the daily headlines and radio bulletins, the real action takes place in the country of metaphor" (Albert J. Gelpi, ed., *Wallace Stevens: The Poetics of Modernism* [London and New York: Cambridge University Press, 1985], pp. 41–52).

Page 205: "fairly substantial income." Wallace Stevens, *Letters of Wallace Stevens,* ed. Holly Stevens (New York: Knopf, 1966), p. 321.

Page 205: "Africanism." "I am using the term 'Africanism' for the denotative and connotative blackness that African peoples have come to signify, as well as the entire range of views, assumptions, readings, and misreadings that accompany Eurocentric learning about these peoples. . . . As a disabling virus within literary discourse, Africanism has become, in the Eurocentric tradition that American education favors, both a way of talking about and a way of policing matters of class, sexual license, and repression, formations and exercises of power, and meditations on ethics and accountability" (Toni Morrison, *Playing in the Dark: Whiteness and the Literary Imagination* [Cambridge, Mass.: Harvard University Press, 1992], pp. 6–7).

XXIV. A POET'S EDUCATION

Page 206: "written by circumstance and environment." Diane Glancy, *Claiming Breath* (Lincoln: University of Nebraska Press, 1992), p. 85.

Page 206: "use of myself as a found object." *Ibid.,* p. 23.

Page 206: "Arkansas backhill culture." *Ibid.,* p. 22.

Page 207: "Before I was eighteen, . . ." Jimmy Santiago Baca, *Working in the Dark: Reflections of a Poet of the Barrio* (Santa Fe: Red Crane Books, 1992), pp. 4–6.

Page 208: "in a world . . . run by men's rules . . . ." *Ibid.,* p. 65.

Page 208: "Every poem is an infant . . . ." *Ibid.,* p. 66.

Page 209: "There was nothing so humiliating . . . ." *Ibid.,* p. 4.

Page 209: *"En boca cerrada no entran moscas . . . ."* Gloria Anzaldúa, *Borderlands/La Frontera: The New Mestiza* (San Francisco: Spinsters/Aunt Lute Books, 1987), p. 54.

Page 210: "the coming together of opposite qualities within." *Ibid.,* p. 19.

Page 210: "In the 1960s, I read my first Chicano novel . . . ." *Ibid.,* pp. 59–61.

Page 211: "After the divorce, I had new territory . . . ." Glancy, pp. 86–87.

XXV. TO INVENT WHAT WE DESIRE

Page 215: "Poetry is not a luxury." Audre Lorde, "Poetry Is Not a Luxury," in her *Sister Outsider: Essays and Speeches* (Freedom, Calif.: Crossing Press, 1984), p. 36.

Page 216: "the intimate face of universal struggle." June Jordan, *Civil Wars* (Boston: Beacon Press, 1981), p. xi.

XXVI. FORMAT AND FORM

Page 217: "*Format:—n.* . . ." Paul Goodman, *Speaking and Language: A Defence of Poetry* (New York: Random House, 1971), pp. 200–1.

Page 218: "Format is not like censorship . . . ." *Ibid.,* pp. 202–3.

Page 219: "works almost in resistance to the form." Richard Hugo, *The Triggering Town: Lectures and Essays on Poetry and Writing* (New York: Norton, 1979), pp. 5 ff.

Page 219: "No worst, there is none . . . ." Gerard Manley Hopkins, *Poems of Gerard Manley Hopkins,* ed. Robert Bridges and W. H. Gardner (London: Oxford University Press, 1952), pp. 106–7.

Page 219: "If we must die, let it not be like hogs . . . ." In Claude McKay, *Selected Poems of Claude McKay* (San Diego: Harcourt Brace Jovanovich, 1981), p. 36. McKay's sonnet, written out by hand, was found in the aftermath of the assault by state troopers on the state prison at Attica, New York, on September 21, 1971, where prisoners protesting conditions had staged a rebellion. A reporter for *Time* ascribed authorship of the poem to one of the prisoners: "Many of the self-styled revolutionaries—transferred to Attica from other prisons because of their militancy—smuggled banned books by such writers as Malcolm X and Bobby Seale into their cells, and held secret political meetings when pretending to be at chapel or engaged in intramural athletics. They passed around clandestine writings of their own; among them was a poem written by an unknown prisoner, crude but touching in its would-be heroic style" (a cut followed with the first four lines of McKay's sonnet copied in a clearly printed handwriting). (See *Time* [September 27, 1971], p. 20.) A member of the Oakland Black Writers Guild recalled that McKay's poem was found on the body of an

African-American soldier killed in World War II (Michelle Cliff, personal communication, 1992).

Page 220: "The camps hold their distance— . . . ." Derek Walcott, "XLI," in his *Midsummer* (New York: Farrar, Straus & Giroux, 1984).

Page 221: "if we are free, all may be free." This draft is in the Manuscript Division of the Library of Congress.

Page 221: "To be a Jew in the twentieth century . . . ." Muriel Rukeyser, *The Collected Poems of Muriel Rukeyser* (New York: McGraw-Hill, 1978), p. 239.

Page 223: "Girl from the realm of birds florid and fleet . . . ." June Jordan, *Moving towards Home: Political Essays* (London: Virago, 1989), pp. 161–71.

Page 223: "tus manos son dos martillos que clavan . . . ." Francisco X. Alarcón, *De amor oscuro: Of Dark Love* (Santa Cruz, Calif.: Moving Parts Press, 1991), n.p.

Page 225: "The deliberate response to format . . . ." Goodman, pp. 215–17.

Page 227: "defenders of privilege." In her essay "The Essential Gesture," Nadine Gordimer speaks of the efforts of some modern writers, impelled by a sense of social responsibility, to "transform the world by style." She is chiefly considering novelists, but her remarks apply to poets as well: "This was and is something that could not serve as the writer's essential gesture in countries such as South Africa and Nicaragua, but it has had its possibilities and sometimes proves its validity where complacency, indifference, accidie, and not conflict, threaten the human spirit. To transform the world by style was the iconoclastic essential gesture tried out by the Symbolists and Dadaists; but whatever social transformation (in shaping a new consciousness) they might have served in breaking old forms was horribly superseded by different means: Europe, the Far, Middle and Near East, Asia, Latin America and Africa overturned by wars; millions of human beings wandering without the basic structure of a roof" (Nadine Gordimer, *The Essential Gesture: Writing, Politics and Places,* ed. and intro. Stephen Clingman [New York: Knopf, 1988], p. 296).

XXVII. TOURISM AND PROMISED LANDS

Page 230: "Even then . . . . ." June Jordan, "Solidarity," in her *Naming Our Destiny: New and Selected Poems* (New York: Thunder's Mouth Press, 1989), p. 171.

Page 232: "This book is not a response to public life . . . ." Thomas Larsen,

"Uneasy Confessions," review of *Truth and Lies That Press for Life: Sixty Los Angeles Poets*, ed. Connie Hersheym (Concord, Mass.: Artifact Press, 1992), in *Poetry Flash* no. 232 (July 1992): 1.

Page 234: "a turning point in human history." *Marxist-Humanism: A Half Century of Its World Development*, XII: *Guide to the Raya Dunayevskaya Collection;* ed. Raya Dunayevskaya (Wayne, Neb.: Wayne State University Library, 1986), p. 59. Available on microfilm from Wayne State University Library.

XXVIII. *WHAT IF?*

Page 235: "When there is no history . . . ." Michael Harper, *Song: I Want a Witness* (Pittsburgh: University of Pittsburgh Press, 1972), p. 1.

Page 235: "The economy of the nation . . . ." Muriel Rukeyser, *The Life of Poetry* (New York: A. A. Wyn, 1949), p. 61.

Page 235: "We must constantly encourage ourselves . . . ." Audre Lorde, "Poetry Is Not a Luxury," in her *Sister Outsider: Essays and Speeches* (Freedom, Calif.: Crossing Press, 1984), pp. 38–39.

Page 236: "To be revolutionary is to be original . . . ." Inés Hernández, "An Open Letter to Chicanas on the Power and Politics of Origin," in *Without Discovery: A Native Response to Columbus,* ed. Ray Gonzalez (Seattle: Broken Moon Press, 1992), p. 161.

Page 236: "The country's uniqueness no longer resides . . . ." These are not the words of a writer in the left-wing press; they were written by Stephen Graubard, editor of *Daedalus: Journal of the American Academy of Arts and Sciences,* an academic-intellectual publication sponsored by an elite institution (see "Political Pharmacology: Thinking about Drugs," *Daedalus* [Summer 1992]: vi–vii).

Page 237: "an icon to be shot down." Octavio Paz, *The Other Voice* (New York: Harcourt Brace Jovanovich, 1990), p. 65.

Page 238: "undergo change or self-destruct." *Ibid.,* p. 156.

Page 238: "has appeared in thirty years." *Ibid.,* p. 119.

Page 238: "Europe and Africa." For some of the work of these poetic movements, see the Selected Bibliography.

Page 238: "What looks the strongest . . . ." Seamus Heaney, "From the Canton of Expectation," in his *Selected Poems 1966–1987* (New York: Noonday Press, 1990), p. 258.

Page 239: "radical juxtaposition with Gibbs's paintings." "Radical juxtaposition" is Gibbs's phrase.

Page 240: "Here is soot Today . . . ." Suzanne Gardinier, *The New World* (Pittsburgh: University of Pittsburgh Press, 1993).

Page 241: "blind sorrow." *Ibid.*

Page 242: "How Europe Underdeveloped Africa." Kamau Brathwaite, in his *MiddlePassages* (New York: New Directions, 1993), pp. 43–48.

Page 247: "For Anna Mae Pictou Aquash . . . ." Joy Harjo, *In Mad Love and War* (Middletown, Conn.: Wesleyan University Press, 1990), pp. 7–8.

Page 249: "In another place, not here . . . ." Dionne Brand, *No Language Is Neutral* (Toronto: Coach House Press, 1990), p. 34.

Selected Bibliography

I want to emphasize "selected." There are many other books of poetry and of prose that could be cited here, I have made this short list for readers who want to follow up on the work of poets whose words appear in the text and are cited in the notes, or on other poets whose words do not appear here but might have done.

ANTHOLOGIES

Brant, Beth, ed. *A Gathering of Spirit: A Collection by North American Indian Women.* (1984). Ithaca, N.Y.: Firebrand Books, 1988.

Bruchac, Joseph, ed. *Breaking Silence: An Anthology of Contemporary Asian American Poets.* Greenfield Center, N.Y.: Greenfield Review Press, 1983.

———. *Songs from This Earth on Turtle's Back: Contemporary American Indian Poetry.* Greenfield Center, N.Y.: Greenfield Review Press, 1983.

Bulkin, Elly, and Joan Larkin, eds. *Lesbian Poetry: An Anthology.* Watertown, Mass.: Persephone Press, 1981.

Chin, Marilyn, and David Wong Louie, eds. *Dissident Song: A Contemporary Asian American Anthology.* Santa Cruz: Quarry West, 1991.

Feinstein, Sascha, and Yusuf Komunyakaa, eds. *The Jazz Poetry Anthology.* Bloomington: Indiana University Press, 1991.

Gonzalez, Ray, ed. *After Atzlan: Latino Poets of the Nineties*. Boston: David R. Godine, 1992.

Hahn, Kimiko, Gale Jackson, and Susan Sherman. *We Stand Our Ground: Three Women, Their Vision, Their Poems*. New York: I-KON, 1988.

Hongo, Garrett, ed. *The Open Boat: Poems from Asian America*. New York: Doubleday/Anchor, 1993.

Klein, Michael, ed., *Poets for Life: Seventy-six Poets Respond to AIDS*. New York: Crown, 1989.

Larkin, Joan, and Carl Morse, eds. *Gay and Lesbian Poetry in Our Time: An Anthology*. New York: St. Martin's Press, 1988.

Majzels, Robert, ed. *The Guerilla Is Like a Poet: An Anthology of Filipino Poetry*. Ontario: Cormorant Books, 1988.

Phillips, J. J., Ishmael Reed, Gundars Strads, and Shawn Wong, eds. *The Before Columbus Foundation Poetry Anthology*. New York: Norton, 1992.

Piercy, Marge, ed. *Early Ripening: American Women's Poetry Now*. New York and London: Pandora, 1987.

Saint, Assoto, ed. *The Road before Us: 100 Gay Black Poets*. New York: Galiens Press, 1991.

Waldman, Anne, ed. *Out of This World: The Poetry Project of St. Mark's Church-in-the-Bowery, 1966–1991*. New York: Crown, 1991.

Yamada, Mitsuye, and Sarie Sachie Hylkema. *Sowing Ti Leaves: Writings by Multi-cultural Women*. Irvine, Calif.: Multi-cultural Writers of Orange County, 1990.

FURTHER WORKS BY POETS CITED

Alarcón, Francisco X. *Snake Poems: An Aztec Incantation*. San Francisco: Chronicle Books, 1992.

―――. *No Golden Gate for Us*. Santa Fe: Pennywhistle Press, 1993.

Baca, Jimmy Santiago. *Black Mesa Poems*. New York: New Directions, 1989.

Brand, Dionne. *Primitive Offensive*. Toronto: Williams-Wallace, 1982.

―――. *Winter Epigrams and Epigrams for Ernesto Cardenal in Defense of Claudia*. Toronto: Williams-Wallace, 1983.

Brant, Beth. *Food and Spirits*. Ithaca, N.Y.: Firebrand Books, 1991.

Brodine, Karen. *Woman Sitting at the Machine, Thinking: Poems 1978–1987*. Seattle: Red Letter Press, 1990.

Carruth, Hayden. *Selected Shorter Poems, 1946–1991.* Port Townsend, Wash.: Copper Canyon Press, 1992.

———. *Suicides and Jazzers.* Ann Arbor: University of Michigan Press, 1992.

———. *Sitting In: Selected Writing on Jazz, Blues, and Related Topics.* Iowa City: University of Iowa Press, (1986), 1993.

Duncan, Robert. *Bending the Bow.* New York: New Directions, 1968.

———. *Ground Work II: In the Dark.* New York: New Directions, 1987.

Esteves, Sandra Maria. *Bluestown Mockingbird Mambo.* Houston: Arte Publico Press, 1990.

Gardinier, Suzanne. *Usahn: Twelve Poems and a Story.* New York: Grand Street, 1990.

Glancy, Diane. *Iron Woman.* New York: New Rivers Press, 1990.

———. *Lone Dog's Winter Count.* Albuquerque: West End Press, 1991.

Goodman, Paul. *Drawing the Line: A Pamphlet.* New York: Random House, 1962.

———. *Growing Up Absurd: Problems of Youth in the Organized System.* New York: Vintage, 1962

———. *The Lordly Hudson.* New York: Macmillan, 1962.

———. *Utopian Essays and Practical Proposals.* New York: Random House, 1962.

———. *Hawkweed.* New York: Vintage, 1967.

Haines, John. *News from the Glacier: Selected Poems 1960–1980.* Middletown, Conn.: Wesleyan University Press, 1982.

Harjo, Joy. *She Had Some Horses.* New York: Thunder's Mouth Press, 1988.

Harper, Michael. *Dear John, Dear Coltrane.* Pittsburgh: University of Pittsburgh Press, 1970.

———. *History Is Your Own Heartbeat.* Urbana: University of Illinois Press, 1972.

———. *Debridement.* New York: Doubleday, 1973.

Hikmet, Nazim. *Rubaiyat,* trans. Randy Blasing and Mutlu Konuk. Providence, R.I.: Copper Beech Press, 1985.

Hugo, Richard. *Making Certain It Goes On: Collected Poems.* New York: Norton, 1984.

Jordan, June. *Technical Difficulties: African American Notes on the State of the Union.* New York: Pantheon, 1992.

————. *Haruko/Love Poems: New and Selected Love Poems*. New York: High Risk Books/Serpent's Tail, 1994.

Kinnell, Galway. *What a Kingdom It Was*. Boston: Houghton Mifflin, 1960.

————. *The Book of Nightmares*. Boston: Houghton Mifflin, 1971.

————. *The Past*. Boston: Houghton Mifflin, 1985.

————. *When One Has Lived for a Long Time Alone*. New York: Knopf, 1990.

Levertov, Denise. *The Poet in the World*. New York: New Directions, 1973. .

————. *Poems 1960–1967*. New York: New Directions, 1983.

————. *Poems 1968–1972*. New York: New Directions, 1987.

————. *New and Selected Essays*. New York: New Directions, 1992.

Lorde, Audre. *Undersong*. New York: Norton, 1992.

————. *The Marvelous Arithmetics of Distance*. New York: Norton, 1993.

McGrath, Thomas. *Letter to an Imaginary Friend, Parts I and II*. Chicago: Swallow Press, 1970.

————. *Letter to an Imaginary Friend, Parts III and IV*, Port Townsend, Wash.: Copper Canyon Press, 1985.

Mura, David. *After We Lost Our Way*. New York: Dutton, 1989.

Pratt, Minnie Bruce. *Rebellion: Essays 1980–1991*, Ithaca, N.Y.: Firebrand Books, 1991.

OTHER WORKS

Agosin, Marjorie. *Zones of Pain/Las Zonas del Dolor*. New York: White Pine Press, 1988.

————. *Circles of Madness: Mothers of the Plaza de Mayo*. Fredonia, N.Y.: White Pine Press, 1992.

Agüeros, Jack. *Correspondence between the Stonehaulers*. Brooklyn, N.Y.: Hanging Loose Press, 1991.

Aguilar, Mila D. *A Comrade Is As Precious As a Rice Seedling*. Latham, N.Y.: Kitchen Table/Women of Color Press, 1987. With an introduction by Audre Lorde.

Allison, Dorothy. *The Women Who Hate Me: Poetry 1980–1990*. Ithaca, N.Y.: Firebrand Books, 1991.

Arteaga, Alfred. *Cantos*. San Jose: Chusma House, 1991.

Ashanti, Baron James. *Nova*. New York: Harlem River Press, 1990.

Césaire, Aimé. *Discourse on Colonialism*. New York and London: Monthly Review Press, 1972.

Cisneros, Sandra. *My Wicked, Wicked Ways*. New York: Turtle Bay Books, 1992.

Cooper, Jane. *Scaffolding*. Gardiner, Maine: Tilbury House, 1993.

———. *Green Notebook, Winter Road*. Gardiner, Maine: Tilbury House, 1994.

Derricotte, Toi. *Captivity*. Pittsburgh: University of Pittsburgh Press, 1989.

Doubiago, Sharon. *Hard Country*. Minneapolis: West End Press, 1982.

———. *The Book of Seeing with One's Own Eyes*. St. Paul: Graywolf Press, 1988.

Dumas, Henry. *Knees of a Natural Man: The Selected Poetry of Henry Dumas*, New York: Thunder's Mouth Press, 1989.

Hamill, Sam. *A Poet's Work: The Other Side of Poetry*. Seattle: Broken Moon Press, 1990.

Hemphill, Essex. *Ceremonies: Prose and Poetry*. New York: Penguin/Plume, 1992.

Hogan, Linda. *Red Clay: Poems and Stories*. Greenfield Center, N.Y.: Greenfield Review Press, 1991.

Ignatow, David. *New and Collected Poems, 1970–1985*. Middletown, Conn.: Wesleyan University Press, 1986.

———. *The One in the Many: A Poet's Memoirs*. Middletown, Conn.: Wesleyan University Press, 1988.

Islas, Arturo. *The Rain God: A Desert Tale*. Palo Alto: Alexandrian Press, 1984.

———. *Migrant Souls: A Novel*. New York: William Morrow, 1990.

Joseph, Lawrence. *Shouting at No One*. Pittsburgh: University of Pittsburgh Press, 1983.

———. *Curriculum Vitae*. Pittsburgh: University of Pittsburgh Press, 1988.

Komunyakaa, Yusuf. *Bien Cai Dau*. Middletown, Conn.: Wesleyan University Press, 1988.

———. *Magic City*. Middletown, Conn.: Wesleyan University Press, 1992.

Laux, Dorianne. *Awake*. Brockport, N.Y.: BOA Editions, 1990.

Lee, Li-Young. *Rose*. Brockport, N.Y.: BOA Editions, 1986.

———. *The City in Which I Love You*. Brockport, N.Y.: BOA Editions, 1990.

Levine, Philip. *New and Selected Poems*. New York: Knopf, 1991.

———. *What Work Is*. New York: Knopf, 1991.

Merwin, W. S. *Writings for an Unfinished Accompaniment*. New York: Knopf, 1973.

———. *Travels*. New York: Knopf, 1993.

Mphalele, Ezekiel. *Voices in the Whirlwind*. New York: Hill and Wang, 1972.

Paley, Grace. *New and Collected Poems*. Gardiner, Maine: Tilbury House, 1992.

Randall, Margaret. *Risking a Somersault in the Air: Conversations with Nicaraguan Writers*. San Francisco: Solidarity Publications, 1984.

———. *Gathering Rage: The Failure of Twentieth Century Revolutions to Develop a Feminist Agenda*. New York: Monthly Review Press, 1993.

Rodriguez, Luís J. *Poems across the Pavement*. Chicago: Chucha Press, 1989.

Sanchez, Sonia. *Home Girls and Hand Grenades*. New York: Thunder's Mouth Press, 1984.

———. *Under a Soprano Sky*. Trenton, N.J.: Africa World Press, 1987.

Whiteman, Roberta Hill. *Star Quilt*. Duluth: Holy Cow! Press, 1984.

Wong, Nellie. *Dreams in Harrison Railroad Park*. Berkeley, Calif.: Kelsey Street Press, 1978.

———. *The Death of Long Steam Lady*. Albuquerque, N.M.: West End Press, 1986.

Many of the small-press editions mentioned here can be obtained through Small Press Distribution Inc., 1814 San Pablo Avenue, Berkeley CA 94702 (telephone: 510–549–3336). SPD issues a semiannual catalogue of the new work from small presses, much of it poetry, with reviews-in-brief.

Acknowledgments

I am deeply in debt to the poets whose words appear in this book, and to the many others whose work is here in spirit because it has given me courage and hope. In particular, I am indebted to two pieces of witness by poets: Muriel Rukeyser's *The Life of Poetry,* written at mid-century soon after the end of World War II, and Audre Lorde's "Poetry Is Not a Luxury," written in the women's liberation movement of the 1970s. These are as alive as ever and deserve to be read by anyone who reads, or writes, poems, or who listens for voices from the past that can speak to the future.

I am grateful to Elly Bulkin, Hayden Carruth, Jane Cooper, and Minnie Bruce Pratt for their critical and sensitive readings of drafts of this book. I thank Miranda Bergman, Enid Dame, Michele Gibbs, and Helen Smelser for work shared and for their responses to parts of the manuscript. Ellen Farmer and Dianna Williamson, always generous and flexible, turned my typescripts into final copy.

I have had three fine editors at W. W. Norton & Company: the late John Benedict, who gave his blessing to an early draft of this book; the late Barry K. Wade, whose finely tuned sensibility and gifted editing I knew all too briefly; and Julia A. Reidhead, who has carried on with care and skill.

During my many years with Norton I have been fortunate to depend on Carol Flechner's keen mind and high standards of editing in preparing my manuscripts for publication. I have been equally fortunate in Antonina Krass's fine book designs, Debra Morton Hoyt's elegant jackets, and Andrew Marasia's meticulous attention to every detail of production. And, in the difficult and sorrowful period of Barry Wade's illness and after, Anna Karvellas has been a steady and active editorial liaison.

I thank here the many people, known and unknown to me, who help build the movements that open new space for the imagination.

Finally, this book and I owe much to seventeen years of conversation with Michelle Cliff.

—A.R.

Permissions
Acknowledgments

by permission of Faber & Faber. From *A Change of World* by Adrienne Rich, 1951. Reprinted by permission of Adrienne Rich.

JIMMY SANTIAGO BACA: From *Immigrants in Our Own Land,* copyright © 1982 by Jimmy Santiago Baca. Reprinted by permission of New Directions Publishing Corporation. From *Working in the Dark: Reflections of a Poet of the Barrio* by Jimmy Santiago Baca, published by Red Crane Books. Reprinted by permission of Red Crane Books.

MIRANDA BERGMAN: Excerpt, letter to Adrienne Rich, reprinted by permission of Miranda Bergman.

ELIZABETH BISHOP: "Chemin de Fer" from *The Complete Poems 1927–1979* by Elizabeth Bishop. Copyright © 1979, 1983 by Alice Helen Methfessel. Reprinted by permission of Farrar, Straus and Giroux, Inc.

WILLIAM BLAKE: From *The Poetry and Prose of William Blake,* edited by David Erdman, published by Doubleday-Anchor, 1970.

DIONNE BRAND: © 1990 Dionne Brand. Reprinted from *No Language Is Neutral* by permission of Coach House Press.

KAMAU BRATHWAITE: Reprinted by permission of Bloodaxe Books Ltd from *Middle Passages* by Kamau Brathwaite (Bloodaxe Books, 1992).

KAREN BRODINE: Reprinted from *Illegal Assembly* © 1980 by Karen Brodine, by permission of Hanging Loose Press.

HAYDEN CARRUTH: Excerpt, letter from Hayden Carruth to Adrienne Rich, 6 April 1992. Permission to reprint granted by Hayden Carruth.

AIMÉ CÉSAIRE: From "On the State of the Union" in *Aimé Césaire: Collected Poetry,* trans./ed. by Eshleman, Smith, published by The University of California Press. Copyright © 1983 The Regents of The University of California. Reprinted by permission of The University of California Press.

SAMUEL TAYLOR COLERIDGE: From *The Letters of Samuel Taylor Coleridge,* edited by E. L. Griggs, 1956, vol. I. By permission of Oxford University Press.

HART CRANE: The lines from "Van Winkle" are reprinted from *The Poems of Hart Crane,* edited by Marc Simon, by permission of Liveright Publishing Corporation. Copyright © 1986 by Marc Simon.

EMILY DICKINSON: From *The Complete Poems of Emily Dickinson*, edited by Thomas H. Johnson. Copyright 1929 by Martha Dickinson Bianchi; copyright © renewed 1957 by Mary L. Hampson. By permission of Little, Brown and Company.

ROBERT DUNCAN: From *Bending the Bow*, copyright © 1968 by Robert Duncan. Reprinted by permission of New Directions Publishing Corporation.

FLORENCE CRANE WOMEN'S PRISON: From *INSIGHT: Serving the Women of Florence Crane Women's Facility*, reprinted by permission of Jacqueline Dixon-Bey and Mary Glover. *Konvict Kitchen* excerpt by Gloria Bolden.

LYNN EMANUEL: From "The Planet Krypton" in *The Dig* by Lynn Emanuel, published by the University of Illinois Press, copyright © 1992. Reprinted by permission of The University of Illinois Press. "The Planet Krypton" was first published in the *Kenyon Review*.

SUZANNE GARDINIER: "To Peace" is reprinted from *The New World*, by Suzanne Gardinier, by permission of the University of Pittsburgh Press. © 1993 by Suzanne Gardinier. The poem beginning "Here is Soot" is from the poem sequence entitled "To the City of Fires" and is reprinted from *The New World*, by Suzanne Gardinier, by permission of the University of Pittsburgh Press. © 1993 by Suzanne Gardinier.

DIANE GLANCY: Reprinted from *Claiming Breath* by Diane Glancy, by permission of the University of Nebraska Press. © 1992 by the University of Nebraska Press.

PAUL GOODMAN: Excerpts from *Speaking and Language: A Defence of Poetry* by Paul Goodman, Random House, 1971. Reprinted by permission of Sally Goodman.

NADINE GORDIMER: Selections by Nadine Gordimer reprinted by permission of Nadine Gordimer.

JUDY GRAHN: "A Woman Is Talking to Death" from *The Work of a Common Woman*, Copyright 1978 by Judy Grahn, published by The Crossing Press, Freedom, California.

JOHN HAINES: Reprinted with permission of the publisher from *In the Forest without Leaves, New Poems: 1980–88*, Story Line Press, 1990, pp. 79–93.

Reprinted by permission of The Charlotte Sheedy Literary Agency. "A Family Resemblance" is reprinted from *Undersong: Chosen Poems Old and New*, Revised Edition, by Audre Lorde, by permission of W. W. Norton & Company, Inc. Copyright © 1992, 1982, 1976, 1974, 1973, 1970, 1968 by Audre Lorde. "Power" is reprinted from *The Black Unicorn: Poems* by Audre Lorde, by permission of W. W. Norton & Company, Inc. and The Charlotte Sheedy Literary Agency. Copyright © 1978 by Audre Lorde. Copyright © 1993 The Estate of Audre Lorde. First published by W. W. Norton & Company, 1992. By permission of Virago Press Ltd.

THOMAS MCGRATH: Selections from "Ordonnance" from *Selected Poems, 1938–1988*. Copyright © 1988 by Thomas McGrath. Used by permission of Copper Canyon Press, P.O. Box 271, Port Townsend, WA 98368.

CLAUDE MCKAY: By permission of Archives of Claude McKay, Carl Cowl, Administrator. From *Selected Poems of Claude McKay* (Harcourt Brace Jovanovich, 1981).

W. S. MERWIN: © 1967 by W. S. Merwin. From "Caesar" which appears in *The Lice*. Reprinted by permission of Georges Borchardt, Inc.

DAVID MURA: From "Notes for a New Poem," which first appeared in *Boston Review* April 1989. Copyright David Mura. Reprinted by permission of David Mura.

ORDINARY WOMEN: Selections from *Ordinary Women*, published by Ordinary Women Books, 1978. Reprinted by permission of Sara Miles.

MINNIE BRUCE PRATT: Selections from "For My Sons," "Justice, Come Down," "The Child Taken from the Mother," "The First Question," "Dreaming a Few Minutes in a Different Element," "Shame," "At Fifteen, the Oldest Son Comes to Visit," "All the Women Caught in Flaring Light," and "Seven Times Going, Seven Times Coming Back" from *Crimes against Nature* by Minnie Bruce Pratt, published by Firebrand Books, Ithaca, New York. Copyright © 1990 by Minnie Bruce Pratt. Reprinted by permission of Firebrand Books. Selections from "Reading Maps: Three" from *We Say We Love Each Other* by Minnie Bruce Pratt, published by Spinsters/Aunt Lute, 1985. Reprinted by permission of Firebrand Books, Ithaca, New York. "Romance" by Minnie Bruce Pratt from *The Sound of One Fork*, copyright 1981 by Minnie Bruce Pratt. Reprinted by permission of Minnie Bruce Pratt.

MURIEL RUKEYSER: From *Willard Gibbs,* © Muriel Rukeyser, 1988, Ox Bow Press, Woodbridge, Connecticut, by permission of William L. Rukeyser. From "Letter to the Front" ("To Be a Jew") by Muriel Rukeyser, from *Out of Silence,* 1992, TriQuarterly Books, Evanston, Illinois, © William L. Rukeyser. "Reading Time: 1 Minute 26 Seconds" and "Homage to Literature" from *Collected Poems, 1978,* McGraw-Hill, New York, © Muriel Rukeyser, by permission of William L. Rukeyser.

WALLACE STEVENS: From *The Collected Poems of Wallace Stevens* by Wallace Stevens. Reprinted by permission of Faber & Faber. From *Collected Poems* by Wallace Stevens, copyright 1954 by Wallace Stevens. Reprinted by permission of Alfred A. Knopf, Inc.

ALLEN TATE: Excerpt from "Sonnets at Christmas" from *Collected Poems 1919–1976* by Allen Tate. Copyright © 1977 by Allen Tate. Reprinted by permission of Farrar, Straus & Giroux, Inc.

LEON TROTSKY: From *Art and Revolution* by Leon Trotsky, copyright © 1970 by Pathfinder Press. Reprinted by permission of Pathfinder Press.

DEREK WALCOTT: From *Midsummer* by Derek Walcott. Reprinted by permission of Faber & Faber. "XLI" from *Midsummer* by Derek Walcott. Copyright © 1984 by Derek Walcott. Reprinted by permission of Farrar, Straus and Giroux, Inc.

WILLIAM CARLOS WILLIAMS: From *The Collected Poems of William Carlos Williams, 1939–1962,* vol. II. Copyright © 1962 by William Carlos Williams. Reprinted by permission of New Directions Publishing Corporation and Carcanet Press Limited.

Index